MLA
Handbook
for Writers
of Research
Papers

MLA Handbook for Writers of Research Papers

Fourth Edition

Joseph Gibaldi

THE MODERN LANGUAGE ASSOCIATION
OF AMERICA
New York   1995

For information about obtaining permission to reprint material from
MLA book publications, send your request by mail (see address below),
e-mail (permissions@mla.org), or fax (212 533-0680).

Library of Congress Cataloging-in-Publication Data

Gibaldi, Joseph, 1942–
    MLA handbook for writers of research papers / Joseph Gibaldi. — 4th ed.
      p.   cm.
    Includes bibliographical references and index.
    ISBN 0-87352-565-5
    1. Report writing—Handbooks, manuals, etc. 2. Research—Handbooks,
manuals, etc. I. Modern Language Association of America. II. Title.
LB2369.G53   1995
808′.02—dc20   94-38577

Book design by Charlotte Staub. Set in Melior and Prestige Elite. Printed on
recycled, acid-free paper

Published by The Modern Language Association of America
10 Astor Place, New York, NY 10003-6981

Contents

Foreword

The *MLA Handbook for Writers of Research Papers* is designed to introduce you to the customs of a community of writers who greatly value scrupulous scholarship and the careful documentation, or recording, of research. Read from beginning to end, the *MLA Handbook* provides a comprehensive picture of how research papers are created. Once you are familiar with the contents, you can use the book as a reference tool. Chapter 1 suggests some of the educational and intellectual purposes of research and describes the first steps in a scholarly project: choosing a topic; using a library; producing a working bibliography, notes, outlines, and drafts; and avoiding plagiarism. Chapter 2 gives practical advice on such matters as spelling, punctuation, and the presentation of names, numbers, titles of works, and quotations. This chapter is meant to help you craft writing that is clear, consistent, and stylistically authoritative. Chapter 3 gives guidelines on the physical format of the paper. The next two chapters cover the MLA's system, or style, of documenting sources: chapter 4 explains how to list sources at the end of a paper, while chapter 5 shows how to cite them in the text of a paper. Chapter 6 describes abbreviations that are useful in documentation and in certain other contexts. Appendix A lists notable reference works in specialized fields; appendix B presents some systems of documentation other than the MLA's. Finally, there are sample pages of a research paper that illustrate MLA style.

Learning the rules the *MLA Handbook* outlines will help you become a writer whose work deserves serious consideration. Similarly, your study of these rules can make you a more discerning reader: knowing how an author is supposed to use sources is essential to judging a text's reliability.

If you are consulting this book for the first time, you may be surprised by its focus on the details of preparing a piece of writing. This concern with details grows out of a respect for the responsibilities writers have to readers—and to other writers. The general practices the *MLA Handbook* describes are followed by writers of studies and reports that serve the needs of many different readers, in government, business, industry, the professions, the academy, and the media. Because research has the power to affect opinions and actions, responsible writers compose their work with great care. They specify when they refer to another author's ideas, facts, and words, whether they want to agree with, object to, analyze, or interpret the source. This kind of documentation tends to discourage the circulation of error, by inviting readers to determine for themselves whether a reference to another text presents a reasonable account of what that text says.

The *MLA Handbook* was developed by the Modern Language Association of America (MLA), an organization of teachers and scholars founded in 1883, when the modern languages were just beginning to gain a place in the college curriculum alongside the classical languages—ancient Greek and Latin. The MLA now has over thirty thousand members and supports a variety of publications and activities designed to strengthen teaching and scholarship in languages and literature. One of the association's best-known publications, the *MLA Handbook* has been widely used by generations of students at colleges and universities throughout the United States and in other countries. The documentation style the book outlines is preferred by a substantial majority of scholarly journals in languages and literature.

The *MLA Handbook* originated nearly fifty years ago. Convinced that commonly agreed-on rules for documenting quotations, facts, opinions, and paraphrases would simplify the task of preparing a manuscript for publication, William Riley Parker, the MLA executive director, compiled and published the "MLA Style Sheet" in 1951 in the association's journal, *PMLA*. The "Style Sheet" gained almost immediate acceptance among MLA members and scholarly publishers both because Parker codified uniform practices among journal editors and university presses and because he encouraged consensus on matters about which there was less agreement. The "Style Sheet" continued to respond to the changing needs of scholars, editors, and publishers and, in time, also addressed the needs of undergraduate students, becoming in 1977 the *MLA Handbook for Writers of Research Papers*. Over the years Walter S. Achtert, John Hurt Fisher, and Joseph Gibaldi contributed to the publication.

The second edition of the *MLA Handbook*, which appeared in 1984, introduced the current simplified set of rules for documentation that allow citations to be placed in the text within parentheses. Although the third edition, produced in 1988, covered some aspects of electronic publication, its treatment of these developments was quickly outdated. The book you hold, the fourth edition, encompasses recent technological changes and thus continues the MLA tradition of adopting new practices in scholarly research and publishing.

You happen to be learning the ways of writers, scholars, libraries, and publishers at a time when preserving the vital legacy of print presents a growing challenge. Librarians and scholars are particularly concerned about preserving the "brittle" books and other documents published or written on the inexpensive acidic paper that began to be used in the mid–nineteenth century. If you have ever tried to save newspaper articles or if you enjoy browsing in secondhand bookstores, you have probably noticed how paper yellows and crumbles with age. Unless steps are taken to preserve the paper of books and periodicals or to reproduce their contents, these documents will be lost forever.

Large-scale photographing of brittle materials has been under way for some time, and the future study of them will be possible primarily through the use of photographs or electronic formats derived from photographs. Resources are insufficient, however, to guarantee the survival of all materials published or written on acidic paper from 1850 to the present, and many documents will disappear before your generation can consult them.

Adapting scholarly practices to electronic media is another historic challenge facing writers, publishers, scholars, and librarians as our society moves from a six-hundred-year-old print era to an electronic era. One important question debated by the members of the MLA committee that oversaw this revision of the handbook concerns how much information readers need in a citation of an electronic work to be able to find the source. A reader who wishes to locate a book can take a few pieces of information—such as the author's name and the title—to a library or bookstore in this country and many others and readily determine whether the volume is available. Publication practices, copyright laws, and the organization of libraries provide an infrastructure that makes locating print publications a relatively simple matter. Consequently, references to print sources can be brief. Because no comparable infrastructure yet exists for electronic publications, citations of them must provide more information than references to print sources normally contain.

A second question the MLA committee discussed concerns the ease with which electronic communications and texts can be changed. This feature of electronic texts is an important strength of the new technology, but it poses problems for the documentation of research. By the time a reader tries to locate an electronic text referred to by an author, the text may have changed and the cited version may no longer exist or may be difficult to find. Sometimes the changes are planned and meant to enhance the publication. Consider, for example, the *MLA International Bibliography*. The association issues this reference work in print, as a CD-ROM, and online. The print volume is published annually, and each installment stands as a permanent record of the books and articles identified when it went to press. The CD-ROM version, however, is updated four times a year, and so the listings change quarterly; the online version is updated even more frequently—ten times a year. (Updating includes adding new entries and correcting errors in existing items.) Therefore, a student who consults an electronic version of the bibliography at different times in the year can end up with different lists of sources for a research assignment.

Regular additions to an electronic database do not pose a substantial problem as long as the user of the database understands that it will change. Greater problems arise from alterations that a writer or a reader cannot anticipate. An electronic document may be modified unpredictably, by its author or other interested parties.

The MLA committee that oversaw this revision of the handbook debated the value of ensuring that readers can get back to the texts a writer read and cited. Some committee members assumed that electronic documents would not—and need not—remain stable. Why, these specialists asked, shouldn't an improved version of a text be substituted for an earlier version whenever improvements are recognized? The other members of the committee replied, Who would determine what constitutes an improvement, and how could readers assess the effects of a change on the substance or wording of a text? After considerable discussion, committee members agreed that electronic texts will and probably should change but that readers must be able to get back to the original texts (or "archival copies") a writer consulted and cited. Ways must be found to archive electronic texts reliably at specific times in their history. A minimal standard is for electronic documents to be dated. In electronic research as in print research, only the ability of readers to verify an author's use of a source can discourage the circulation of error. How this important goal will be achieved remains to be seen.

The fourth edition of the *MLA Handbook* covers the new media while continuing to supply authoritative guidelines on traditional publications. As you will see, the rules for citing electronic material that the MLA committee established are not presented as definitive, and they will surely change as the technology and practices governing electronic communication evolve.

Because the MLA is a membership association, all its projects are communal efforts. The collaborative work on the *MLA Handbook* is particularly far-reaching; the various editions have benefited for over forty years from the contributions of MLA committees and staff members, editors, scholars, librarians, teachers, and students. Overseeing the development of this edition were the members of the *MLA Handbook* Revision Committee: Wayne C. Booth, Marshall J. Brown, Anne Ruggles Gere, James L. Harner, Susan Kallenbach, John W. Kronik, and Ian Lancashire. They brought to their work wisdom and experience, a respect for old and new technologies, and a strong commitment to the students who will use this book. The views of the members of the MLA Committee on Computers and Emerging Technologies in Teaching and Research also helped shape the revision.

A number of MLA staff members aided in the planning, writing, and design of this edition of the handbook. Joseph Gibaldi, director of book acquisitions and development, did the lion's share of the revision, working with Martha Noel Evans, director of the MLA book publication program. Members of the MLA editorial department, headed by Judy Goulding, made several specific contributions. Elizabeth Holland enlarged and improved the section on punctuation, Eric Wirth was the principal copyeditor, Judith Altreuter coordinated the book's design, and Roslyn Schloss provided many useful comments on the manuscript. Daniel J. Uchitelle, director of information services, and Bettina J. Huber, director of research, analyzed electronic publications and communication practices.

Of central importance in the development of the section on library research were the following librarians, who generously supplied information about resources and services in college and university libraries: Mary Beth Aust-Keefer, Paul Burnham, William Calhoon, Nancy Carter, Paul Doty, Kathryn Franco, Ellen Gilbert, Francisca Goldsmith, Susan Hockey, Robert Hohl, Kay Klayman, Naomi Lederer, Rosemary Little, Mary Sue Livingston, S. David Mash, Carol McAllister, James McPhee, Jill Miller, Elaine Misko, Ann Okerson, Val Ontell, Rona Ostrow, Catherine Palmer, Sarah Philips, John Price-Wilkins, Sharon Propas, Anne Marie Secord, Linda Sharp, Victoria Swinney, Susan Szasz, Linda TerHaar, Virginia Tiefel, Alan Wallace, Helene Williams, and James Wyatt.

The MLA also owes special thanks to library staff members at Fairleigh Dickinson University, Florham-Madison; the University of Findlay; Kean College; the New York Public Library; New York University; the University of North Carolina, Chapel Hill; Northern Illinois University; and Union County College. Finally, I acknowledge the contributions of the many teachers who have assigned the *MLA Handbook* to students and who sent suggestions for improvements that we incorporated in this edition.

As you learn to guide your research by the rules outlined in the *MLA Handbook*, you will take your place in a community of writers who are sure to influence the development of new rules. In time, you too may identify ways of improving future editions of this book.

Phyllis Franklin
Executive Director
Modern Language Association

1 Research and Writing

1.1. THE RESEARCH PAPER AS A FORM OF EXPLORATION

During your school career, you have probably written many personal essays that presented your thoughts, feelings, and opinions and that did not refer to any other source of information or ideas. Some subjects and assignments, however, require us to go beyond our personal knowledge and experience. We undertake research when we wish to explore an idea, probe an issue, solve a problem, or make an argument that compels us to turn to outside help. We then seek out, investigate, and use materials beyond our personal resources. The research paper presents the findings and conclusions of such an inquiry.

The research paper is generally based on primary research, secondary research, or a combination of the two. Primary research is the study of a subject through firsthand observation and investigation, such as analyzing a literary or historical text, conducting a survey, or carrying out a laboratory experiment. Primary sources include statistical data, historical documents, and works of literature and art. Secondary research is the examination of studies that other researchers have made of a subject. Examples of secondary sources are books and articles about political issues, historical events, scientific debates, or literary works.

Most academic papers depend at least partly on secondary research. No matter what your subject of study, learning to investigate, review, and productively use the information, ideas, and opinions of other researchers will play a major role in your development as a student. The sorts of activities that constitute a research paper—identifying, locating, assessing, and assimilating others' research and then developing and expressing your own ideas clearly and persuasively—are at the center of the educational experience.

These skills are by no means just academic. Like the research papers you write in school, many reports and proposals required in business, government, and other professions rely on secondary research. Learning how to write a research paper, then, can help prepare you for assignments in your professional career. It is difficult to think of any profession that would not require you to consult sources of information about a specific subject, to combine this information with your ideas, and to present your thoughts, findings, and conclusions effectively.

Research increases your knowledge and understanding of a subject. Sometimes research will confirm your ideas and opinions; sometimes it will challenge and modify them. But almost always it will help to shape your thinking. Unless your instructor specifically directs you otherwise, a research paper should not just review publications and extract a series of quotations from them. Rather, you should look for sources that provide new information, that helpfully survey the various positions already taken on the subject, that lend authority to your viewpoint, that expand or nuance your ideas, or that furnish negative examples against which you wish to argue. As you use and scrupulously acknowledge sources, however, always remember that the main purpose of doing research is not to summarize the work of others but to assimilate and build on it and to arrive at your own understanding of the subject.

A book like this cannot present all the profitable ways of doing research. Because this handbook emphasizes the mechanics of preparing effective papers, it may give you the mistaken impression that the process of researching and writing a research paper follows a fixed pattern. The truth is that different paths can and do lead to successful research papers. Some researchers may pursue a more or less standard sequence of steps, but others may find themselves working less sequentially. In addition, certain projects lend themselves to a standard approach, whereas others may call for different strategies. Keeping in mind that researchers and projects differ, this book discusses activities that nearly all writers of research papers perform, such as selecting a suitable topic, using the library, compiling a working bibliography, taking notes, outlining, and writing.

If you are writing your first research paper, you may feel overwhelmed by the many tasks discussed here. This handbook is designed to help you learn to manage a complex process efficiently. As you follow the book's advice on how to locate and document sources, how to format your paper, and so forth, you may be tempted to see doing a paper as a mechanical exercise. Actually, a research paper is an adventure, an intellectual adventure rather like solving a mystery: it is a form of exploration leading to discoveries that are new—at least to you if not to others. The mechanics of the paper, important though they are, should never override the intellectual challenge of pursuing a question that interests *you*. This quest should guide your research and writing. Even if you are just learning how to prepare a research paper, you may still experience the excitement of pursuing and developing ideas that is one of the great satisfactions of research and scholarship.

1.2. THE RESEARCH PAPER AS A FORM OF WRITING

A research paper is a form of written communication. Like other kinds of nonfiction writing—letters, memos, reports, essays, articles, books—it should present information and ideas clearly and cogently. You should not let the mechanics of gathering source materials, taking notes, and documenting sources make you forget to apply the knowledge and skills you have acquired through previous writing experiences.

This handbook is not about expository writing. (See 1.11 for a selected list of useful books on composition, usage, language, and style.) It is, instead, a guide for the preparation of research papers. No set of conventions for preparing a manuscript can replace lively and intelligent writing, however, and no amount of research and documentation can compensate for a poor presentation of ideas. While you must fully document the facts and opinions you draw from your research, the documentation should only support your statements and provide concise information about the sources cited; it should not overshadow your own ideas or distract the reader from them.

1.3. SELECTING A TOPIC

Your instructor may let you choose what to write about in your paper or may assign a topic. Even if the topic is assigned, you will probably need to decide which specific idea to explore or which approach to use. Selecting an appropriate topic is seldom a simple matter. Even after you discover a subject that attracts your interest, you may well find yourself revising your choice, modifying your approach, or changing topics altogether after you have begun research.

Remember the time allotted to you and the expected length of the paper. "Twentieth-century world politics" would obviously be too broad a subject for a ten-page term paper. You may prefer to begin with a fairly general topic and then to refine it, by thought and research, into a more specific one that can be fully explored. Try to narrow your topic by focusing on an aspect of the subject or an approach to it. A student initially interested in writing on Shakespeare's poetic imagery, for instance, might decide, after careful thought and reading, to focus on the blood imagery in *Macbeth*; the topic "violence in the media" could likewise be narrowed to "the effects of cartoon violence on preschool children." When you begin to focus on a topic, you should check your library's resources to see whether enough work has been done on the subject to permit adequate research and whether the pertinent source materials are readily available.

In general, then, give yourself plenty of time to think through and rethink your choice of a topic. Look for a subject or issue that will continue to engage you throughout the research and writing. Preliminary reading is essential to evaluating topics. Consult some general reference works, such as encyclopedias, as well as books and articles in the areas that you are considering. Before settling on a final topic, make sure you understand the amount and depth of research required and the type of paper expected. If necessary, your instructor can clarify the assignment or help you choose a topic.

1.4. USING THE LIBRARY AND OTHER INFORMATION SOURCES

1.4.1. Introduction to the Library

Since most of your research papers will draw on the published work of experts, you should become thoroughly acquainted with the libraries to which you have access. Many academic libraries offer programs of orientation and instruction to meet the needs of all students, beginning researchers as well as graduate students. Ask about introductory pamphlets or handbooks, guided tours, lectures, and courses on using the library. Be sure to take full advantage of the services your library provides.

Nearly all public and academic libraries have desks staffed by professional reference librarians who can tell you about the available instructional programs and help you locate sources. Consulting a librarian at key points in your research may save you considerable time and effort. Often librarians prepare and hand out informative bulletins that describe library resources and services.

For a comprehensive introduction to the library, consult such books as Jean Key Gates, *Guide to the Use of Libraries and Information Sources* (7th ed., New York: McGraw, 1994), and Thomas Mann, *A Guide to Library Research Methods* (New York: Oxford UP, 1987). Useful for finding reference works in literary studies are James L. Harner,

5

Literary Research Guide (2nd ed., New York: MLA, 1993), and Nancy L. Baker and Nancy Huling, *A Research Guide for Undergraduate Students: English and American Literature* (4th ed., New York: MLA, 1996).

1.4.2. The Central Catalog or Central Information System

a. The Online Central Catalog

A typical academic library has its catalog of holdings online—that is, stored in a computer. You search the catalog by typing information and commands on the keyboard of a computer terminal; the terminal's monitor displays the results of the search. There is as yet no standard system for online catalogs. Systems differ, for example, in how users access information and in what appears on the screen. Online catalog systems also vary considerably in the assistance they provide. Most offer on-screen help. (If your library has a card catalog for part or all of its holdings, see 1.4.2c.)

When using an online catalog, you can locate a book in a number of ways. The most common are by author, by title, and by subject. If you enter the author's full name, the screen displays a list of all the books the library has by that author. Entering the title produces a list of all the books the library has with that title. If you have no author or title in mind, you can enter a subject to produce a list of books about it. (To find out the subjects by which the catalog is organized, see *Library of Congress Subject Headings* or the list your library follows.)

The online catalog can help you locate a book even if you lack some of the information you would ordinarily use for the search. If you know only the beginning of the title—for example, only *Advertising, Competition*, instead of *Advertising, Competition, and Public Policy: A Simulation Study*—you can enter what you know, and the screen will display all titles that begin with those words. If you know only an author's last name, you can obtain a list of all authors with that last name.

The computer-stored catalog also allows you to initiate more sophisticated searches, such as by keyword or subject. You can, for example, call up a list of all works that contain the word "competition" somewhere in their titles. A subject search using "competition" will produce the titles of all works whose subject descriptions include the word. In addition, some online catalogs allow you to limit your search in various ways. You may ask for titles published during a certain range of years (e.g., 1990 to the present) or titles located only in one part of your library (e.g., the main collection). You may be able, too, to limit your search to specific media (e.g., books, serials, archival materials, manuscripts, musical scores, films, video or sound recordings). This feature will let you find out, say, whether your library has any videotapes about mythology or the Civil War.

Some online catalogs permit searching according to Boolean logic (named after the nineteenth-century British mathematician and logician George Boole). In this kind of searching, you customize your search request with the operators *and*, *or*, and *not*. For instance, suppose you are interested in studies on the relation between nutrition and cancer. A search using "nutrition" alone or "cancer" alone would yield a list of all works having anything to do with the subject of the search, and you would have to pick out the items dealing with the two subjects together. In contrast, a Boolean search using "nutrition *and* cancer" excludes all works that are not about both subjects. Likewise, if you would like to see which authors besides Goethe wrote about the Faust theme, you can give a command such as "Faust *not* Goethe." In addition to narrowing lists of titles, Boolean searching is useful for expanding them. For example, if you wish to research solar heating, you might enter a command like "solar *or* sun," which will produce more titles than would just "solar."

When you access a title, the screen shows something like the example in figure 1. The top lines of the screen image contain the author's name and date of birth (Geherin, David, 1943–), the full title of the book (*The American Private Eye: The Image in Fiction*), and complete publication information (the book was published by the Frederick Ungar Publishing Company in New York City in 1985). Then follows the call number, the designation by which the book is shelved in the library. The next section tells you that the library possesses one copy of the work, which is located on an open shelf (the "stack"), and that the copy is in the library and not on loan. The following lines describe the physical characteristics of the book (it has 11 pages of front matter—material before the main text—and 228 pages of text and measures 22 centimeters in height), indicate that it contains an index and a bibliography, show the subject entries under which the book is cataloged, and give the Library of Congress catalog card number, the International Standard Book Numbers for the cloth and paperback versions of the book, and the Research Libraries Information Network identification number.

```
AUTHOR: Geherin, David, 1943-

TITLE: The American Private Eye: The Image in
Fiction

IMPRINT: New York: F. Ungar Pub. Co., 1985

CALL NUMBER: PS374.D4G39 1985

LOCATION            COPY              Status

   Stack             #1           In Library

PHYSICAL FEATURES: xi, 228 p.: 22cm.

NOTES: Includes index * Bibliography: p. 211-
21.

SUBJECTS: Detective and mystery stories,
American--History and criticism * Detectives
in literature * American fiction--20th
century--History and criticism.

LC CARD: 84015251

ISBN: 0804422435 * 0804461848 (pbk.)

RLIN ID NO.: 85-B34382
```

Fig. 1. An entry from an online central catalog.

b. Information Needed for Research and Writing

For the purposes of researching and writing your paper, you normally will not use most of the information that appears in the catalog entry. You need to know the call number, of course, to locate the book in the library (see 1.4.4); and, for your paper's works-cited list, you also need to know the author, title, and relevant publication information (see ch. 4, on information required for compiling the list of works cited). Following is the entry in the works-cited list for the title given above:

```
Geherin, David. The American Private Eye: The Image in
     Fiction. New York: Ungar, 1985.
```

Transcribe this information carefully. Some online catalogs give users the option of printing out or downloading onto computer diskettes the bibliographic data displayed on the screen. This feature not only saves researchers the time and effort of copying the information but also eliminates the possibility of transcription errors. You should, of course, verify the information you derive from the catalog against the source; errors sometimes occur during cataloging.

c. The Card Catalog and Other Catalogs

Your library's central catalog may exist, in whole or in part, in some form besides online. For example, a version of the online catalog may be available on a CD-ROM (a compact disc containing computer data). Sometimes libraries list only recent books online and retain printed files for older books on microfilm or microfiche, in bound volumes, or on cards kept in drawers. If your library keeps a print catalog as well as an online catalog, be sure to consult each, since titles in one may not be in the other.

In some libraries, especially public ones, the central catalog is primarily in the form of cards. Books in a card catalog are usually listed by author, title, and subject. Although author cards, title cards, and subject cards may be arranged alphabetically in a single catalog, most card catalogs are divided into two sections (author and title cards in one, subject cards in the other) or, more rarely, into three sections (one each for authors, titles, and subjects). Finally, your library may have special catalogs for publications other than books, such as serials (newspapers, magazines, scholarly journals) or audiovisual materials.

d. The Central Information System

Increasingly, online catalogs are evolving into central information systems. Such systems ordinarily combine various catalogs (of books, serials, audiovisual materials) and commonly incorporate a number of bibliographic databases, such as *National Newspaper Index*, *Readers' Guide to Periodical Literature*, *Business Periodicals Index*, *Humanities Index*, *Social Sciences Index*, and *General Science Index*, and other kinds of reference works like those discussed in the next section. A central information system might also be part of a network that gives access to the catalogs of a number of libraries. For instance, the system in your school might permit you to search the holdings of local public libraries or of other schools. If your library is part of a network such as the Online Computer Library Center (OCLC) or the Research Libraries Information Network (RLIN), you may be able to locate sources recorded in the catalogs of thousands of other libraries. (See 1.4.5 for comments on using the Internet to search library catalogs.)

Computer technology makes it possible for you to use a central information system even if you are not physically in the library. There may be connections with the library at various locations on your campus. With a personal computer and a modem (a telephone hookup), you might also be able to access information in the system from locations both on and off the campus.

1.4.3. Reference Works

This section provides a brief introduction to the range of general and specialized reference works you should know about. For a more comprehensive listing by subject area, see appendix A.

a. Types of Reference Works

Indexes. Indexes guide you to material in newspapers, magazines, and journals as well as to writings in book collections. *The New York Times Index* lists news stories and feature articles in the *New York Times*. *National Newspaper Index* covers the *Christian Science Monitor*, *Los Angeles Times*, *New York Times*, *Wall Street Journal*, and *Washington Post*. *Canadian News Index* provides citations to the major newspapers in Canada. *Readers' Guide to Periodical Literature* indexes the contents of magazines. *Essay and General Literature Index* lists essays and articles published in books. Most subject areas have their own specialized indexes, such as *Art Index*, *Business Periodicals Index*, *Education Index*, *General Science Index*, *Humanities Index*, *Index to Legal Periodicals*, *The Philosopher's Index*, and *Social Sciences Index*.

Bibliographies. Bibliographies are lists of related books and other materials. Serial bibliographies in specific disciplines include such works as *Bibliography of Agriculture*, *Bibliography and Index of Geology*, and *MLA International Bibliography* (for the field of language and literature). *Bibliographic Index* contains citations to bibliographies that are published as books or pamphlets, as parts of books, or in periodicals. (For sample citations from a bibliography, see 1.4.3c.)

Collections of abstracts. Abstracts are summaries of journal articles and other literature. Collections of abstracts include *Biological Abstracts*, *Chemical Abstracts*, *Historical Abstracts*, *Linguistics and Language Behavior Abstracts*, *Physics Abstracts*, *Psychological Abstracts*, and *Sociological Abstracts*. Summaries of doctoral dissertations are available in *Dissertation Abstracts International*.

Guides to research. There are guides intended to direct you to the most important sources of information and scholarship in the area you are researching. Whereas indexes, bibliographies, and collections of abstracts tend to strive for comprehensiveness and objectivity in presenting information, guides to research are usually selective and evaluative. Some research guides cover entire fields and have titles like *Guide to the Literature of Art History*, *Guide to the Literature of Pharmacy and the Pharmaceutical Sciences*, *Philosophy: A Guide to the Reference Literature*, and *A Guide to English and American Literature*; other guides to research may be devoted to specific subjects (e.g., *The English Romantic Poets: A Review of Research and Criticism*). To learn of guides that might be useful to your project, consult the latest edition of the American Library Association's *Guide to Reference Books* or your instructor or a librarian.

Dictionaries. Dictionaries are alphabetically arranged works that provide information, usually in concise form, about words or topics. Two of the most authoritative dictionaries of words are *Webster's Third New International Dictionary of the English Language* and, especially for the history of a word's meanings and usages, *The Oxford English Dictionary*. Major fields of study have specialized dictionaries, such as *A Dictionary of Botany*, *Computer Dictionary*, *Black's Law Dictionary*, *Dorland's Illustrated Medical Dictionary*, *The New Grove Dictionary of Music and Musicians*, *A Dictionary of Philosophy*, *The Interpreter's Dictionary of the Bible*, and *A Dictionary of the Social Sciences*.

Encyclopedias. Encyclopedias are works, usually alphabetically arranged, that give introductory information about subjects. Popular general encyclopedias are *Academic American Encyclopedia*, *The Encyclopedia Americana*, and *The New Encyclopaedia Britannica*. Specialized encyclopedias include *Encyclopedia of World Art*, *Encyclopedia of Economics*, *The Film Encyclopedia*, *An Encyclopedia of World History*, *The New Princeton Encyclopedia of Poetry and Poetics*, *Encyclopedia of Psychology*, and *McGraw-Hill Encyclopedia of Science and Technology*.

Biographical sources. Information on living persons is collected in *Current Biography*, *The International Who's Who*, and *Who's Who in America*. Sources for persons no longer living are *Dictionary of American Biography* (for the United States), *Dictionary of Canadian Biography*, *Dictionary of National Biography* (for Great Britain), and *Webster's New Biographical Dictionary*.

Yearbooks. Yearbooks present information about individual years in the past. Examples are *The Americana Annual*, *Britannica Book of the Year*, and *The Europa World Year Book*.

Atlases. Atlases are collections of maps. *The National Atlas of the United States of America* is the official atlas of the United States; *The Times Atlas of the World* covers regions and nations of the entire world.

Gazetteers. Gazetteers provide geographic information. Examples are *The Columbia Lippincott Gazetteer of the World* and *Webster's New Geographical Dictionary.*

Statistical data sources. Collections of statistics are often published by governmental agencies. Such works include the following annual publications: *Statistical Abstract of the United States*, issued by the United States Bureau of the Census, and *Statistical Yearbook* and *Demographic Yearbook*, both published by the United Nations.

b. Publication Forms of Reference Works: Print and Electronic

Your library probably has most—and may even have all—of its reference works in print form. There may be a reference room in which many such works are located. General reference books, like dictionaries, encyclopedias, biographical sources, yearbooks, atlases, and gazetteers, may all be shelved together in one place, while specialized reference books may be grouped according to subject area—biology, business, literature, psychology, and so forth. Indexes, bibliographies, and collections of abstracts that are published annually are probably lined up on appropriate shelves, with volumes available for each year. Printed versions of reference works are perhaps easiest for the beginning researcher to use.

Many publishers of reference works issue their publications not only as books but also in electronic form, as databases. The most widely used databases at present are those available either online or on CD-ROM. (See the most recent edition of the two-volume *Gale Directory of Databases*: volume 1 describes thousands of online databases; volume 2 covers CD-ROMs and other portable databases.)

Online databases. An online database is stored in a powerful computer. The researcher accesses information in an online database by means of a computer terminal that usually has a telecommunication link to a service like Dialog, Data-Star, or BRS. Online searching may be available in the library and may also be conducted outside the library through a personal computer and a modem. Searching online databases may entail paying a fee. If your library provides access to online databases, consult a librarian for further information.

CD-ROM databases. A CD-ROM database is stored on a small disc. The researcher uses a standard personal computer to access information in the CD-ROM database; there is no need of an external computer service or a telecommunication connection. The disc is usually preinstalled in a computer in the library and, like print publications, is available for public use free of charge. Some libraries make selected CD-ROM databases available as part of the central information system.

Online and CD-ROM databases have a number of distinct advantages over print versions of reference works. Much more information is generally available in a database. Whereas the print version of an annual bibliography covers research and scholarship for only one year, the electronic version of the work typically covers several years. Let us say, then, that you want to find out what was written on a subject during the last five years. With the print version of an annual bibliography, you would need to consult five volumes—in effect, conduct five searches. With the electronic version, you would need to do just one search.

In addition, information is more current in electronic formats. The printed volume of an annual reference work is published once a year. A CD-ROM version of the same work will usually be updated and issued to subscribers several times a year. An online database is normally an ongoing, continually updated project and is, therefore, the most up-to-date of the three forms.

In using printed sources, moreover, you have to copy the information you wish. Electronic databases allow you to print out or download information. You can transfer downloaded data from your own computer disk to your research paper without the risk of introducing errors through copying by hand. Since database compilers sometimes make errors, however, you need to verify the information derived from a database against the source.

Most important of all, you can search electronic versions of a reference work in many more ways than you can the printed version.

c. Searching a Reference Database

Every field of study has standard reference works. One such work is the *MLA International Bibliography*. The printed library edition of this work is published annually as two clothbound books. The first contains listings in five areas: literature in English, literature in other languages, linguistics, general literature and related topics, and folklore. The second book provides a subject index to the first.

Like other such reference works, the *MLA International Bibliography* is also available online and on CD-ROM. The following description suggests ways in which you might search this bibliography using the CD-ROM version available, as of this writing, from SilverPlatter Information, Inc. The SilverPlatter disc contains all citations published in annual volumes of the bibliography from 1981 to the present. Therefore, while an annual print volume of the *MLA International Bibliography* lists around fifty thousand titles, the CD-ROM version offers information on hundreds of thousands of titles.

The standard ways of searching this database and similar ones are through author, title, and subject. For example, if you want to know what writings by Toni Morrison or Deborah Tannen have been published in the fields covered by this bibliography, all you need do is enter the author's name. Or if you know only the title of a work—like "Black Matter(s)" or *Talking Voices*—you can call forth complete bibliographic information about it from the database. If you remember only part of the title (e.g., the word "city"), you can request a listing of all titles containing that term.

In addition, since every work added to this bibliography is accompanied by at least one descriptor, or index term, you can also search the database by subject. Thus, if you ask for studies that discuss, for instance, "detective fiction," the system will search through its files and present you with all titles that have "detective fiction" as a descriptor.

Databases like the SilverPlatter CD-ROM version of the *MLA International Bibliography* also permit you to expand or narrow your searches usefully. While you are trying to decide on a topic, you may want to do expanded searches to get a broad sense of possibilities. The index and thesaurus of this database can be particularly helpful when you are developing a suitable research topic. If you have a vague notion to write on detective fiction, you can take a look at the bibliography's index to find related subjects. Here you will encounter not only "detective fiction" but also "detective drama," "detective film," "detective magazines," "detective novel," and "detective story," among others. The thesaurus, a more extensive and detailed list, yields other terms that might suggest a specific topic, such as "American detective fiction," "English detective novel," "French detective," "hard-boiled detective fiction," and "woman detective."

Also useful for expanded searches is this database's truncation feature. By truncating a word root or term with an asterisk, you can retrieve all variants of it. If you wish, for example, to write a paper on feminism but cannot decide what aspect to focus on, you can enter as a search term "femini*" and receive records on, among others, "feminine," "femininity," "feminist literary theory and criticism," "feminist movement," and "feminist writers." Finally, you can use the Boolean operator *or* to expand your search. Entering "Arthur Conan Doyle *or* Sherlock Holmes" will furnish more titles than either "Arthur Conan Doyle" or "Sherlock Holmes" by itself would.

After you have selected a topic for your paper, you will probably want to perform more restricted searches. For instance, if you have narrowed your topic from "detective fiction" to "the English detective novel," consulting the latter term in this database's index or thesaurus will help you locate only the titles specifically relevant to your project. The Boolean operators *not* and *and* also limit the field of titles accessed. If you are interested in finding studies on versions of the story of Othello other than Shakespeare's, enter "Othello *not* Shakespeare." Or if you would like to identify studies that compare Shakespeare's play with *Otello*, Giuseppe Verdi's operatic adaptation of it, keying "Othello *and* Otello" rather than just "Othello" will result in a shorter, more focused list of sources.

The *MLA International Bibliography* in its SilverPlatter CD-ROM version offers other ways to narrow searches. You can retrieve titles from a single publication source, such as articles on *Othello* that have appeared in *Shakespeare Quarterly* since 1981. The database also allows you to limit your search according to language of publication (e.g., Japanese, Spanish), publication type (e.g., book, journal article), and publication year. You can obtain a list, for example, of books on Goethe's *Faust* that were written in German and published in 1988 or later.

This brief discussion far from exhausts the searching possibilities provided by this database and similar ones. SilverPlatter supplies a typical user's manual that extensively describes the features of the database as well as the codes and procedures for accessing information. Typically, too, the database allows you to print out and download information. It also gives you a choice of how to view, print, or download data. You may prefer to select the complete record, which includes title, author, source, international standard numbers, language of publication, publication type, publication year, descriptors, update code, and accession number (see fig. 2). Or you can select a shortened citation that gives only title, author, source, and accession number (see fig. 3).

The advantage of the short form is that it saves time and space while providing the information necessary both for locating the material and for creating an entry for your works-cited list. You can easily convert the bibliographic data in figure 3 to MLA documentation style (see ch. 4):

Tannen, Deborah. "Repetition in Conversation: Toward a
    Poetics of Talk." <u>Language</u> 63 (1987): 574-605.

```
TI: Repetition in Conversation: Toward a
Poetics of Talk

AU: Tannen,-Deborah

SO: Language:-Journal-of-the-Linguistic-
Society-of-America, Pittsburgh, PA
(Language). 1987 Sept., 63:3, 574-605.

IS: ISSN 0023-8260

LA: English

PT: journal-article

PY: 1987

DE: English-language-Modern; pragmatics-;
repetition-; in conversation-; relationship
to poetic-language

UD: 8701

AN: 87-3-6464
```

Fig. 2. A complete citation from a bibliographic database.

```
TI: Repetition in Conversation: Toward a
Poetics of Talk

AU: Tannen,-Deborah

SO: Language:-Journal-of-the-Linguistic-
Society-of-America, Pittsburgh, PA
(Language). 1987 Sept., 63:3, 574-605.

AN: 87-3-6464
```

Fig. 3. A shortened citation from a bibliographic database.

1.4.4. Location of Library Materials

The call numbers in your library probably follow one of two systems of classification: the Dewey decimal system or the Library of Congress system. Learning your library's system will help you not only to find books but also to know their contents from their call numbers.

The Dewey decimal system classifies books under ten major headings:

000	General works
100	Philosophy and psychology
200	Religion
300	Social sciences
400	Language
500	Natural sciences and mathematics
600	Technology and applied sciences
700	Fine arts
800	Literature
900	Geography and history

The Library of Congress system divides books into twenty major groups:

A	General works
B	Philosophy, psychology, and religion
C	General history
D	World history
E–F	American history
G	Geography and anthropology
H	Social sciences
J	Political science
K	Law
L	Education
M	Music
N	Fine arts
P	Language and literature
Q	Science
R	Medicine
S	Agriculture
T	Technology
U	Military science
V	Naval science
Z	Bibliography and library science

Library books are kept either on open shelves, to which the public has direct access, or in closed stacks. To obtain a book in closed stacks, you usually have to present a call slip to a library staff member, who will locate the book for you. Regardless of the classification system used, all libraries keep some books separate from the main collection. If a book is kept in a special area, the central catalog should indicate the location. For example, the word *Reserved* in a catalog entry indicates a book required in a course and stored in a special section, at the instructor's request, so that the volume stays available for students in the course. A book shelved in the reference section, designated by *R* or *Ref*, must also remain in the library. Some libraries have additional special collections, such as rare books or government documents, that are kept separate from the main collection.

Libraries also commonly set aside areas for other types of materials—current periodicals, pamphlets, clippings, and nonprint materials, like pictures, maps, films, slides, and audio and video recordings. Consult the library directory or a librarian for locations.

1.4.5. Other Library Resources and Services

Microforms—greatly reduced photographic copies of printed matter—are also usually kept in a special section of the library. Common types of microforms are microfilm, microfiche, and microcard. Libraries use microforms to store such materials as back copies of periodicals (newspapers, magazines, scholarly journals), the card catalog for older books not yet on the central online catalog, and rare books. To use microforms, you need a special magnifying reader. Library staff members can assist you in locating microform materials and operating the readers.

Most libraries have agreements with other libraries that permit the quick and inexpensive exchange of research materials regionally, statewide, or nationally. If your library does not have the source you need, ask whether the item can be obtained through an interlibrary loan. To find out which libraries own your title, you can consult such databases as the Online Computer Library Center (OCLC) or the Research Libraries Information Network (RLIN). Or you can consult print sources like *The National Union Catalog* or, if you need a periodical, *Union List of Serials* and *New Serial Titles*.

Photocopying machines are common in libraries. Some schools have computer centers located in the library as well. In such centers, students can use personal computers linked to high-quality printers and offering software for such tasks as word processing, financial analysis, database management, desktop publishing, drawing, and drafting. Some centers even have the equipment for multimedia production, involving photography, audio, and video.

Other computer terminals are commonly located at various sites in the library. In contrast to the personal computers furnished for individual use, these terminals give direct access to the central catalog and often other databases, too, whether online or on CD-ROM. Your library may also provide a link to computer services, like Dialog, or to information networks, such as the Internet.

A vast international computer network, the Internet allows users to communicate electronically with individuals and groups, to search the files of other cooperating computers, and to transfer files between computers. Through the Internet, a researcher can search and retrieve files from thousands of library catalogs and other databases. A number of reference and text databases are available on the Internet. Among reference sources are dictionaries; thesauri; compilations of famous quotations; collections of facts and statistics, such as United States census data; summaries of news stories; and material from the Educational Resources Information Center (ERIC), the bibliographic database for education. Electronic texts on the Internet include historical documents (e.g., Declaration of Independence, United States Constitution, Gettysburg Address), literary works (e.g., texts by Shakespeare, Emily Brontë, Frederick Douglass), and religious works (e.g., King James Bible, Koran, Torah).

Internet users may also derive articles and other information from electronic journals and newsletters and from the many electronic bulletin boards and discussion lists. Examples of electronic journals and newsletters are the *Bryn Mawr Classical Review*, *Postmodern Culture*, *Psycoloquy*, *Clionet: An Electronic Journal of History*, and the *Electronic Hebrew Users Newsletter* (or *E-HUG*); electronic bulletin boards and discussion lists cover almost every area of interest. If your library allows access to the Internet, consult a librarian for further information. If you wish to learn more about the Internet, see the most recent editions of such works as Brendan P. Kehoe, *Zen and the Art of the Internet: A Beginner's Guide* (Englewood Cliffs: Prentice); Ed Krol, *The Whole Internet: User's Guide and Catalog* (Sebastopol: O'Reilly); Richard J. Smith and Mark Gibbs, *Navigating the Internet* (Indianapolis: Sams); and Harley Hahn and Rick Stout, *The Internet Complete Reference* (Berkeley: Osborne-McGraw).

19

Obviously, the more you know about the library and the materials and services it provides, the more successful you will be in gathering information and ideas for your research paper.

1.5. COMPILING A WORKING BIBLIOGRAPHY

As you discover where to look for information and opinions on your topic, you will want to keep a list of books, articles, and other sources that seem promising for your paper. Such a record is called a working bibliography. Your preliminary reading will probably provide the first titles for this list. Other titles will emerge when you consult the library catalog, as well as indexes, bibliographies, and other reference works mentioned in the preceding section. If you read carefully through the bibliography and notes of each book and article you consult, more often than not you will discover additional important sources. Your working bibliography will frequently change during your research as you add new titles and eliminate those that do not prove useful and as you explore and emphasize some aspects of your subject in preference to others. The working bibliography will eventually evolve into the list of works cited that appears at the end of the research paper.

Many instructors recommend that students use index cards to compile the working bibliography. Writing each source on a separate index card allows greater flexibility than does listing sources on a sheet of paper. For example, as you research, you can arrange and rearrange sources on cards however you wish (e.g., in alphabetical order, in chronological order by date of publication, in order of relevance to your topic); index cards also permit you to divide sources into groups (e.g., those already consulted and those not yet consulted, those most useful and those less so).

You can achieve similar results with a personal computer. Create a computer file for the working bibliography, and enter titles as you proceed with your research. Whenever you wish to add new works to the list, to remove works you no longer think helpful, or to correct entries already stored, you retrieve the file, make the changes, and save the revised file for future use. As with index cards, you will be able to arrange, rearrange, and group sources. At any point, you can print the file to review it or to use it for research.

When you add sources to your working bibliography, be sure you have all the publication information needed for the works-cited list. The information to be recorded depends on the kind of source used.

BOOK (see 4.6)

1. Author's full name (last name first)
2. Full title (including any subtitle)
3. Editor or translator (if there is one)
4. Edition (if the book is a second or later edition)
5. Number of the volume and the total number of volumes (if the book is a multivolume work)
6. Series name (if the book is part of a series)
7. City of publication (note only the first city if several are listed)
8. Publisher
9. Year of publication

Budden, Julian. <u>The Operas of Verdi</u>. Rev. ed. 3 vols.

    Oxford: Clarendon, 1992.

ARTICLE IN A SCHOLARLY JOURNAL (see 4.7.1–4)

1. Author's name
2. Title of the article
3. Title of the journal
4. Volume number (and issue number, if needed—see 4.7.2)
5. Year of publication
6. Inclusive page numbers of the article (i.e., the number of the page on which the article begins, a hyphen, and the number of the page on which the article ends)

Vartanov, Anri. "Television as Spectacle and Myth."

    <u>Journal of Communication</u> 41 (1991): 162-71.

NEWSPAPER OR MAGAZINE ARTICLE (see 4.7.5–6)

1. Author's name
2. Title of the article
3. Title of the periodical
4. Date of publication
5. Inclusive page numbers of the article or the initial page number followed by a plus sign, as appropriate

Shea, Christopher. "The Limits of Free Speech." <u>Chronicle</u>

    <u>of Higher Education</u> 1 Dec. 1993: A37-38.

(See ch. 4 for complete information on compiling the works-cited list
of the research paper.)

In addition to keeping a record of the data you will need for the
works-cited list, note for each title in the working bibliography exactly
where you found the bibliographic information, in case you need to
recheck the information or to borrow the work from another library
(before accepting a request for an interlibrary loan, a library often
requires a printed or electronic citation of the requested work). Always
also record the call number or any other identifying information
needed to locate the work. The sample bibliography card in figure 4
contains not only all the information needed for the final bibliography
(author's name, full title, and relevant publication information) but
also information useful for research: the origin of the reference (1985
MLA International Bibliography, vol. 1, item 7414) and the call number (PS 374.D4.G39). Here is how the entry might look in a working
bibliography maintained in a computer file:

```
Geherin, David. The American Private Eye: The Image in
      Fiction. New York: Ungar, 1985. ['85 MLA Bib. 1:
      7414; PS 374.D4.G39]
```

You will delete reference origins and call numbers when you convert
your working bibliography into the list of works cited.

Once you have the source work in hand, carefully verify the publication facts against your records—even if you printed out or downloaded

Fig. 4. A card in a researcher's working bibliography.

the data. Add any missing information that you will need for the works-cited list, and correct any part of your records that does not match the data obtained from the work. For a book, check the author's name, title, subtitle (if any), edition (if relevant), editor or translator (if there is one), volume number and number of volumes, series name (if the book is part of a series), city of publication, publisher, and year of publication. (This information normally appears on the title and copyright pages of the book.) For an article in a periodical, check the author's name, title of the article, title of the periodical, date of publication, and, as appropriate, inclusive page numbers or initial page number. If the periodical is a scholarly journal, check the volume number (and, if needed, issue number) as well. (Volume numbers and dates of publication normally appear on the title pages of journals.) Recording and verifying all the information about your sources when you first consult them will spare you many last-minute problems and frustrations.

Eventually, you will transform your working bibliography into a works-cited list. If your working bibliography is composed of index cards, you will need to type up entries for the works you cite, putting each entry in correct form, incorporating all the appropriate bibliographic information, and listing the items in alphabetical order by authors' last names. If your working bibliography is in a computer file, edit the entries to remove unnecessary information (e.g., origin of reference, call number), and arrange them alphabetically by author. When you have finished the final draft of your paper, transfer the edited bibliography file to the end of the file containing the paper.

There is computer software for preparing works-cited lists. Several programs can arrange entries in alphabetical order; some programs automatically put bibliographic information into MLA style. Since bibliography files are essential to researching and writing the paper, be certain to save these files on your working disk and to keep copies of them not only on paper but also on a backup disk.

If compiled with care and attention, the working bibliography will be invaluable to you throughout the preparation of your paper. It will, on the one hand, function as an efficient tool for finding and acquiring information and ideas and, on the other, provide all the data you will need for your list of works cited.

1.6. TAKING NOTES

Students writing their first research papers often find it difficult to evaluate sources. Not all sources are equally reliable or of equal quality. You should not assume that something is truthful or trustworthy just because it is published. Some material may be based on incorrect or outdated information, on poor logic, or on narrow opinions held by the author. Weigh what you read against your own knowledge and intelligence as well as against other treatments of the subject. Consult *Book Review Index* and *Book Review Digest* to see how a book was received by experts in the field that the work covers. If you are working with historical documents or literary texts that exist in various versions, make certain you use reliable editions. For example, versions of Shakespeare's plays published during his lifetime and shortly after his death sometimes differ drastically. The task of a modern scholarly editor is to compare, analyze, and evaluate these variations and produce an edition that is as historically authoritative as possible. Therefore, if you want to use, say, an electronic text of a Shakespeare play, look for one that, at a minimum, clearly states who the editor of the text is and when the edition was published. Ask your instructor for advice if you have any doubts about the reliability of a source.

Once you determine that material is reliable and useful, you will want to take notes on it. Although everyone agrees that note-taking is essential to research, probably no two researchers use exactly the same methods. Some take notes on a set of index cards different from those used for the working bibliography; others write in notebooks, beginning each entry on a fresh page; still others favor letter-size or legal-size sheets clipped together according to one system or another. Using a word processor might save you time and should improve the accuracy with which you transcribe material, including quotations, from your sources into the text of your paper. Whatever your preference, take down first the author's full name and the complete title of the source—enough information to enable you to locate the source easily in your working bibliography.

There are, generally speaking, three methods of note-taking: summary, paraphrase, and quotation. Summarize if you want to record only the general idea of large amounts of material. If you require detailed notes on specific sentences and passages but do not need the exact wording, you may wish to paraphrase—that is, to restate the material in your own words. But when you believe that some sentence or passage in its original wording might make an effective addition to your paper, transcribe that material exactly as it appears, word for word, comma for comma. Whenever you quote verbatim from a work, be sure to use quotation marks scrupulously in your notes to distinguish the quotation from summary and paraphrase. Keep an accurate record of the page numbers of all material you summarize, paraphrase, or quote. When a quotation continues to another page, carefully note where the page break occurs, since only a portion of what you transcribe may find its way into your paper.

Using a word processor to store notes is handy, but while doing research, you may find yourself in a situation—for example, working in the library—where you do not have access to a computer. Then you will need to write your notes by hand and transfer them into your computer later.

Strategies of storing and retrieving notes with a computer vary. For a short paper for which you have taken few notes, you may place all notes in a single file and draw material from it whenever you want. For a longer paper that makes use of numerous sources, you may create a new file for each source. (See 1.9 for advice on using note files during writing.)

Another strategy is to write summaries and paraphrases of the source by hand and to enter into computer files only quotations, which you can electronically copy into the text of your paper as you write. At the least, this strategy will eliminate the time and effort and, more important, the possibility of error involved in transcribing quoted words more than once. Of course, when you download quotations from a database to your computer disk, you never transcribe them at all. Finally, since note files are essential to your paper, be certain to save them on your working disk and to keep copies of them both on paper and on a backup disk.

In taking notes, seek to steer a middle course between recording too much and recording too little. In other words, try to be both thorough and concise. Above all, strive for accuracy, not only in copying words for direct quotation but also in summarizing and paraphrasing authors' ideas. Careful note-taking will help you avoid the problem of plagiarism.

1.7. PLAGIARISM

You probably have heard of lawsuits about plagiarism in the publishing and recording industries. You may also have had classroom discussions about academic plagiarism. Derived from the Latin word *plagiarius* ("kidnapper"), *plagiarism* refers to a form of cheating that has been defined as "the false assumption of authorship: the wrongful act of taking the product of another person's mind, and presenting it as one's own" (Alexander Lindey, *Plagiarism and Originality* [New York: Harper, 1952] 2). To use another person's ideas or expressions in your writing without acknowledging the source is to plagiarize. Plagiarism, then, constitutes intellectual theft and often carries severe penalties, ranging from failure in a course to expulsion from school.

Plagiarism in student writing is often unintentional, as when an elementary school pupil, assigned to do a report on a certain topic, goes home and copies down, word for word, everything on the subject in an encyclopedia. Unfortunately, some students continue to use such "research methods" in high school and even in college without realizing that these practices constitute plagiarism. At all times during research and writing, guard against the possibility of inadvertent plagiarism by keeping careful notes that distinguish between your musings and thoughts and the material you gather from others. A writer who fails to give appropriate acknowledgment when repeating another's wording or particularly apt term, paraphrasing another's argument, or presenting another's line of thinking is guilty of plagiarism. You may certainly use other persons' words and thoughts in your research paper, but the borrowed material must not appear to be your creation. Suppose, for example, that you want to use the material in the following passage, which appears on page 625 of an essay by Wendy Martin in the book *Columbia Literary History of the United States*.

> Some of Dickinson's most powerful poems express her firmly held conviction that life cannot be fully comprehended without an understanding of death.

If you write the following sentence without any documentation, you commit plagiarism.

```
Emily Dickinson strongly believed that we cannot
understand life fully unless we also comprehend death.
```

But you may present the material if you cite your source.

As Wendy Martin has suggested, Emily Dickinson strongly
believed that we cannot understand life fully unless we
also comprehend death (625).

The source is indicated, in accordance with MLA style, by the name
of the author and by a page reference in parentheses. The name refers
the reader to the corresponding entry in the works-cited list, which
appears at the end of the paper.

Martin, Wendy. "Emily Dickinson." <u>Columbia Literary</u>
<u>History of the United States</u>. Emory Elliott, gen.
ed. New York: Columbia UP, 1988. 609-26.

Two more examples follow:

ORIGINAL SOURCE

Everyone uses the word *language* and everybody these days talks
about *culture.* . . . "Languaculture" is a reminder, I hope, of the
necessary connection between its two parts. . . . (Michael Agar,
Language Shock: Understanding the Culture of Conversation
[New York: Morrow, 1994] 60)

PLAGIARISM

At the intersection of language and culture lies a
concept that we might call "languaculture."

ORIGINAL SOURCE

Humanity faces a quantum leap forward. It faces the deepest
social upheaval and creative restructuring of all time. Without
clearly recognizing it, we are engaged in building a remarkable
civilization from the ground up. This is the meaning of the
Third Wave.

Until now the human race has undergone two great waves of
change, each one largely obliterating earlier cultures or civiliza-
tions and replacing them with ways of life inconceivable to those
who came before. The First Wave of change—the agricultural revolution—took thousands of years to play itself out. The Second
Wave—the rise of industrial civilization—took a mere hundred
years. Today history is even more accelerative, and it is likely that
the Third Wave will sweep across history and complete itself in a

few decades. (Alvin Toffler, *The Third Wave* [1980; New York: Bantam, 1981] 10)

PLAGIARISM

```
There have been two revolutionary periods of change in
history: the agricultural revolution and the industrial
revolution. The agricultural revolution determined the
course of history for thousands of years; the industrial
civilization lasted about a century. We are now on the
threshold of a new period of revolutionary change, but
this one may last for only a few decades.
```

In the first example, the student borrowed a specific term ("langua-culture") without acknowledgment; in the second example, the student presented another's line of thinking without giving credit. The students could have avoided the charge of plagiarism by rewording slightly and inserting appropriate parenthetical documentation.

```
At the intersection of language and culture lies a
concept that Michael Agar has called "languaculture"
(60).
```

```
According to Alvin Toffler, there have been two
revolutionary periods of change in history: the
agricultural revolution and the industrial revolution.
The agricultural revolution determined the course of
history for thousands of years; the industrial
civilization lasted about a century. We are now on the
threshold of a new period of revolutionary change, but
this one may last for only a few decades (10).
```

In each revision, the author's name refers the reader to the full description of the work in the works-cited list at the end of the paper, and the parenthetical documentation identifies the location of the borrowed material in the work.

```
Agar, Michael. Language Shock: Understanding the Culture
of Conversation. New York: Morrow, 1994.
```

Toffler, Alvin. <u>The Third Wave</u>. 1980. New York:

Bantam, 1981.

In writing your research paper, then, you must document everything that you borrow—not only direct quotations and paraphrases but also information and ideas. Of course, common sense as well as ethics should determine what you document. For example, you rarely need to give sources for familiar proverbs ("You can't judge a book by its cover"), well-known quotations ("We shall overcome"), or common knowledge ("George Washington was the first president of the United States"). But you must indicate the source of any appropriated material that readers might otherwise mistake for your own. If you have any doubt about whether or not you are committing plagiarism, cite your source or sources.

Finally, two issues related to plagiarism do not deal with outside sources. The first arises when a student submits in a course a paper done for a previous course. Although obviously not the same as stealing someone else's ideas, this practice nonetheless qualifies as a kind of self-plagiarism and constitutes another form of cheating. If you want to rework a paper that you prepared for another course, ask your current instructor for permission to do so.

The other issue concerns collaborative work, such as a group project you carry out with other students. Joint participation in research and writing is common and, in fact, encouraged in many courses and in many professions, and it does not constitute plagiarism provided that credit is given for all contributions. One way to give credit, if roles were clearly demarcated or were unequal, is to state exactly who did what. Another way, especially if roles and contributions were merged and truly shared, is to acknowledge all concerned equally. Ask your instructor for advice if you are not certain how to acknowledge collaboration.

1.8. OUTLINING

1.8.1. Working Outline

Some writers like to work from an outline; others do not. For research papers, outlining can be a particularly useful intermediate activity between research and writing. In fact, many instructors require each student to hand in an outline with the final draft. Others require a draft outline earlier, asking the student to submit not only a topic for the paper but also a tentative list of subtopics for research. They then suggest that this working outline be continually revised—items dropped, added, modified—as the research progresses.

You may find a series of outlines valuable whether or not your instructor requires them, especially if you are a beginning writer of research papers. An outline will help you to get an overview of your paper and, perhaps more important, to figure out how each section of the paper relates to the others. Thus, developing an outline can help you to see the logical progression of your argument.

A word processor is useful for preparing a working outline, which may well pass through many and sometimes quite different versions. Word-processing programs commonly have an outlining feature that offers several formats with automatic numbering and lettering. It is probably best to create a different computer file for each version of an outline. For example, assign the first version a label like "outline1," and save the file when it is finished. When you are ready to revise the outline, create a new file for the second version ("outline2"), copy the first-draft file into the new file, and revise. If you become dissatisfied with the way the second version or a subsequent one is progressing, you can discard it, return to an earlier draft, which is stored untouched on the disk, and begin revising in another direction. Printing out each new version will let you compare it more easily with other versions.

A working outline will make it easier for you to keep track of all important aspects of your subject and to focus your research on relevant topics. Continual revision of the working outline, moreover, will encourage you to change your thinking and your approach as new information modifies your understanding of the subject.

1.8.2. Thesis Statement

As you get closer to writing, you can begin to shape the information you have at hand into a unified, coherent whole by framing a thesis statement for your paper: a single sentence that formulates both your topic and your point of view. In a sense, the thesis statement is your answer to the central question or problem you have raised. Writing this statement will enable you to see where you are heading and to remain on a productive path as you plan and write. Try out different possibilities until you find a statement that seems right for your purpose. Moreover, since the experience of writing may well alter your original plans, do not hesitate to revise the thesis statement as you write the paper. A word processor, through its storage and retrieval capabilities, can help you build efficiently on previous drafts of a thesis statement.

Two factors are important to the shaping of a thesis statement—your purpose and your audience:

- What purpose will you try to achieve in the paper? Do you want to describe something, explain something, argue for a certain point of view, or persuade your reader to think or do something?
- What audience are you writing for? Is your reader a specialist on the subject? someone likely to agree or disagree with you? someone likely to be interested or uninterested in the subject?

The answers to these questions should to a large extent give your research the appropriate slant or point of view not just in your thesis statement but also in the final outline and the paper itself.

Many instructors require students to submit thesis statements for approval some two or three weeks before the papers are due. If you have difficulty writing one, talk with your instructor about the research you have done and about what you want to say; given this information, your instructor can probably help you frame an appropriate thesis statement.

The following sample is a thesis statement for section 1.4 of this book:

Students who wish to write successful research papers must know as much as possible about the resources and services of the library, such as its central catalog or central information system, the reference works in the collection, and the location of materials.

1.8.3. Final Outline

After you have a satisfactory thesis statement, you can transform your working outline into a final one. This step will help you organize your ideas and the accumulated research into a logical, fluent, and effective paper. Again, many instructors request that final outlines be submitted with papers.

Start by carefully reviewing all your notes to see how strongly they will support the various points in the working outline. Next, read over your working outline *critically* and delete everything that is irrelevant to the thesis statement or that might weaken your argument.

Eliminating material may be painful since you might have a natural desire to use everything you have collected and to impress your readers (especially teacher readers) with all the work you have done and with all you now know on the subject. But you should resist these temptations, for the inclusion of irrelevant or repetitive material will detract from the effectiveness of your paper. Keep your thesis statement and your audience in mind. Include only the ideas and information that will help you accomplish what you set out to do and that will lead your readers to care about your investigation, your presentation, and your conclusions.

As you continue to read, reread, and think about the ideas and information you have decided to use, you will begin to see new connections between items, and patterns of organization will suggest themselves. Bring related material together under general headings, and arrange these sections so that one logically connects with another. Then order the subjects under each heading so that they, too, proceed logically. Finally, plan an effective introduction and a conclusion appropriate to the sequence you have worked out.

Common organizing principles are chronology (useful for historical discussions—e.g., how the Mexican War developed); cause and effect (e.g., what consequences a scientific discovery will have); process (e.g., how a politician got elected); and logic, deductive or inductive. A deductive line of argument moves from the general to the specific (e.g., from the problem of violence in the United States to violence involving handguns), and an inductive one moves from the specific to the general (e.g., from violence involving handguns to the problem of violence in the United States).

As you choose an organizational plan, keep in mind the method or methods you will use in developing your paper. For example, do you plan to define, classify, or analyze something? to use descriptive details or give examples? to compare or contrast one thing with another? to argue for a certain point of view? The procedures you intend to adopt will influence the way you arrange your material, and they should be evident in your outline.

It is also a good idea to indicate in the outline, specifically and precisely, the quotations and reference sources you will use. All this planning will take a good deal of time and thought, and you may well make several preliminary outlines before arriving at the one you will follow. But the time and thought will be well spent. The more planning you do, the easier and more efficient the writing will be.

If the final outline is only for your use, its form has little importance. If it is to be submitted, your instructor will probably discuss the
various forms of outline—for example, the topic outline (which uses
only short phrases throughout) and the sentence outline—and tell you
which to use. Whatever the form, maintain it consistently.

The descending parts of an outline are normally labeled in the following order:

I.
   A.
      1.
         a.
           (1)
              (a)
              (b)
           (2)
         b.
      2.
   B.
II.

Logic requires that there be a *II* to complement a *I*, a *B* to complement
an *A*, and so forth.

The following sample is a topic outline of section 1.4 of this book:

Using the Library and Other Information Sources

I. Introduction to the library
   A. Programs of orientation and instruction
      1. Pamphlets, handbooks, other materials distributed by the
         library
      2. Orientation tours, lectures, courses
   B. Books about the library (examples: Gates, Mann, Harner, Baker
      and Huling)
II. The central catalog or central information system
   A. The online central catalog
      1. Definition and description
      2. Searching the online catalog
         a. Searching by author, title, subject, keywords
         b. Limiting the search
         c. Using Boolean logic
      3. Information accessed from the online catalog
   B. Information needed for research and writing

C. The card catalog and other catalogs
D. The central information system
III. Reference works
   A. Types of reference works
      1. Indexes
      2. Bibliographies
      3. Collections of abstracts
      4. Guides to research
      5. Dictionaries
      6. Encyclopedias
      7. Biographical sources
      8. Yearbooks
      9. Atlases
     10. Gazetteers
     11. Statistical data sources
   B. Publication forms of reference works: print and electronic
   C. Searching a reference database (example: *MLA International Bibliography*)
IV. Location of library materials
   A. Classification systems
      1. Dewey decimal system
      2. Library of Congress system
   B. Main collection (open shelves, closed stacks)
   C. Special sections (reserved books; reference works; special collections; periodicals, nonprint materials, etc.)
V. Other library resources and services
   A. Microforms: microfilm, microfiche, microcard
   B. Interlibrary loans
   C. Photocopying
   D. Computer centers
   E. Access to databases and computer services
   F. Access to information networks (e.g., Internet)
Conclusion—knowledge of the library and successful research papers

If you stored your notes in your computer, a helpful intermediate activity between outlining and writing is to incorporate your notes into your outline. Using this strategy, you should create a separate file for each major topic of your outline and shift relevant material, in appropriate order, from the note files into the various topic files. Then, as you write, you can call up the topic files one by one and blend material from them into the text of the paper. Be sure to save and to back up your outline files.

1.9. WRITING DRAFTS

Do not expect the first draft of your paper to be the finished product. The successful research paper is usually the culmination of a series of drafts. Habits, capacities, and practices of writers differ widely. Some individuals write slowly and come close to a final draft the first time through. Others prefer to work in stages and expect to undertake several drafts. In any case, review and rewriting are always necessary. Plan ahead and leave plenty of time for revision.

You might start by trying to set down all your ideas in the order in which you want them to appear. Do not be too concerned if the writing in the first draft is hasty and fairly rough. Attempt to stay focused by following your outline closely. Revise the outline, of course, whenever new ideas occur to you and it no longer works. After you complete a rough draft, read it over and try to refine it.

In revising, you may add, eliminate, and rearrange material. If a section in the first draft seems unclear or sketchy, you may have to expand it by writing another sentence or two or even a new paragraph. Similarly, to improve the fluency and coherence of the paper, you may need to add transitions between sentences or paragraphs or to define connections or contrasts. Delete any material that is irrelevant, unimportant, repetitive, or dull and dispensable. If the presentation of ideas seems illogical or confusing, you may find that you can clarify it by rearranging phrases, clauses, sentences, or paragraphs.

In later drafts, you should concern yourself with the more mechanical kinds of revision. For example, strive for more precise and economical wording. Try, in addition, to vary your sentence patterns as well as your choice of words. Finally, correct all technical errors, using a standard writing guide to check punctuation, grammar, and usage and consulting a standard dictionary for the spelling and meaning of words. Your last draft, carefully proofread and corrected, is the text of your research paper.

If you do not own a computer, see whether your school has personal computers available for student use. With a word processor, you can store a first draft—or just a portion of one—and later retrieve and revise it. If you create a different file for each draft, you can return to a preceding draft whenever you wish.

Word processing makes it easy to insert words into, or delete words from, your text and to shift a word or a block of words from one part of the text to another. Moreover, you can produce a printed version of a revision without having to retype the whole new draft. A word processor can also center titles, format pages, and relieve you of other mechanical tasks. For example, the global revision feature of word processing permits you to search for and automatically change text. Thus, if you realize you misspelled the same word several times in your draft, you can correct all the misspellings with a single command.

Word processors similarly allow for more efficient transitions between the various activities related to the research paper. After developing an outline, for instance, you can copy it into a new file, where the outline can serve as the basis for your writing of the text. Or if you created a file of notes for each major topic in your outline (see 1.8.3), you can copy into the text file each topic file in sequence as you write. If your paper will be short and you have taken few notes, you may choose to copy the entire note file into the text file. Using this approach, you can scroll up and down the file and transfer what you want into the text of the paper. If your paper will be longer and you have created a separate file for each of numerous sources, you can readily transfer material (e.g., an effective quotation) from the note files to the text file. You might find it easier to print out all your notes before writing and to decide in advance which portions you want to use in the paper. In this way, when you retrieve note files, you will know exactly what parts you are seeking. Another way to proceed is to use split screens or multiple windows to read the note files as you write the paper. Last, when you have completed your final draft, you can simply add the file containing the works-cited list to the end of the paper. With practice and planning, then, as you write your paper you can use a word processor strategically to draw on outline, note, and bibliography files that you created earlier in the project.

Word processing has certain limitations, however. Since no more than a fixed number of lines of text are visible on a computer screen, you may find it difficult to get a sense of your whole project. Some writers like to print out text regularly to see better how the writing is developing from paragraph to paragraph and from page to page. Use spelling and usage checkers cautiously, for they are only as effective as the dictionaries they contain. On the one hand, a spelling checker will call your attention to words that are correctly spelled if they are not in its dictionary. On the other, it will not point out misspellings that match words in the dictionary—for example, *their* used for *there* or *its* for *it's*.

Finally, in working on a computer file, you run the risk of losing it, through either a technical mistake or equipment failure. Be sure to save your work frequently (after writing a page or so), not just when you finish with it or leave the computer. It is also a good idea to keep a paper copy of text you write and to create a backup disk in case something happens to the disk you are using to prepare the paper. Most important of all, leave yourself ample time to cope with any mechanical problems that may arise.

1.10. LANGUAGE AND STYLE

Effective writing depends as much on clarity and readability as on content. The organization and development of your ideas, the unity and coherence of your presentation, and your command of sentence structure, grammar, and diction are all important, as are the mechanics of writing—capitalization, spelling, punctuation, and so on. The key to successful communication is using the right language for the audience you are addressing. In all writing, the challenge is to find the words, phrases, clauses, sentences, and paragraphs that express your thoughts and ideas precisely and that make them interesting to others.

Because good scholarship requires objectivity, careful writers of research papers avoid language that implies unsubstantiated or irrelevant generalizations about such personal qualities as age, economic class, ethnicity, sexual orientation, political or religious belief, race, or sex. Discussions about this subject have generally focused on wording that could be labeled sexist. For example, many writers no longer use *he*, *him*, or *his* to express a meaning that includes women or girls: "If a young artist is not confident, he can quickly become discouraged." This use of *he*, *him*, or *his* can often be avoided through a revision that recasts the sentence into the plural or that eliminates the pronoun: "If young artists are not confident, they can quickly become discouraged" or "A young artist who is not confident can quickly become discouraged." Another technique is to make the discussion refer to a person who is identified, so that there is a reason to use a specific singular pronoun. *He or she* and *her or him* are cumbersome alternatives to be used sparingly. Many authors now also avoid terms that unnecessarily integrate a person's sex with a job or role. For instance, *anchorman*, *policewoman*, *stewardess*, and *poetess* are commonly replaced with *anchor*, *police officer*, *flight attendant*, and *poet*, which can apply to both men and women. For advice on current practices, consult your instructor or one of the guides to nonsexist language listed below.

1.11. GUIDES TO WRITING

A good dictionary is an essential tool for all writers. Your instructor will probably recommend a standard American dictionary such as *The American Heritage College Dictionary*, *Merriam-Webster's Collegiate Dictionary*, or *Random House Webster's College Dictionary*. Because dictionaries vary in matters like word division and spelling preference, you should, to maintain consistency, use the same one throughout your project.

You should also keep on hand at least one reliable guide to writing. A selected list of writing guides appears below, classified under four headings. Your instructor can help you choose among these titles.

Handbooks of Composition

Baker, Sheridan. *The Complete Stylist and Handbook*. 3rd ed. New York: Harper, 1984.

———. *The Practical Stylist*. 7th ed. New York: Harper, 1990.

Beene, Lynn, and William Vande Kopple. *The Riverside Handbook*. Boston: Houghton, 1992.

Booth, Wayne C., and Marshall W. Gregory. *The Harper and Row Rhetoric: Writing as Thinking / Thinking as Writing*. New York: Harper, 1987.

Corbett, Edward P. J., and Sheryl L. Finkle. *The Little English Handbook: Choices and Conventions*. 6th ed. New York: Harper, 1992.

Crews, Frederick. *The Random House Handbook*. 6th ed. New York: Random, 1992.

Fowler, H. Ramsey, and Jane E. Aaron. *The Little, Brown Handbook*. 5th ed. New York: Harper, 1992.

Gere, Anne R. *Writing and Learning*. 3rd ed. New York: Macmillan, 1992.

Guth, Hans P. *New English Handbook*. 3rd ed. Belmont: Wadsworth, 1990.

Hacker, Diana. *The Bedford Handbook for Writers*. 4th ed. Boston: Bedford–St. Martin's, 1994.

Heffernan, James A. W., and John E. Lincoln. *Writing: A College Handbook*. 4th ed. New York: Norton, 1994.

Hodges, John C., Winifred Bryan Horner, Suzanne Strobeck Webb, and Robert Keith Miller. *Harbrace College Handbook*. 12th ed. Fort Worth: Harcourt, 1994.

Leggett, Glenn, C. David Mead, and Melinda G. Kramer. *Prentice Hall Handbook for Writers*. 11th ed. Englewood Cliffs: Prentice, 1991.

Lunsford, Andrea, and Robert Connors. *The St. Martin's Handbook*. 3rd ed. New York: St. Martin's, 1995.

Marius, Richard, and Harvey S. Wiener. *The McGraw-Hill College Handbook*. 4th ed. New York: McGraw, 1994.

McPherson, Elisabeth, and Gregory Cowan. *Plain English Please: A Rhetoric*. 5th ed. New York: Random, 1986.

Mulderig, Gerald P., and Langdon Elsbree. *The Heath Handbook of Composition*. 13th ed. Lexington: Heath, 1995.

Troyka, Lynn Quitman. *Simon and Schuster Handbook for Writers*. 3rd ed. Englewood Cliffs: Prentice, 1993.

Watkins, Floyd C., and William B. Dillingham. *Practical English Handbook*. 9th ed. Boston: Houghton, 1992.

Dictionaries of Usage

Bernstein, Theodore. *The Careful Writer: A Modern Guide to English Usage*. New York: Atheneum, 1965.

Bryant, Margaret M. *Current American Usage: How Americans Say It and Write It*. New York: Funk, 1962.

Copperud, Roy H. *American Usage and Style: The Consensus*. New York: Van Nostrand, 1980.

Evans, Bergen, and Cornelia Evans. *A Dictionary of Contemporary American Usage*. New York: Random, 1957.

Follett, Wilson. *Modern American Usage: A Guide*. Ed. Jacques Barzun. New York: Hill, 1966.

Fowler, H[enry] W. *A Dictionary of Modern English Usage*. Ed. Ernest Gowers. 2nd ed. New York: Oxford UP, 1965.

Mager, Nathan H., and Sylvia K. Mager. *Prentice Hall Encyclopedic Dictionary of English Usage*. 2nd ed. Englewood Cliffs: Prentice, 1992.

Morris, William, and Mary Morris. *Harper Dictionary of Contemporary Usage*. 2nd ed. New York: Harper, 1985.

Nicholson, Margaret. *A Dictionary of American-English Usage Based on Fowler's* Modern English Usage. New York: Oxford UP, 1957.

Weiner, Edmund S., and Joyce M. Hawkins. *The Oxford Guide to the English Language*. New York: Oxford UP, 1984.

Guides to Nonsexist Language

American Psychological Association. "Guidelines to Reduce Bias in Language." *Publication Manual of the American Psychological Association*. 4th ed. Washington: Amer. Psychological Assn., 1994. 46–60.

Frank, Francine Wattman, and Paula A. Treichler, with others. *Language, Gender, and Professional Writing: Theoretical Approaches and Guidelines for Nonsexist Usage*. New York: MLA, 1989.

International Association of Business Communication. *Without Bias: A Guidebook for Nondiscriminatory Communication*. Ed. J. E. Pickens, P. W. Rao, and L. C. Roberts. 2nd ed. New York: Wiley, 1982.

Maggio, Rosalie. *The Nonsexist Word Finder: A Dictionary of Gender-Free Usage*. 1987. Boston: Beacon, 1989.

Miller, Casey, and Kate Swift. *The Handbook of Nonsexist Writing*. 2nd ed. New York: Harper, 1988.

Schwartz, Marilyn, and the Task Force of the Association of American University Presses. *Guidelines for Bias-Free Writing*. Bloomington: Indiana UP, 1995.

Sorrels, Bobbye D. *The Nonsexist Communicator: Solving the Problems of Gender and Awkwardness in Modern English*. Englewood Cliffs: Prentice, 1983.

Warren, Virginia L. "Guidelines for the Nonsexist Use of Language." *American Philosophical Association Proceedings* 59 (1986): 471–84.

Books on Style

Barzun, Jacques. *Simple and Direct: A Rhetoric for Writers*. Rev. ed. New York: Harper, 1984.

Beardsley, Monroe C. *Thinking Straight: Principles of Reasoning for Readers and Writers*. 4th ed. Englewood Cliffs: Prentice, 1975.

Cook, Claire Kehrwald. *Line by Line: How to Edit Your Own Writing*. Boston: Houghton, 1985.

Eastman, Richard M. *Style: Writing and Reading as the Discovery of Outlook*. 3rd ed. New York: Oxford UP, 1984.

Elbow, Peter. *Writing without Teachers*. New York: Oxford UP, 1973.

———. *Writing with Power: Techniques for Mastering the Writing Process*. New York: Oxford UP, 1981.

Gibson, Walker. *Tough, Sweet, and Stuffy: An Essay on Modern American Prose Styles*. Bloomington: Indiana UP, 1966.

Gowers, Ernest. *The Complete Plain Words*. Ed. Sidney Greenbaum and Janet Whitcut. Rev. ed. Boston: Godine, 1990.

Lanham, Richard A. *Style: An Anti-textbook*. New Haven: Yale UP, 1974.

Smith, Charles K. *Styles and Structures: Alternative Approaches to College Writing*. New York: Norton, 1974.

Strunk, William, Jr., and E. B. White. *The Elements of Style*. 3rd ed. New York: Macmillan, 1979.

Williams, Joseph M. *Style: Ten Lessons in Clarity and Grace*. 4th ed. New York: Harper, 1994.

———. *Style: Toward Clarity and Grace*. Chicago: U of Chicago P, 1990.

2 The Mechanics of Writing

Although the scope of this book precludes a detailed discussion of grammar, usage, style, and related aspects of writing, this chapter addresses mechanical questions that you will likely encounter in writing research papers.

1. Spelling
2. Punctuation
3. Italics (underlining)
4. Names of persons
5. Numbers
6. Titles of works in the research paper
7. Quotations
8. Capitalization and personal names in languages other than English

2.1. SPELLING

2.1.1. Consistency

Spelling, including hyphenation, should be consistent throughout the research paper—except in quotations, which must retain the spelling of the original, whether correct or incorrect. You can best ensure consistency by always adopting the spelling that your dictionary gives first in any entry with variant spellings.

2.1.2. Word Division

To save time and avoid possible errors, do not divide words at the ends of lines. If a word you are about to type on a typewriter will not fit on the line, you may leave the line short and begin the word on the next line. The "word-wrap" feature of word-processing programs performs this operation automatically. If you choose to divide a word, consult your dictionary about where the break should occur.

2.1.3. Foreign Words

If you quote material in a foreign language, you must reproduce all accents and other marks exactly as they appear in the original (*école*, *frère, tête, leçon, Fähre, año*). If you need marks that are not available on your word processor or typewriter, write them in by hand. On the use of foreign words in an English text, see 2.3.2; on capitalization and personal names in languages other than English, see 2.8.

2.2. PUNCTUATION

2.2.1. The Purpose of Punctuation

The primary purpose of punctuation is to ensure the clarity and readability of writing. Punctuation clarifies sentence structure, separating some words and grouping others. It adds meaning to written words and guides the understanding of readers as they move through sentences. The rules set forth here cover many of the situations you will encounter in writing research papers. For the punctuation of quotations in your text, see 2.7. For the punctuation of parenthetical references and bibliographies, see chapters 4 and 5. See also the individual listings in the index for specific punctuation marks.

2.2.2. Commas

a. Use a comma before a coordinating conjunction (*and, but, for, nor, or, yet,* or *so*) joining independent clauses in a sentence.

```
Congress passed the bill, and the president signed it
into law.
```

```
The poem is ironic, for the poet's meaning contrasts
with her words.
```

```
Take along a tape recorder, or you risk misquoting your
interviewee.
```

```
Other wars were longer, but few were as costly in human
lives.
```

b. Use commas to separate words, phrases, and clauses in a series.

WORDS

Boccaccio's tales have inspired plays, films, operas,
and paintings.

PHRASES

Alfred the Great established a system of fortified
towns, reorganized the military forces, and built a
fleet of warships.

CLAUSES

In the Great Depression, millions lost their jobs,
businesses failed, and charitable institutions closed
their doors.

But use semicolons when items in a series have internal commas.

Pollsters focused their efforts on Columbus, Ohio; Des
Moines, Iowa; and Saint Louis, Missouri.

c. Use a comma between coordinate adjectives—that is, adjectives
that separately modify the same noun.

Critics praise the novel's unaffected, unadorned style.
(The adjectives *unaffected* and *unadorned* each modify *style*.)

The new regime imposed harsh, repressive laws. (The adjectives *harsh* and *repressive* each modify *laws*.)

But note:

Most of the characters are average city dwellers. (The
adjective *average* modifies *city dwellers*.)

A famous photo shows Marianne Moore in a black
tricornered hat. (The adjective *black* modifies *tricornered hat*.)

d. Use commas to set off a parenthetical comment, or an aside, if it
is brief and closely related to the rest of the sentence. (For punctuation of longer, more intrusive, or more complex parenthetical elements, see 2.2.5.)

The Tudors, for example, ruled for over a century.

```
The vernacular, after all, was the language of everyday
life.
```

```
Tonight's performance, I'm sorry to say, has been
canceled.
```

e. Use commas to set off a nonrestrictive modifier—that is, a modifier that is not essential to the meaning of the sentence. A nonrestrictive modifier, unlike a restrictive one, could be dropped without changing the main sense of the sentence. Modifiers in the following three categories are either nonrestrictive or restrictive. (For the use of parentheses and dashes around complex nonrestrictive modifiers, see 2.2.5b.)

Words in apposition:

NONRESTRICTIVE

```
The color of the costume, blue, acquires symbolic
meaning in the story.
```

```
The theme song of the campaign, "Happy Days Are Here
Again," is indelibly associated with the Great Depression.
```

```
Isabel Allende, the Chilean novelist, will appear at the
arts forum tonight.
```

RESTRICTIVE

```
The color blue acquires symbolic meaning in the story.
```

```
The campaign song "Happy Days Are Here Again" is
indelibly associated with the Great Depression.
```

```
The Chilean novelist Isabel Allende will appear at the
arts forum tonight.
```

Clauses that begin with *who*, *whom*, *whose*, *which*, and *that*:

NONRESTRICTIVE

```
Scientists, who must observe standards of objectivity
in their work, can contribute usefully to public-
policy debates.
```

The Italian sonnet, which is exemplified in Petrarch's Canzoniere, developed into the English sonnet.

RESTRICTIVE

Scientists who receive the Nobel Prize sometimes contribute usefully to public-policy debates.

The sonnet that is exemplified in Petrarch's Canzoniere developed into the English sonnet.

Note that some writers prefer to use *which* to introduce nonrestrictive clauses and *that* to introduce restrictive clauses.

Adverbial phrases and clauses:

NONRESTRICTIVE

The novel takes place in China, where many languages are spoken.

The ending is sad, as the narrator hinted it would be.

RESTRICTIVE

The novel takes place in a land where many languages are spoken.

The ending is as the narrator hinted it would be.

f. Use a comma after a long introductory phrase or clause.

PHRASE

After years of anxiety over the family's finances, Linda Loman looks forward to the day the mortgage will be paid off.

CLAUSE

Although she was virtually unknown in her day, scholars have come to recognize the originality of her work.

g. Use commas to set off alternative or contrasting phrases.

The king remains a tragic figure, however appalling his actions.

A determined, even obsessed, taxi driver tells of his ambitions.

It is Julio, not his mother, who sets the plot in motion.

But note:

Several cooperative but autonomous republics were formed. (The conjunction *but* links *cooperative* and *autonomous*, making a comma inappropriate.)

h. Do not use a comma between subject and verb.

Many of the characters who dominate the early chapters and then disappear [no comma] are portraits of the author's friends.

i. Do not use a comma between verb and object.

The agent reported to the headquarters staff [no comma] that the documents had been traced to an underground garage.

j. Do not use a comma between the parts of a compound subject, compound object, or compound verb.

COMPOUND SUBJECT

A dozen wooden chairs [no comma] and a window that admits a shaft of light complete the stage setting.

COMPOUND OBJECT

Ptolemy devised a system of astronomy accepted until the sixteenth century [no comma] and a scientific approach to the study of geography.

COMPOUND VERB

He composed several successful symphonies [no comma] but won the most fame for his witticisms.

48

k. Do not use a comma between two parallel subordinate elements.

Nona thought of the crew members, who worked from dawn to
dusk [no comma] but whose lives seemed free and joyful.

She broadens her analysis by exploring the tragic
elements of the play [no comma] and by integrating the
hunting motif with the themes of death and resurrection.

The farmhouse stood on top of a hill [no comma] and just
beyond the Silver Creek bridge.

l. Use a comma in a date whose order is month, day, and year. If such a date comes in the middle of a sentence, include a comma after the year.

Martin Luther King, Jr., was born on January 15, 1929,
and died on April 4, 1968.

But commas are not used with dates whose order is day, month, and year.

Martin Luther King, Jr., was born on 15 January 1929 and
died on 4 April 1968.

m. Do not use a comma between a month and a year or between a season and a year.

The events of July 1789 are as familiar to the French as
those of July 1776 are to Americans.

I passed my oral exams in spring 1993.

2.2.3. Semicolons

a. Use a semicolon between independent clauses not linked by a conjunction.

The coat is tattered beyond repair; still, Akaky hopes
the tailor can mend it.

b. Use semicolons between items in a series when the items contain commas.

Present at the symposium were Henri Guillaume, the art
critic; Sam Brown, the <u>Daily Tribune</u> reporter; and Maria
Rosa, the conceptual artist.

2.2.4. Colons

The colon is used between two parts of a sentence when the first part
creates a sense of anticipation about what follows in the second.

a. Use a colon to introduce a list, an elaboration of what was just
said, or the formal expression of a rule or principle.

LIST

The reading list includes three Latin American novels:
<u>The Death of Artemio Cruz</u>, <u>One Hundred Years of
Solitude</u>, and <u>The Green House</u>.

ELABORATION

The plot is founded on deception: the three main
characters have secret identities.

RULE OR PRINCIPLE

Many books would be briefer if their authors followed
the logical principle known as Occam's razor:
Explanations should not be multiplied unnecessarily. (A
rule or principle after a colon should begin with a capital letter.)

But a verb or preposition that performs the same introductory function
as a colon makes the colon unnecessary.

The novels on the reading list include <u>The Death of
Artemio Cruz</u>, <u>One Hundred Years of Solitude</u>, and <u>The
Green House</u>. (The verb *include* performs the introductory function.)

The reading list includes such novels as <u>The Death of
Artemio Cruz</u>, <u>One Hundred Years of Solitude</u>, and <u>The
Green House</u>. (The preposition *as* performs the introductory function.)

b. Use a colon to introduce a quotation that is independent from the structure of the main sentence:

> In The Awakening, Mme Ratignolle exhorts Robert Lebrun
> to stop flirting with Edna: "She is not one of us; she
> is not like us."

A quotation that is integral to the sentence structure is generally preceded by no punctuation or, if a verb of saying (*says, exclaims, notes, writes*) introduces the quotation, by a comma. A colon is used after a verb of saying, however, if the verb introduces certain kinds of formal literary quotations, such as long quotations set off from the main text (see 2.7.2–4, 2.7.7).

2.2.5. Dashes and Parentheses

Dashes make a sharper break in the continuity of the sentence than commas do, and parentheses make a still sharper one. To indicate a dash in typing, use two hyphens, with no space before, between, or after. (Some word processors have a dash, and you may use it instead of hyphens.) Your writing will be smoother and more readable if you use dashes and parentheses sparingly. Limit the number of dashes in a sentence to two paired dashes or one unpaired dash.

a. Use dashes or parentheses to enclose a sentence element that interrupts the train of thought.

> Soaring in a balloon--inventors first performed this
> feat in 1783--is a way to recapture the wonder that
> early aviators must have felt.

> The "hero" of the play (the townspeople see him as
> heroic, but he is the focus of the author's satire)
> introduces himself as a veteran of the war.

b. Use dashes or parentheses to set off a parenthetical element that contains a comma and that might be misread if set off with commas.

> The colors of the costume--blue, scarlet, and yellow--
> acquire symbolic meaning in the story.

51

The Italian sonnet (which is exemplified in Petrarch's
Canzoniere, along with other kinds of poems) developed
into the English sonnet.

c. Use a dash to introduce words that summarize a preceding series.

Ruthlessness and acute sensitivity, greed and
compassion--the main character's contradictory qualities
prevent any simple interpretation of the film.

A dash may also be used instead of a colon to introduce a list or an elaboration of what was just said (see 2.2.4a).

2.2.6. Hyphens

Compound words of all types—nouns, verbs, adjectives, and so on—are written as separate words (*hard drive, hard labor*), with hyphens (*hard-and-fast, hard-boiled*), and as single words (*hardcover, hardheaded*). The dictionary shows how to write many compounds. A compound not in the dictionary should usually be written as separate words unless a hyphen is needed to prevent readers from misunderstanding the relation between the words. Following are some rules to help you decide whether you need a hyphen in compounds and other terms that may not appear in the dictionary.

a. Use a hyphen in a compound adjective beginning with an adverb such as *better, best, ill, lower, little,* or *well* when the adjective precedes a noun.

better-prepared ambassador
best-known work
ill-informed reporter
lower-priced tickets
well-dressed announcer

But do not use a hyphen when the compound adjective comes after the noun it modifies.

The ambassador was better prepared than the other
delegates.

b. Do not use a hyphen in a compound adjective beginning with an adverb ending in -*ly* or with *too, very,* or *much.*

```
thoughtfully presented thesis
very contrived plot
too hasty judgment
much maligned performer
```

c. Use a hyphen in a compound adjective ending with the present participle (e.g., *loving*) or the past participle (e.g., *inspired*) of a verb when the adjective precedes a noun.

```
sports-loving throng
fear-inspired loyalty
hate-filled speech
```

d. Use a hyphen in a compound adjective formed by a number and a noun when the adjective precedes a noun.

```
twelfth-floor apartment
second-semester courses
early-thirteenth-century architecture
```

e. Use hyphens in other compound adjectives before nouns to prevent misreading.

`continuing-education program` (The hyphen indicates that the term refers to a program of continuing education and not to an education program that is continuing.)

`Portuguese-language student` (The hyphen makes it clear that the term refers to a student who is studying Portuguese and not to a language student who is Portuguese.)

f. Do not use hyphens in familiar unhyphenated compound terms, such as *social security, high school, liberal arts,* and *show business,* when they appear before nouns as modifiers.

```
social security tax
high school reunion
liberal arts curriculum
show business debut
```

g. Use hyphens to join coequal nouns.

```
writer-critic
scholar-athlete
author-chef
```

But do not use a hyphen in a pair of nouns in which the first noun modifies the second.

```
father figure
opera lover
```

h. In general, do not use hyphens after prefixes (e.g., *anti-*, *co-*, *multi-*, *non-*, *over-*, *post-*, *pre-*, *re-*, *semi-*, *sub-*, *un-*, *under-*).

```
antiwar           overpay          semiretired
coworker          postwar          subsatellite
multinational     prescheduled     underrepresented
nonjudgmental     reinvigorate     unenlarged
```

But sometimes a hyphen is called for after a prefix:

`post-Victorian` (Use a hyphen before a capital letter.)

`re-cover` (The hyphen distinguishes this verb, meaning "cover again,"
   from *recover*, meaning "get back.")

`anti-icing` (Without the hyphen, the doubled vowel would make the
   term hard to recognize.)

2.2.7. Apostrophes

A principal function of apostrophes is to indicate possession. They are also used to form contractions (*can't*, *wouldn't*), which are rarely acceptable in research papers, and the plurals of the letters of the alphabet (*p's and q's, three A's*).

a. To form the possessive of a singular noun, add an apostrophe and an *s*.

```
the zebra's stripes
a poem's meter
the dean's list
```

b. To form the possessive of a plural noun ending in *s*, add only an apostrophe.

```
photographers' props
firefighters' trucks
tourists' luggage
```

c. To form the possessive of an irregular plural noun not ending in *s*, add an apostrophe and an *s*.

```
children's entertainment
the media's role
women's studies
```

d. To form the possessive of nouns in a series, add a single apostrophe and an *s* if the ownership is shared.

```
Palmer and Colton's book on European history
Fred, Lucinda, and Nan's house
```

But if the ownership is separate, place an apostrophe and an *s* after each noun.

```
Fred's, Lucinda's, and Nan's coats
```

e. To form the possessive of any singular proper noun, add an apostrophe and an *s*.

```
Venus's beauty
Dickens's reputation
Descartes's philosophy
Marx's precepts
```

f. To form the possessive of a plural proper noun, add only an apostrophe.

```
the Vanderbilts' estate
the Dickenses' economic woes
```

g. Do not use an apostrophe to form the plural of an abbreviation or a number.

```
PhDs                    1990s
MAs                     fours
VCRs                    SAT score in the 1400s
IRAs
```

2.2.8. Quotation Marks

a. Place quotation marks around a word or phrase used in a special sense or purposefully misused.

```
A silver dome concealed the robot's "brain."
```

```
Their "friend" brought about their downfall.
```

But note:

```
Their so-called friend brought about their downfall. (So-
called makes quotation marks unnecessary.)
```

b. Use quotation marks for a translation of a foreign word or phrase.

```
Et ux., a legal abbreviation for the Latin et uxor, means
"and wife."
```

```
The first idiomatic Spanish expression I learned was
irse todo en humo ("to go up in smoke").
```

You may use single quotation marks for a translation that follows the original directly, without intervening words or punctuation.

```
The word text derives from the Latin verb texere 'to
weave.'
```

2.2.9. Square Brackets

Use square brackets around a parenthesis within a parenthesis, so that the levels of subordination can be easily distinguished. Insert square brackets by hand if they are not available on your word processor or typewriter.

```
The sect known as the Jansenists (after Cornelius Jansen
[1585-1638]) faced opposition from both the king and the
pope.
```

```
The labors of Heracles (Hercules) included the slaying
of the Nemean lion (so called because Hera [Juno] sent
it to destroy the Nemean plain).
```

For square brackets around an interpolation in a quotation, see 2.7.6. For square brackets around missing or unverified data in documentation, see 4.6.25.

2.2.10. Slashes

The slash, or diagonal, is rarely necessary in formal prose. Other than in quotations of poetry (see 2.7.3), the slash has a place mainly between two terms paired as opposites or alternatives and used together as a noun.

```
The writer discussed how fundamental oppositions like
good/evil, East/West, and aged/young affect the way
cultures view historical events.
```

But use a hyphen when such a compound precedes and modifies a noun.

```
nature-nurture conflict
either-or situation
East-West relations
```

2.2.11. Periods, Question Marks, and Exclamation Points

A sentence can end with a period, a question mark, or an exclamation point. Periods end declarative sentences. (For the use of periods with ellipsis points, see 2.7.5.) Question marks follow interrogative sentences. Exclamation points should be avoided in research writing.

Place a question mark inside a closing quotation mark if the quoted passage is a question. Place a question mark outside if the quotation ends a sentence that is a question. If a question mark occurs where a comma or period would normally be required, omit the comma or period. Note the use of the question mark and other punctuation marks in the following sentences:

> The professor asked, "Who can tell me the capital of
> Thailand?"

> Why did Sally say, "I never want to see him again"?

> "What have you done to my car?" his uncle demanded.

2.3. ITALICS (UNDERLINING)

Italic is a style of type in which the characters slant to the right (*Casablanca*). In research papers and manuscripts submitted for publication, words that would be italicized in print are usually underlined.

> <u>Casablanca</u>

Many word-processing programs and computer printers permit the reproduction of italic type. In material that will be graded, edited, or typeset, the type style of every letter and punctuation mark must be easily recognizable. Italic type is sometimes not distinctive enough for this purpose, and you can avoid ambiguity by using underlining when you intend italics. If you wish to use italics rather than underlining, check your instructor's preferences. (For the use of italics for titles, see 2.6.2.)

2.3.1. Words and Letters Referred to as Words and Letters

Underline words and letters that are referred to as words and letters.

> Shaw spelled <u>Shakespeare</u> without the final <u>e</u>.

> The word <u>albatross</u> derives from the Spanish and
> Portuguese word <u>alcatras</u>.

2.3.2. Foreign Words in an English Text

In general, underline foreign words used in an English text.

> The Renaissance courtier was expected to display
> sprezzatura, or nonchalance, in the face of adversity.

The numerous exceptions to this rule include quotations entirely in another language ("Julius Caesar said, 'Veni, vidi, vici'"); non-English titles of short works (poems, short stories, essays, articles), which are placed in quotation marks and not underlined ("El sueño," the title of a poem by Quevedo); proper names (Marguerite de Navarre); and foreign words anglicized through frequent use. Since American English rapidly naturalizes words, use a dictionary to decide whether a foreign expression requires italics. Following are some adopted foreign words, abbreviations, and phrases commonly not underlined:

ad hoc	et al.	laissez-faire
cliché	etc.	lieder
concerto	genre	raison d'être
e.g.	hubris	versus

2.3.3. Emphasis

Italics for emphasis ("Booth *does* concede, however . . .") is a device that rapidly becomes ineffective. It is rarely appropriate in research writing.

2.4. NAMES OF PERSONS

2.4.1. First and Subsequent Uses of Names

In general, the first time you use a person's name in the text of your research paper, state it fully and accurately, exactly as it appears in your source.

> Arthur George Rust, Jr.
> Victoria M. Sackville-West

Do not change Arthur George Rust, Jr., to Arthur George Rust, for example, or drop the hyphen in Victoria M. Sackville-West. In subsequent references to the person, you may give the last name only (Rust, Sackville-West)—unless, of course, you refer to two or more persons with the same last name—or you may give the most common form of the name (e.g., Garcilaso for Garcilaso de la Vega). In casual references to the very famous—say, Mozart, Shakespeare, or Michelangelo—it is not necessary to give the full name initially.

In some languages (e.g., Chinese, Hungarian, Japanese, Korean, and Vietnamese), surnames precede given names; consult reference works for guidance on these names. For rules concerning names of persons in other languages, see 2.8.

2.4.2. Titles of Persons

In general, do not use formal titles (Mr., Mrs., Miss, Ms., Dr., Professor, Reverend) in referring to men or women, living or dead (Churchill, not Mr. Churchill; Einstein, not Professor Einstein; Hess, not Dame Hess; Montagu, not Lady Montagu). A few women in history are traditionally known by their titles as married women (e.g., Mrs. Humphry Ward, Mme de Staël). Treat other women's names the same as men's.

FIRST USE	SUBSEQUENT USES
Emily Dickinson	Dickinson (not Miss Dickinson)
Harriet Beecher Stowe	Stowe (not Mrs. Stowe)
Margaret Mead	Mead (not Ms. Mead)

The appropriate way to refer to persons with titles of nobility can vary. For example, the full name and title of Henry Howard, earl of Surrey, should be given at first mention, and thereafter Surrey alone may be used. In contrast, for Benjamin Disraeli, first earl of Beaconsfield, it is sufficient to give Benjamin Disraeli initially and Disraeli subsequently. Follow the example of your sources in citing titles of nobility.

2.4.3. Names of Authors and Fictional Characters

It is common and acceptable to use simplified names of famous authors (Vergil for Publius Vergilius Maro, Dante for Dante Alighieri). Also acceptable are pseudonyms of authors.

Molière (Jean-Baptiste Poquelin)
Voltaire (François-Marie Arouet)

George Sand (Amandine-Aurore-Lucie Dupin)

George Eliot (Mary Ann Evans)

Mark Twain (Samuel Clemens)

Stendhal (Marie-Henri Beyle)

Novalis (Friedrich von Hardenberg)

Refer to fictional characters in the same way that the work of fiction does. You need not always use their full names, and you may retain titles (Dr. Jekyll, Mme Defarge).

2.5. NUMBERS

2.5.1. Arabic Numerals

Although there are still a few well-established uses for roman numerals (see 2.5.7), virtually all numbers not spelled out are commonly represented today by arabic numerals. If your keyboard does not have the number *1*, use a small letter el (*l*), not capital *I*, for the arabic numeral.

2.5.2. Use of Words or Numerals

If you are writing about literature or another subject that involves infrequent use of numbers, you may spell out numbers written in one or two words and represent other numbers by numerals (*one, thirty-six, ninety-nine, one hundred, fifteen hundred, two thousand, three million*, but *2½, 101, 137, 1,275*).

If your project is one that calls for frequent use of numbers—say, a paper on a scientific subject or a study of statistical findings—use numerals for all numbers that precede technical units of measurement (*16 amperes, 5 milliliters*). In such a project, also use numerals for numbers that are presented together and that refer to similar things, such as in comparisons or reports of experimental data. Spell out other numbers if they can be written in one or two words. In the following example of statistical writing, neither "ten years" nor "six-state region" is presented with related figures, so the numbers are spelled out, unlike the other numbers in the sentence.

```
In the ten years covered by the study, the number of
participating institutions in the United States doubled,
reaching 90, and membership in the six-state region rose
from 4 to 15.
```

But do not begin a sentence with a numeral, including a date. Always use numerals in the following instances:

WITH ABBREVIATIONS OR SYMBOLS

```
6 lbs.            4:20 p.m.            3%
8 KB              $9                   2"
```

IN ADDRESSES

```
4401 13th Avenue
```

IN DATES

```
1 April 1995
April 1, 1995
```

IN DECIMAL FRACTIONS

```
8.3
```

IN PAGE REFERENCES

```
page 7
```

For large numbers, you may use a combination of numerals and words.

```
4.5 million
```

Express related numbers in the same style.

```
only 5 of the 250 delegates
exactly 3 automobiles and 129 trucks
from 1 billion to 1.2 billion
```

2.5.3. Commas in Numbers

Commas are usually placed between the third and fourth digits from the right, the sixth and seventh, and so on.

```
1,000
20,000
7,654,321
```

Following are some of the exceptions to this practice:

PAGE AND LINE NUMBERS

```
On page 1014 . . .
```

ADDRESSES

```
At 4132 Broadway . . .
```

FOUR-DIGIT YEAR NUMBERS

```
In 1999 . . .
```

But commas are added in year numbers of five or more figures.

```
In 20,000 BC . . .
```

2.5.4. Percentages and Amounts of Money

Treat percentages and amounts of money like other numbers: use numerals with the appropriate symbols.

```
1%              $5.35              68¢
45%             $35
100%            $2,000
```

In discussions involving infrequent use of numbers, you may spell out a percentage or an amount of money if you can do so in three words or fewer (*five dollars, forty-five percent, two thousand dollars, sixty-eight cents*). Do not combine spelled forms of numbers with symbols.

2.5.5. Dates

Be consistent in writing dates: use either the day-month-year style (*22 July 1995*) or the month-day-year style (*July 22, 1995*) but not both. (If you begin with the month, be sure to add a comma after the day and also after the year, unless another punctuation mark goes there, such as a period or a question mark.) Do not use a comma between month and year (*August 1993*).

Spell out centuries in lowercase letters.

```
the twentieth century
```

Hyphenate centuries when they are used as adjectives before nouns.

```
eighteenth-century thought

nineteenth- and twentieth-century literature
```

Decades are usually written out without capitalization (*the nineties*), but it is acceptable to express them in figures (*the 1990s*). Whichever form you use, be consistent.

The abbreviation *BC* follows the year, but *AD* precedes it.

```
19 BC

AD 565
```

Instead of *BC* and *AD,* some writers prefer to use *BCE*, "before the common era," and *CE*, "common era," both of which follow the year.

2.5.6. Inclusive Numbers

In a range of numbers, give the second number in full for numbers through ninety-nine.

```
2-3              21-48
10-12            89-99
```

For larger numbers, give only the last two digits of the second number, unless more are necessary.

```
96-101           923-1003
103-04           1003-05
395-401          1608-774
```

In a range of years, write both in full unless they are within the same century.

```
1898-1901        1898-99
```

2.5.7. Roman Numerals

Use capital roman numerals for the primary divisions of an outline (see 1.8) and after the names of individuals in a series.

```
Richard III
John D. Rockefeller IV
John Paul II
```

Use lowercase roman numerals for citing pages of a book that are so numbered (e.g., the pages in a preface). Your instructor may prefer that you use roman numerals to designate acts and scenes of plays (see 5.4.8, on citing literary works).

2.6. TITLES OF WORKS IN THE RESEARCH PAPER

2.6.1. Capitalization and Punctuation

Always take the title of a work from the title page, not from the cover or from the top of a page. Do not reproduce any unusual typographical characteristics, such as special capitalization or lowercasing of letters. Here are examples of how titles are sometimes presented on title pages:

> MODERNISM & NEGRITUDE

> **BERNARD BERENSON**
> The Making of a Connoisseur

> Turner's early sketchbooks

These titles should appear in a research paper as follows:

<u>Modernism and Negritude</u>

<u>Bernard Berenson: The Making of a Connoisseur</u>

<u>Turner's Early Sketchbooks</u>

The rules for capitalizing titles are strict. In both titles and subtitles, capitalize the first words, the last words, and all principal words, including those that follow hyphens in compound terms. Therefore, capitalize the following parts of speech:

- Nouns (e.g., *flowers* and *Europe* as in *The Flowers of Europe*)
- Pronouns (e.g., *our* as in *Save Our Children*, *that* as in *The Mouse That Roared*)
- Verbs (e.g., *watches* as in *America Watches Television*, *is* as in *What Is Literature?*)
- Adjectives (e.g., *ugly* as in *The Ugly Duckling*, *that* as in *Who Said That Phrase?*)
- Adverbs (e.g., *slightly* as in *Only Slightly Corrupt*, *down* as in *Go Down, Moses*)
- Subordinating conjunctions (e.g., *after, although, as if, as soon as, because, before, if, that, unless, until, when, where, while* as in *One If by Land* and *Anywhere That Chance Leads*)

Do not capitalize the following parts of speech when they fall in the middle of a title:

- Articles (*a, an, the* as in *Under the Bamboo Tree*)
- Prepositions (e.g., *against, between, in, of, to* as in *The Merchant of Venice* and "A Dialogue between the Soul and Body")
- Coordinating conjunctions (*and, but, for, nor, or, so, yet* as in *Romeo and Juliet*)
- The *to* in infinitives (as in *How to Play Chess*)

Use a colon and a space to separate a title from a subtitle, unless the title ends in a question mark, an exclamation point, or a dash. Include other punctuation only if it is part of the title.

The following examples illustrate how to capitalize and punctuate a variety of titles. For a discussion of which titles to underline and which to place in quotation marks, see 2.6.2–3.

<u>Death of a Salesman</u>

<u>The Teaching of Spanish in English-Speaking Countries</u>

<u>Storytelling and Mythmaking: Images from Film and Literature</u>

<u>Life As I Find It</u>

<u>What Are You Doing in My Universe?</u>

<u>Whose Music? A Sociology of Musical Language</u>

<u>Where Did You Go? Out. What Did You Do? Nothing.</u>

```
"Ode to a Nightingale"
"Italian Literature before Dante"
"What Americans Stand For"
"Why Fortinbras?"
```

When the first line of a poem serves as the title of the poem, reproduce the line exactly as it appears in the text.

```
Dickinson's poem "I heard a Fly buzz--when I died--"
contrasts the everyday and the momentous.
```

For rules concerning capitalization of titles in languages other than
English, see 2.8. See 2.6.4 for titles and quotations within titles.

2.6.2. Underlined Titles

In general, underline the titles of works published independently (for
works published within larger works, see 2.6.3). Titles to be underlined
include the names of books, plays, long poems published as books,
pamphlets, periodicals (newspapers, magazines, and journals), films,
radio and television programs, compact discs, audiocassettes, record
albums, ballets, operas, instrumental musical compositions (except
those identified simply by form, number, and key; see 2.6.5), paintings, works of sculpture, ships, aircraft, and spacecraft. In the following examples, note that the underlining is not broken between words.
While there is no need to underline the spaces between words, a continuous line is easier to create on a typewriter, and it guards against
the error of failing to underline the punctuation within a title.

```
The Awakening  (book)
The Importance of Being Earnest  (play)
The Waste Land  (long poem published as a book)
New Jersey Driver Manual  (pamphlet)
Wall Street Journal  (newspaper)
Time  (magazine)
It's a Wonderful Life  (film)
Star Trek  (television program)
Sgt. Pepper's Lonely Hearts Club Band  (compact disc, audio-
    cassette, record album)
```

<u>The Nutcracker</u> (ballet)

<u>Rigoletto</u> (opera)

Berlioz's <u>Symphonie fantastique</u> (instrumental composition
  identified by name)

Chagall's <u>I and My Village</u> (painting)

French's <u>The Minute Man</u> (sculpture)

HMS <u>Vanguard</u> (ship)

<u>Spirit of St. Louis</u> (aircraft)

2.6.3. Titles in Quotation Marks

Use quotation marks for the titles of works published within larger
works. Such titles include the names of articles, essays, short stories,
short poems, chapters of books, and individual episodes of television
and radio programs. Also use quotation marks for songs and for
unpublished works, such as lectures and speeches.

"Rise in Aid to Education Is Proposed" (newspaper article)

"Sources of Energy in the Next Century" (magazine article)

"Etruscan" (encyclopedia article)

"The Fiction of Langston Hughes" (essay in a book)

"The Lottery" (short story)

"Kubla Khan" (poem)

"The American Economy before the Civil War" (chapter in a
  book)

"The Trouble with Tribbles" (episode of the television program
  Star Trek)

"Mood Indigo" (song)

"Preparing for a Successful Interview" (lecture)

2.6.4. Titles and Quotations within Titles

Underline a title normally indicated by underlining when it appears
within a title enclosed in quotation marks.

"<u>Romeo and Juliet</u> and Renaissance Politics" (an article about
  a play)

"Language and Childbirth in <u>The Awakening</u>" (an article about a novel)

Enclose in single quotation marks a title normally indicated by quotation marks when it appears within another title requiring quotation marks.

"Lines after Reading 'Sailing to Byzantium'" (a poem about a poem)

"The Uncanny Theology of 'A Good Man Is Hard to Find'" (an article about a short story)

Also place single quotation marks around a quotation that appears within a title requiring quotation marks.

"Emerson's Strategies against 'Foolish Consistency'" (an article with a quotation in its title)

Do not underline or enclose in quotation marks a normally underlined title when it appears within another underlined title.

<u>Approaches to Teaching Murasaki Shikibu's</u> The Tale of Genji (a book about a novel)

<u>From</u> The Lodger <u>to</u> The Lady Vanishes<u>: Hitchcock's Classic British Thrillers</u> (a book about films)

Use quotation marks around a title normally indicated by quotation marks when it appears within an underlined title.

<u>"The Lottery" and Other Stories</u> (a book of short stories)

<u>New Perspectives on "The Eve of St. Agnes"</u> (a book about a poem)

If a period is required after an underlined title that ends with a quotation mark, place the period before the quotation mark.

The study appears in <u>New Perspectives on "The Eve of St. Agnes."</u>

2.6.5. Exceptions

The convention of using underlining and quotation marks to indicate titles does not apply to the names of sacred writings (including all books and versions of the Bible); of laws, acts, and similar political documents; of instrumental musical compositions identified by form, number, and key; of series, societies, buildings, and monuments; and of conferences, seminars, workshops, and courses. These terms all appear without underlining or quotation marks.

SACRED WRITINGS

Bible	Gospels
King James Version	Talmud
Old Testament	Koran
Genesis	Upanishads

LAWS, ACTS, AND SIMILAR POLITICAL DOCUMENTS

Magna Carta
Declaration of Independence
Bill of Rights
Treaty of Trianon

INSTRUMENTAL MUSICAL COMPOSITIONS IDENTIFIED BY FORM, NUMBER, AND KEY

Beethoven's Symphony no. 7 in A, op. 92
Vivaldi's Concerto for Two Trumpets and Strings in C, RV539

SERIES

Bollingen Series
University of North Carolina Studies in Comparative Literature
Masterpiece Theatre

SOCIETIES

American Medical Association
Renaissance Society of America

BUILDINGS AND MONUMENTS

Moscone Center

Sears Tower

Arch of Constantine

CONFERENCES, SEMINARS, WORKSHOPS, AND COURSES

Strengthening the Cooperative Effort in Biomedical
    Research: A National Conference for Universities and
    Industry
Geographic Information Analysis Workshop
MLA Annual Convention
Introduction to Calculus
Anthropology 102

Words designating the divisions of a work are also not underlined or put within quotation marks, nor are they capitalized when used in the text.

preface	bibliography	act 4
introduction	appendix	scene 7
list of works	index	stanza 20
cited	chapter 2	canto 32

2.6.6. Shortened Titles

If you cite a title often in the text of your paper, you may, after stating the title in full at least once, use a shortened form (preferably a familiar or obvious one) or an abbreviation (e.g., "Nightingale" for "Ode to a Nightingale," FCC for Federal Communications Commission; for standard abbreviations of literary and religious works, see 6.7).

2.7. QUOTATIONS

2.7.1. Use of Quotations

Quotations are effective in research papers when used selectively. Quote only words, phrases, lines, and passages that are particularly interesting, vivid, unusual, or apt, and keep all quotations as brief as possible. Overquotation can bore your readers and might lead them to conclude that you are neither an original thinker nor a skillful writer.

The accuracy of quotations in research writing is extremely important. They must reproduce the original sources exactly. Unless indicated in brackets or parentheses (see 2.7.6), changes must not be made in the spelling, capitalization, or interior punctuation of the source. You must construct a clear, grammatically correct sentence that allows you to introduce or incorporate a quotation with complete accuracy. Alternatively, you may paraphrase the original and quote only fragments, which may be easier to integrate into the text. If you change a quotation in any way, make the alteration clear to the reader, following the rules and recommendations below.

2.7.2. Prose

If a prose quotation runs no more than four lines and requires no special emphasis, put it in quotation marks and incorporate it in the text.

```
"It was the best of times, it was the worst of times,"
wrote Charles Dickens of the eighteenth century.
```

You need not always reproduce complete sentences. Sometimes you may want to quote just a word or phrase as part of your sentence.

```
For Charles Dickens the eighteenth century was both "the
best of times" and "the worst of times."
```

You may put a quotation at the beginning, middle, or end of your sentence or, for the sake of variety or better style, divide it by your own words.

```
Joseph Conrad writes of the company manager in Heart of
Darkness, "He was obeyed, yet he inspired neither love
nor fear, nor even respect."
```

or

> "He was obeyed," writes Joseph Conrad of the company
> manager in <u>Heart of Darkness</u>, "yet he inspired neither
> love nor fear, nor even respect."

If a quotation ending a sentence requires a parenthetical reference, place the sentence period after the reference. (For more information on punctuating quotations, see 2.7.7.)

> For Charles Dickens the eighteenth century was both "the
> best of times" and "the worst of times" (35).

> "He was obeyed," writes Joseph Conrad of the company
> manager in <u>Heart of Darkness</u>, "yet he inspired neither
> love nor fear, nor even respect" (87).

If a quotation runs to more than four typed lines, set it off from your text by beginning a new line, indenting one inch (or ten spaces if you are using a typewriter) from the left margin, and typing it double-spaced, without adding quotation marks. A colon generally introduces a quotation displayed in this way, though sometimes the context may require a different mark of punctuation or none at all. If you quote only a single paragraph or part of one, do not indent the first line more than the rest. A parenthetical reference to a prose quotation set off from the text follows the last line of the quotation.

> At the conclusion of <u>Lord of the Flies</u>, Ralph and the
> other boys realize the horror of their actions:
>
> > The tears began to flow and sobs shook him. He
> > gave himself up to them now for the first time
> > on the island; great, shuddering spasms of
> > grief that seemed to wrench his whole body. His
> > voice rose under the black smoke before the
> > burning wreckage of the island; and infected by
> > that emotion, the other little boys began to
> > shake and sob too. (186)

If you need to quote two or more paragraphs, indent the first line of each paragraph an additional quarter inch (or three spaces on a type-writer). If the first sentence quoted does not begin a paragraph in the

source, however, do not indent it the additional amount. Indent only
the first lines of the successive paragraphs.

2.7.3. Poetry

If you quote part or all of a single line of verse that does not require
special emphasis, put it in quotation marks within your text. You may
also incorporate two or three lines in this way, using a slash with a
space on each side (/) to separate them.

```
Bradstreet frames the poem with a sense of mortality:
"All things within this fading world hath end" (1).

Reflecting on the "incident" in Baltimore, Cullen
concludes, "Of all the things that happened there /
That's all that I remember" (11-12).
```

Verse quotations of more than three lines should begin on a new
line. Unless the quotation involves unusual spacing, indent each line
one inch (or ten spaces on a typewriter) from the left margin and double-space between lines, adding no quotation marks that do not appear
in the original. A parenthetical reference for a verse quotation set off
from the text follows the last line of the quotation (as in quotations of
prose); a parenthetical reference that will not fit on the line should
begin a new line, flush with the right margin of the page.

```
Elizabeth Bishop's "In the Waiting Room" is rich in
 evocative detail:
                 It was winter. It got dark
                 early. The waiting room
                 was full of grown-up people,
                 arctics and overcoats,
                 lamps and magazines. (6-10)
```

A line that is too long to fit within the right margin should be continued on the next line and the continuation indented an additional
quarter inch (or three spaces). You may reduce the indentation of the
quotation to less than one inch (or ten spaces) from the left margin
if doing so will eliminate the need for such continuations. If the spa-
tial arrangement of the original lines, including indentation and spac-

ing within and between them, is unusual, reproduce it as accurately as possible.

> E. E. Cummings concludes the poem with this vivid
> description of a carefree scene, reinforced by the
> carefree form of the lines themselves:
>
>> it's
>> spring
>> and
>>> the
>>>> goat-footed
>> balloonMan   whistles
>> far
>> and
>> wee (16-24)

When a verse quotation begins in the middle of a line, the partial line should be positioned where it is in the original and not shifted to the left margin.

> In a poem on Thomas Hardy ("T. H."), Molly Holden recalls
> her encounter with a "young dog fox" one morning:
>
>>   I remember
>> he glanced at me in just that way, independent
>> and unabashed, the handsome sidelong look
>> that went round and about but never directly
>> met my eyes, for that would betray his soul.
>> He was not being sly, only careful. (43-48)

2.7.4. Drama

If you quote dialogue between two or more characters in a play, set the quotation off from your text. Begin each part of the dialogue with the appropriate character's name indented one inch (or ten spaces if you are using a typewriter) from the left margin and written in all capital letters: HAMLET. Follow the name with a period, and start the quotation. Indent all subsequent lines in that character's speech an additional quarter inch (or three spaces). When the dialogue shifts to another character, start a new line indented one inch (or ten spaces) from the left margin. Maintain this pattern throughout the entire quotation. For the other aspects of formatting, follow the recommendations above for quoting prose and poetry (2.7.2–3).

```
Marguerite Duras's screenplay for Hiroshima mon amour
suggests at the outset the profound difference between
observation and experience:
            HE. You saw nothing in Hiroshima. Nothing.
            SHE. I saw everything. Everything. . . . The
                hospital, for instance, I saw it. I'm sure
                I did. There is a hospital in Hiroshima. How
                could I help seeing it?
            HE. You did not see the hospital in Hiroshima.
                You saw nothing in Hiroshima. (2505-06)
```

```
A short time later Lear loses the final symbol of his
former power, the soldiers who make up his train:
            GONERIL.                    Hear me, my lord.
                What need you five-and-twenty, ten or five,
                To follow in a house where twice so many
                Have a command to tend you?
            REGAN.                            What need one?
            LEAR. O, reason not the need! (2.4.254-58)
```

2.7.5. Ellipsis

In quoting a passage, you will frequently want to omit words, phrases, or sentences in the original that are not useful to your paper. Whenever you omit material from a quoted passage, you should be guided by two principles: fairness to the author quoted and the grammatical integrity of your writing.

A quotation should never be presented in a way that could cause a reader to misunderstand the sentence structure of the original source. If you quote only a word or a phrase, it will be obvious that you left out some of the original sentence.

```
In his inaugural address, John F. Kennedy spoke of a
"new frontier."
```

But if omitting material from the original sentence or sentences leaves a quotation that appears to be a sentence or a series of sentences, you must use ellipsis points, or spaced periods, to indicate that your quotation does not completely reproduce the original.

For an ellipsis *within* a sentence, use three periods with a space before each and a space after the last (. . .).

ORIGINAL

Medical thinking, trapped in the theory of astral influences, stressed air as the communicator of disease, ignoring sanitation or visible carriers. (Barbara W. Tuchman, *A Distant Mirror: The Calamitous Fourteenth Century* [1978; New York: Ballantine, 1979] 101–02)

QUOTATION WITH AN ELLIPSIS IN THE MIDDLE

```
In surveying various responses to plagues in the
Middle Ages, Barbara W. Tuchman writes, "Medical
thinking . . . stressed air as the communicator of
disease, ignoring sanitation or visible carriers."
```

QUOTATION WITH AN ELLIPSIS IN THE MIDDLE AND A PARENTHETICAL REFERENCE

```
In surveying various responses to plagues in the
Middle Ages, Barbara W. Tuchman writes, "Medical
thinking . . . stressed air as the communicator of
disease, ignoring sanitation or visible carriers"
(101-02).
```

When the ellipsis coincides with the end of your sentence, use three periods with a space before each following a sentence period—that is, four periods, with no space before the first or after the last.

QUOTATION WITH AN ELLIPSIS AT THE END

```
In surveying various responses to plagues in the
Middle Ages, Barbara W. Tuchman writes, "Medical
```

```
thinking, trapped in the theory of astral influences,
stressed air as the communicator of disease. . . ."
```

If a parenthetical reference follows the ellipsis at the end of your sentence, use three periods with a space before each, and place the sentence period after the final parenthesis.

QUOTATION WITH AN ELLIPSIS AT THE END, FOLLOWED BY A
PARENTHETICAL REFERENCE

```
In surveying various responses to plagues in the
Middle Ages, Barbara W. Tuchman writes, "Medical
thinking, trapped in the theory of astral influences,
stressed air as the communicator of disease . . ."
(101-02).
```

Four periods can also indicate the omission of a whole sentence or more or even of a paragraph or more. Remember, however, that grammatically complete sentences must both precede and follow the four periods.

ORIGINAL

Presidential control reached its zenith under Andrew Jackson, the extent of whose attention to the press even before he became a candidate is suggested by the fact that he subscribed to twenty newspapers. Jackson was never content to have only one organ grinding out his tune. For a time, the *United States Telegraph* and the *Washington Globe* were almost equally favored as party organs, and there were fifty-seven journalists on the government payroll. (William L. Rivers, *The Mass Media: Reporting, Writing, Editing*, 2nd ed. [New York: Harper, 1975] 7)

QUOTATION OMITTING A SENTENCE OR MORE

```
In discussing the historical relation between politics
and the press, William L. Rivers notes, "Presidential
control reached its zenith under Andrew Jackson. . . .
For a time, the United States Telegraph and the
Washington Globe were almost equally favored as party
organs, and there were fifty-seven journalists on the
government payroll" (7).
```

The omission of words and phrases from quotations of poetry is indicated by three or four spaced periods (as in quotations of prose). The omission of a line or more in the middle of a poetry quotation that is set off from the text, however, is indicated by a line of spaced periods approximately the length of a complete line of the quoted poem.

ORIGINAL

In Worcester, Massachusetts,
I went with Aunt Consuelo
to keep her dentist's appointment
and sat and waited for her
in the dentist's waiting room.
It was winter. It got dark
early. The waiting room
was full of grown-up people,
arctics and overcoats,
lamps and magazines.
(Elizabeth Bishop, "In the Waiting Room," lines 1–10)

QUOTATION OMITTING A LINE OR MORE IN THE MIDDLE

Elizabeth Bishop's "In the Waiting Room" is rich in evocative detail:

      In Worcester, Massachusetts,

      I went with Aunt Consuelo

      to keep her dentist's appointment

      . . . .

      It was winter. It got dark

      early. (1-3, 6-7)

QUOTATION WITH AN ELLIPSIS AT THE END

Elizabeth Bishop's "In the Waiting Room" is rich in evocative detail:

      In Worcester, Massachusetts,

      I went with Aunt Consuelo

      to keep her dentist's appointment

      and sat and waited for her

      in the dentist's waiting room.

      It was winter. It got dark

```
early. The waiting room
was full of grown-up people. . . . (1-8)
```

2.7.6. Other Alterations of Sources

Occasionally, you may decide that a quotation will be unclear or confusing to your reader unless you provide supplementary information. For example, you may need to insert material missing from the original, to add *sic* (from the Latin for "thus" or "so") to assure readers that the quotation is accurate even though the spelling or logic might make them think otherwise, or to underline words for emphasis. While such contributions to a quotation are permissible, you should keep them to a minimum and make sure to distinguish them from the original, usually by explaining them in parentheses after the quotation or by putting them in square brackets within the quotation.

A comment or an explanation that immediately follows the closing quotation mark appears in parentheses.

```
Shaw admitted, "Nothing can extinguish my interest in
Shakespear" (sic).
```

```
Lincoln specifically advocated a government "for the
people" (emphasis added).
```

A comment or an explanation that goes inside the quotation must appear within square brackets, not parentheses. (If your keyboard does not include square brackets, insert them by hand.)

```
He claimed he could provide "hundreds of examples [of
court decisions] to illustrate the historical tension
between church and state."
```

```
Milton's Satan speaks of his "study [pursuit] of revenge."
```

Similarly, if a pronoun in a quotation seems unclear, you may add an identification in square brackets.

```
Why she would hang on him [Hamlet's father]
As if increase of appetite had grown
By what it fed on. . . .
```

2.7.7. Punctuation with Quotations

Whether set off from the text or run into it, quoted material is usually preceded by a colon if the quotation is formally introduced and by a comma or no punctuation if the quotation is an integral part of the sentence structure.

```
Shelley held a bold view: "Poets are the unacknowledged
legislators of the World" (794).

Shelley thought poets "the unacknowledged legislators of
the World" (794).

"Poets," according to Shelley, "are the unacknowledged
legislators of the World" (794).
```

Do not use opening and closing quotation marks to enclose quotations set off from the text. Use double quotation marks around quotations incorporated into the text, single quotation marks around quotations within those quotations.

```
In "Memories of West Street and Lepke," Robert Lowell, a
conscientious objector (or "C.O."), recounts meeting a
Jehovah's Witness in prison: "'Are you a C.O.?' I asked
a fellow jailbird. / 'No,' he answered, 'I'm a J.W.'"
(38-39).
```

Except for changing internal double quotation marks to single ones when you incorporate quotations into your text, you should reproduce internal punctuation exactly as in the original. The closing punctuation, though, depends on where the quoted material appears in your sentence. Suppose, for example, that you want to quote the following sentence: "You've got to be carefully taught." If you begin your sentence with this line, you have to replace the closing period with a punctuation mark appropriate to the new context.

```
"You've got to be carefully taught," wrote Oscar
Hammerstein II about how racial prejudice is perpetuated.
```

If the quotation ends with a question mark or an exclamation point, however, the original punctuation is retained and no comma is required.

"How can I describe my emotions at this catastrophe, or
how delineate the wretch whom with such infinite pains
and care I had endeavoured to form?" wonders the doctor
in Mary Shelley's <u>Frankenstein</u> (42).

"What a wonderful little almanac you are, Celia!"
Dorothea Brooke responds to her sister (7).

By convention, commas and periods that directly follow quotations go inside the closing quotation marks, but a parenthetical reference should intervene between the quotation and the required punctuation. Thus, if a quotation ends with a period, the period appears after the reference.

N. Scott Momaday's <u>House Made of Dawn</u> begins with an
image that also concludes the novel: "Abel was
running" (7).

If a quotation ends with both single and double quotation marks, the comma or period precedes both.

"Read 'Kubla Khan,'" he told me.

All other punctuation marks—such as semicolons, colons, question marks, and exclamation points—go outside a closing quotation mark, except when they are part of the quoted material.

ORIGINAL

I believe taxation without representation is tyranny!

QUOTATIONS

He attacked "taxation without representation" (32).
Did he attack "taxation without representation"?
What dramatic events followed his attack on "taxation
without representation"!

but

He declared, "I believe taxation without representation
is tyranny!"

If a quotation ending with a question mark or an exclamation point concludes your sentence and requires a parenthetical reference, retain the original punctuation within the quotation mark and follow with the reference and the sentence period outside the quotation mark.

```
In Mary Shelley's Frankenstein, the doctor wonders, "How
can I describe my emotions at this catastrophe, or how
delineate the wretch whom with such infinite pains and
care I had endeavoured to form?" (42).
```

```
Dorothea Brooke responds to her sister, "What a
wonderful little almanac you are, Celia!" (7).
```

2.8. CAPITALIZATION AND PERSONAL NAMES IN LANGUAGES OTHER THAN ENGLISH

The following section contains recommendations for writing personal names and for capitalizing in French, German, Italian, Spanish, and Latin. If you need such rules for other languages or if you need information on transliterating from languages that do not use the Latin alphabet, such as Russian or Chinese, consult *The MLA Style Manual*.

2.8.1. French

Personal Names

With some exceptions, French *de* following a first name or a title such as *Mme* or *duc* is not used with the last name alone.

```
La Boétie, Etienne de
La Bruyère, Jean de
Maupassant, Guy de
Nemours, duc de
Ronsard, Pierre de
Scudéry, Madeleine de
```

When the last name has only one syllable, however, *de* is usually retained.

```
de Gaulle, Charles
```

The preposition also remains, in the form *d'*, when it elides with a last name beginning with a vowel.

```
d'Arcy, Pierre
d'Arsonval, Arsène
```

The forms *du* and *des*—combinations of *de* with *le* and *les*—are always used with last names and are capitalized.

```
Des Périers, Bonaventure
Du Bartas, Guillaume de Salluste
```

A hyphen is frequently used between French given names, as well as between their initials (Marie-Joseph Chénier, M.-J. Chénier). Note that *M.* (for *Monsieur*) and *P.* (for *Père*) before names may be abbreviated titles equivalent to *Mr.* and *Father* (M. René Char, P. J. Reynard).

Capitalization

In prose and verse, French capitalization is the same as English except that the following terms are not capitalized in French unless they begin sentences or, sometimes, lines of verse: (1) the subject pronoun *je* 'I,' (2) the names of months and days of the week, (3) the names of languages, (4) adjectives derived from proper nouns, (5) titles preceding personal names, and (6) the words for a street, a square, a lake, a mountain, and so on, in most place-names.

```
Un Français m'a parlé anglais près de la place de
la Concorde.

Hier j'ai vu le docteur Maurois qui conduisait une
voiture Ford.

Le capitaine Boutillier m'a dit qu'il partait pour Rouen
le premier jeudi d'avril avec quelques amis normands.
```

In a title or a subtitle, capitalize the first word and all proper nouns.

```
L'ami du peuple
Du côté de chez Swann
Le grand Meaulnes
La guerre de Troie n'aura pas lieu
Nouvelle revue d'onomastique
```

Some instructors follow other rules. When the title of a work begins with an article, they also capitalize the first noun and any preceding adjectives. In titles of series and periodicals, they capitalize all major words: *Nouvelle Revue d'Onomastique*.

2.8.2. German

Personal Names

German *von* is generally not used with the last name alone, but there are some exceptions, especially in English contexts, where the *von* is firmly established by convention.

```
Droste-Hülshoff, Annette von
Kleist, Heinrich von
```

but

```
Von Braun, Wernher
Von Trapp, Maria
```

Alphabetize a German name with an umlaut (the mark over the vowel in *ä, ö, ü*) without regard to the umlaut. Do not substitute a two-letter combination for a vowel with an umlaut; for example, do not convert *ü* to *ue*.

Capitalization

In prose and verse, German capitalization differs considerably from English. Always capitalized in German are all nouns—including adjectives, infinitives, pronouns, prepositions, and other parts of speech used as nouns—as well as the pronoun *Sie* 'you' and its possessive, *Ihr* 'your,' and their inflected forms. Not capitalized unless they begin sentences or, usually, lines of verse are (1) the subject pronoun *ich* 'I,' (2) the names of languages and of days of the week used as adjectives, adverbs, or complements of prepositions, and (3) adjectives and adverbs formed from proper nouns, except when the proper nouns are names of persons and the adjectives and adverbs refer to the persons' works or deeds.

```
Ich glaube an das Gute in der Welt.
```

```
Er schreibt, nur um dem Auf und Ab der Buch-Nachfrage zu
entsprechen.

Fahren Sie mit Ihrer Frau zurück?

Ein französischer Schriftsteller, den ich gut kenne,
arbeitet sonntags immer an seinem neuen Buch über die
platonische Liebe.

Der Staat ist eine der bekanntesten Platonischen
Schriften.
```

In letters and ceremonial writings, the pronouns *du* and *ihr* 'you' and their derivatives are capitalized.

In a title or a subtitle, capitalize the first word and all words normally capitalized.

```
Thomas Mann und die Grenzen des Ich
Ein treuer Diener seines Herrn
Zeitschrift für vergleichende Sprachforschung
```

2.8.3. Italian

Personal Names

The names of many Italians who lived before or during the Renaissance are alphabetized by first name.

```
Bonvesin da la Riva
Cino da Pistoia
Dante Alighieri
Iacopone da Todi
Michelangelo Buonarroti
```

But other names of the period follow the standard practice.

```
Boccaccio, Giovanni
Cellini, Benvenuto
Stampa, Gaspara
```

The names of members of historic families are also usually alphabetized by last name.

```
Este, Beatrice d'
Medici, Lorenzo de'
```

In modern times, Italian *da*, *de*, *del*, *della*, and *di* are used with the last name. They are usually capitalized and are treated as an integral part of the name, even though a space may separate the prepositional from the nominal part of the name.

```
D'Annunzio, Gabriele
Del Buono, Oreste
Della Casa, Giovanni
De Sanctis, Francesco
Di Costanzo, Angelo
```

Capitalization

In prose and verse, Italian capitalization is the same as English except that in Italian centuries and other large divisions of time are capitalized (*il Seicento*) and the following terms are not capitalized unless they begin sentences or, usually, lines of verse: (1) the subject pronoun *io* 'I,' (2) the names of months and days of the week, (3) the names of languages, (4) nouns, adjectives, and adverbs derived from proper nouns, (5) titles preceding personal names, and (6) the words for a street, a square, and so on, in most place-names.

```
Un italiano parlava francese con uno svizzero in piazza
di Spagna.

Il dottor Bruno ritornerà dall'Italia giovedì otto
agosto e io partirò il nove.
```

In a title or a subtitle, capitalize only the first word and all words normally capitalized.

```
L'arte tipografica in Urbino
Bibliografia della critica pirandelliana
Collezione di classici italiani
Dizionario letterario Bompiani
Studi petrarcheschi
```

2.8.4. Spanish

Personal Names

Spanish *de* is not used before the last name alone.

```
Las Casas, Bartolomé de
Madariaga, Salvador de
Rueda, Lope de
Timoneda, Juan de
```

Spanish *del*, formed from the fusion of the preposition *de* and the definite article *el*, must be used with the last name.

```
Del Río, Angel
```

A Spanish surname may include both the paternal name and the maternal name, with or without the conjunction *y*. The surname of a married woman usually includes her paternal surname and her husband's paternal surname, connected by *de*. Alphabetize Spanish names by the full surnames (consult your sources or a biographical dictionary for guidance in distinguishing surnames and given names).

```
Carreño de Miranda, Juan
Cervantes Saavedra, Miguel de
Díaz del Castillo, Bernal
Larra y Sánchez de Castro, Mariano José
López de Ayala, Pero
Matute, Ana María
Ortega y Gasset, José
Quevedo y Villegas, Francisco Gómez de
Sinues de Marco, María del Pilar
Zayas y Sotomayor, María de
```

Even persons commonly known by the maternal portions of their surnames, such as Galdós and Lorca, should be indexed under their full surnames.

```
García Lorca, Federico
Pérez Galdós, Benito
```

Capitalization

In prose and verse, Spanish capitalization is the same as English except that the following terms are not capitalized in Spanish unless they begin sentences or, sometimes, lines of verse: (1) the subject pronoun *yo* 'I,' (2) the names of months and days of the week, (3) nouns and adjectives derived from proper nouns, (4) titles preceding personal names, and (5) the words for a street, a square, and so on, in most place-names.

El francés hablaba inglés en la plaza Colón.

Ayer yo vi al doctor García en un coche Ford.

Me dijo don Jorge que iba a salir para Sevilla el primer
martes de abril con unos amigos neoyorkinos.

In a title or a subtitle, capitalize only the first word and words normally capitalized.

Breve historia del ensayo hispanoamericano

Extremos de América

La gloria de don Ramiro

Historia verdadera de la conquista de la Nueva España

Revista de filología española

Trasmundo de Goya

Some instructors follow other rules. In titles of series and periodicals, they capitalize all major words: *Revista de Filología Española*.

2.8.5. Latin

Personal Names

Roman male citizens generally had three names: a praenomen (given name), a nomen (clan name), and a cognomen (family or familiar name). Men in this category are usually referred to by nomen, cognomen, or both; your source or a standard reference book such as *The Oxford Classical Dictionary* will provide guidance.

Brutus (Marcus Iunius Brutus)

Calpurnius Siculus (Titus Calpurnius Siculus)

Cicero (Marcus Tullius Cicero)

```
Lucretius  (Titus Lucretius Carus)
Plautus  (Titus Maccius Plautus)
```

Roman women usually had two names—a nomen (the clan name in the feminine form) and a cognomen (often derived from the father's cognomen): Livia Drusilla (daughter of Marcus Livius Drusus). Sometimes a woman's cognomen indicates her chronological order among the daughters of the family: Antonia Minor (younger daughter of Marcus Antonius). Most Roman women are referred to by nomen: Calpurnia, Clodia, Octavia, Sulpicia. Some, however, are better known by cognomen: Agrippina (Vipsania Agrippina).

When citing Roman names, use the forms most common in English.

```
Horace  (Quintus Horatius Flaccus)
Julius Caesar  (Gaius Iulius Caesar)
Juvenal  (Decimus Iunius Iuvenalis)
Livy  (Titus Livius)
Ovid  (Publius Ovidius Naso)
Quintilian  (Marcus Fabius Quintilianus)
Terence  (Publius Terentius Afer)
Vergil  (Publius Vergilius Maro)
```

Finally, some medieval and Renaissance figures are best known by their adopted or assigned Latin names.

```
Albertus Magnus  (Albert von Bollstädt)
Comenius  (Jan Amos Komenský)
Copernicus  (Niklas Koppernigk)
Paracelsus  (Theophrastus Bombast von Hohenheim)
```

Capitalization

Although practice varies, Latin most commonly follows the English rules for capitalization, except that *ego* 'I' is not capitalized.

```
Semper ego auditor tantum? Numquamne reponam / Vexatus
totiens rauci Theseide Cordi?

Quidquid id est, timeo Danaos et dona ferentes.

Nil desperandum.

Quo usque tandem abutere, Catilina, patientia nostra?
```

In a title or a subtitle, however, capitalize only the first word and all words normally capitalized.

De senectute

Liber de senectute

Medievalia et humanistica

3 The Format of the Research Paper

If your instructor has specific requirements for the format of a research paper, check them before preparing your final draft. The recommendations presented in this chapter are the most common.

3.1. PRINTING OR TYPING

If you composed your paper on a computer, use a high-quality printer. Do not justify the lines of your paper. If you are using a typewriter, make certain the ribbon produces dark, clear type. Always choose a standard, easily readable typeface. Print or type on only one side of the paper; do not use the other side for any purpose. Instructors who accept handwritten work similarly require neatness, legibility, dark blue or black ink, and the use of only one side of the paper. Be sure to keep a copy of the paper.

3.2. PAPER

Use only white, 8½- by 11-inch paper of good quality. Do not submit work typed on erasable paper, which smudges easily. If you find erasable paper convenient to use for your final draft, submit a high-quality photocopy to your instructor.

3.3. MARGINS

Except for page numbers, leave margins of one inch at the top and bottom and on both sides of the text. (For placement of page numbers, see 3.6.) Indent the first word of a paragraph one-half inch (or five spaces if you are using a typewriter) from the left margin. Indent set-off quotations one inch (or ten spaces) from the left margin. (For examples, see 2.7 and the sample first page of a research paper at the end of this book.)

3.4. SPACING

A research paper must be double-spaced throughout, including quotations, notes, and the list of works cited. In a handwritten paper, skip every other ruled line. (See the sample pages of a research paper at the end of this book.)

3.5. HEADING AND TITLE

A research paper does not need a title page. Instead, beginning one inch from the top of the first page and flush with the left margin, type your name, your instructor's name, the course number, and the date on separate lines, double-spacing between the lines. Double-space again and center the title. Double-space also between the lines of the title, and double-space between the title and the first line of the text (see fig. 5). Do not underline your title or put it in quotation marks or type it in all capital letters. Follow the rules for capitalization in 2.6.1, and underline only the words that you would underline in the text (see 2.3, 2.6.2).

Local Television Coverage of International News Events

The Attitude toward Violence in <u>A Clockwork Orange</u>

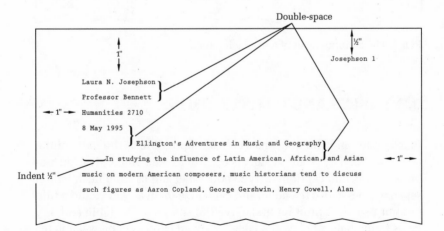

Fig. 5. The top of the first page of a research paper.

The Use of the Words <u>Fair</u> and <u>Foul</u> in Shakespeare's
    <u>Macbeth</u>
Romanticism in England and the <u>Scapigliatura</u> in Italy

Do not use a period after your title or after any heading in the paper
(e.g., *Works Cited*).

If your teacher requires a title page, format it according to the
instructions you are given.

3.6. PAGE NUMBERS

Number all pages consecutively throughout the manuscript in the
upper right-hand corner, one-half inch from the top and flush with the
right margin. Type your last name before the page number, as a pre-
caution in case of misplaced pages. Word processors with automatic
page numbering will save you the time and effort of numbering every
page. Do not use the abbreviation *p.* before a page number or add a
period, a hyphen, or any other mark or symbol. Position the first line
of text one inch from the top of the page (see fig. 6).

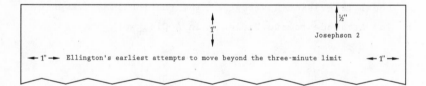

Fig. 6. The running head of a research paper.

3.7. TABLES AND ILLUSTRATIONS

Place tables and illustrations as close as possible to the parts of the
text to which they relate. A table is usually labeled *Table*, given an arabic numeral, and captioned. Type both label and caption flush left on
separate lines above the table, and capitalize them as you would a title
(do not use all capital letters). Give the source of the table and any
notes immediately below the table. To avoid confusion between notes
to the text and notes to the table, designate notes to the table with low-

ercase letters rather than with numerals. Double-space throughout, making dividing lines as needed (see fig. 7).

Table 1

Earned Degrees in Modern Foreign Languages Conferred by

   Institutions of Higher Education in the United States[a]

Year	Bachelor's Degrees	Master's Degrees	Doctor's Degrees
1980-81	10,052	2,023	561
1981-82	9,577	1,917	502
1982-83	9,335	1,605	454
1983-84	9,158	1,641	429
1984-85	9,675	1,613	389
1985-86	9,810	1,656	427
1986-87	9,847	1,694	406
1987-88	9,790	1,795	383
1988-89	10,500	1,823	392
1989-90	11,096	1,932	476

Source: United States, Dept. of Education, Office of

   Educational Research and Improvement, National Center

   for Education Statistics, Digest of Education

   Statistics, 1993 (Washington: GPO, 1993) table 276.

   [a] These figures include degrees conferred in a single modern foreign language or a combination of modern foreign languages and exclude degrees in linguistics, Latin, classical Greek, and some not commonly taught modern languages.

Fig. 7. A table in a research paper.

Any other type of illustrative visual material—for example, a photograph, map, line drawing, graph, or chart—should be labeled *Figure* (usually abbreviated *Fig.*), assigned an arabic numeral, and given a title or caption: "Fig. 1. Mary Cassatt, *Mother and Child*, Wichita Art Museum, Wichita." A label and title or caption ordinarily appear directly below the illustration and have the same one-inch margins as the text of the paper (see fig. 8).

If your research papers have many illustrations, you will probably want to become familiar with the various kinds of drafting software, for the creation of tables, graphs, drawings, and so forth, on a computer. These programs automatically number tables and illustrations, set them appropriately into the text, and generate a listing of all tables and illustrations created for the paper.

Musical illustrations are labeled *Example* (usually abbreviated *Ex.*), assigned an arabic numeral, and given a title or caption: "Ex. 1. Pyotr Ilich Tchaikovsky, Symphony no. 6 in B, op. 74 (*Pathétique*), finale." A label and title or caption ordinarily appear directly below the example and have the same one-inch margins as the text of the paper (see fig. 9).

Fig. 1. Manticore, woodcut from Edward Topsell, The History of Four-Footed Beasts and Serpents . . . (London, 1658) 344; rpt. in Konrad Gesner, Curious Woodcuts of Fanciful and Real Beasts (New York: Dover, 1971) 8.

Fig. 8. A figure in a research paper.

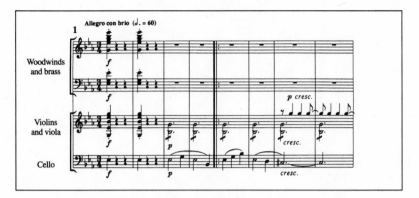

Ex. 1. Ludwig van Beethoven, Symphony no. 3 in E flat,
op. 55 (Eroica), first movement, opening.

Fig. 9. A musical example in a research paper.

3.8. CORRECTIONS AND INSERTIONS

Proofread and correct your research paper carefully before submitting
it. If you find a mistake in the final copy and you are using a word
processor, recall the file, make the appropriate revisions, and reprint
the corrected page or pages. Be sure to save the changed file. Some
writers find such software as spelling checkers and usage checkers
helpful when used with caution (see 1.9). If you are not using a computer and if your instructor permits brief corrections, write them
neatly and legibly in ink directly above the lines involved, using
carets (∧) to indicate where they go. Do not use the margins or write a
change below the line it affects. If corrections on any page are numerous or substantial, retype the page.

3.9. BINDING

Pages of your research paper may get misplaced or lost if they are left
unattached or merely folded down at a corner. Although a plastic
folder or some other kind of binder may seem an attractive finishing
touch, most instructors find such devices a nuisance in reading and
commenting on students' work. Many prefer that a paper be secured
with a simple paper clip, which can be easily removed and restored.

4 Documentation: Preparing the List of Works Cited

4.1. DOCUMENTING SOURCES

Nearly all research builds on previous research. Researchers commonly begin a project by studying past work in the area and deriving relevant information and ideas from their predecessors. This process is largely responsible for the continual expansion of human knowledge. In presenting their work, researchers generously acknowledge their debts to predecessors by carefully documenting each source, so that earlier contributions receive appropriate credit.

As you prepare your paper, you should similarly seek to build on the work of previous writers and researchers. And whenever you draw on another's work, you must also document your source by indicating what you borrowed—whether facts, opinions, or quotations—and where you borrowed it from. If you have not already done so, read carefully the earlier section on plagiarism (1.7) to learn what you must document in your paper.

4.2. MLA STYLE

In MLA documentation style, you acknowledge your sources by keying brief parenthetical citations in your text to an alphabetical list of works that appears at the end of the paper. The parenthetical citation that concludes the following sentence is typical of MLA style.

```
Ancient writers attributed the invention of the
monochord to Pythagoras, who lived in the sixth century
BC (Marcuse 197).
```

The citation "(Marcuse 197)" tells readers that the information in the sentence was derived from page 197 of a work by an author named Marcuse. If readers want more information about this source, they can turn to the works-cited list, where, under the name Marcuse, they would find the following information.

```
Marcuse, Sibyl. A Survey of Musical Instruments. New
York: Harper, 1975.
```

This entry states that the work's author is Sibyl Marcuse and its title is *A Survey of Musical Instruments*. The remaining information relates, in shortened form, that the work was published in New York City by Harper and Row in 1975.

A citation in MLA style contains only enough information to enable readers to find the source in the works-cited list. If the author's name is mentioned in the text, only the page number appears in the citation: "(197)." If more than one work by the author is in the list of works cited, a shortened version of the title is given: "(Marcuse, *Survey* 197)." (See ch. 5 for a fuller discussion of parenthetical citations in MLA style.)

MLA style is not the only way to document sources. Many disciplines have their own documentation systems. MLA style is widely used in the humanities. Although generally simpler and more economical than other documentation styles, it shares with most others its central feature: parenthetical citations keyed to a works-cited list. If you learn MLA documentation style at an early stage in your school career, you will probably have little difficulty in adapting to other styles.

Documentation styles differ according to discipline because they are shaped by the kind of research and scholarship undertaken. For example, in the sciences, where timeliness of research is crucial, the date of publication is usually given prominence. Thus, in the style recommended by the American Psychological Association (APA), a typical citation includes the date of publication (as well as the abbreviation *p.* before the page number). Compare APA and MLA parenthetical citations for the same source.

APA

(Marcuse, 1975, p. 197)

MLA

(Marcuse 197)

In the humanities, where most important scholarship remains relevant for a substantial period, publication dates receive less attention: though always stated in the works-cited list, they are omitted in parenthetical references. An important reason for this omission is that many humanities scholars like to keep their texts as readable and as free of disruptions as possible.

In an entry in an APA-style works-cited list, the date (in parentheses) immediately follows the name of the author (whose first name is written only as an initial), just the first word of the title is capitalized, and the publisher's full name is provided. In APA style, the first line of the entry is indented; second and subsequent lines are flush with the left margin.

APA

>   Marcuse, S. (1975). <u>A survey of musical instruments</u>. New York: Harper and Row.

By contrast, in an MLA-style entry, the author's name appears in full, every important word of the title is capitalized, the publisher's name is shortened, and the publication date is placed at the end. In MLA style, the first line of the entry is flush with the left margin, and second and subsequent lines are indented. This format helps readers locate authors' names in the alphabetical listing.

MLA

>   Marcuse, Sibyl. <u>A Survey of Musical Instruments</u>. New
>   York: Harper, 1975.

Chapters 4 and 5 offer an authoritative and comprehensive presentation of MLA style. For descriptions of other systems of documentation, including one using endnotes and footnotes, see appendix B.

4.3. THE LIST OF WORKS CITED AND OTHER SOURCE LISTS

Although the list of works cited appears at the end of your paper, you need to draft the section in advance, so that you will know what information to give in parenthetical references as you write. For example, you have to include shortened titles if you cite two or more works by the same author, and you have to add initials or first names if two of the cited authors have the same last name: "(K. Roemer 123–24)," "(M. Roemer 67)." This chapter therefore explains how to prepare a list of works cited, and the next chapter demonstrates how to document sources where you use them in your text.

As the heading *Works Cited* indicates, this list contains all the works that you will cite in your text. The list simplifies documentation by permitting you to make only brief references to these works in the text. For example, when you have the following entry in your list of works cited, a citation such as "(Thompson 32–35)" fully identifies your source to readers (provided that you cite no other work by an author with the same last name).

```
Thompson, Stith. The Folktale. New York: Dryden, 1946.
```

Other names for such a listing are *Bibliography* (literally, "description of books") and *Literature Cited*. Usually, however, the broader title *Works Cited* is most appropriate, since research papers often draw on not only books and articles but also films, recordings, television programs, and other nonprint sources.

Titles used for other kinds of source lists include *Annotated Bibliography*, *Works Consulted*, and *Selected Bibliography*. An annotated bibliography, also called *Annotated List of Works Cited*, contains descriptive or evaluative comments on the sources. (For more information on such listings, see James L. Harner, *On Compiling an Annotated Bibliography*, rev. ed. [New York: MLA, 1991].)

```
Thompson, Stith. The Folktale. New York: Dryden, 1946. A
    comprehensive survey of the most popular folktales,
    including their histories and their uses in
    literary works.
```

The title *Works Consulted* indicates that the list is not confined to works cited in the paper. The heading *Selected Bibliography*, or *Selected List of Works Consulted*, is appropriate for lists suggesting readings in the field.

4.4. PLACEMENT OF THE LIST OF WORKS CITED

The list of works cited appears at the end of the paper. Begin the list on a new page and number each page, continuing the page numbers of the text. For example, if the text of your research paper ends on page 10, the works-cited list begins on page 11. The page number appears in the upper right-hand corner, half an inch from the top and flush with the right margin. Center the title, *Works Cited*, an inch from the top of the page. Double-space between the title and the first entry. Begin each entry flush with the left margin; if an entry runs more than one line, indent the subsequent line or lines one-half inch (or five spaces if you are using a typewriter) from the left margin. Double-space the entire list, both between and within entries (see fig. 10). Continue the list on as many pages as necessary.

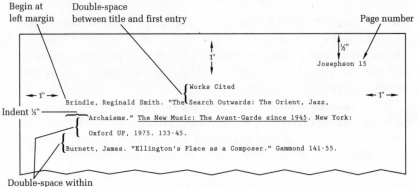

Fig. 10. The top of the first page of a works-cited list.

4.5. ARRANGEMENT OF ENTRIES

In general, alphabetize entries in the list of works cited by the author's last name, using the letter-by-letter system. In this system, the alphabetical order of names is determined by the letters before the commas that separate last names and first names. Spaces and other punctuation marks are ignored. The letters following the commas are considered only when two or more last names are identical. The following examples are alphabetized letter by letter. (For more information on alphabetizing foreign names, see 2.8.)

```
Descartes, René
De Sica, Vittorio

MacDonald, George
McCullers, Carson

Morris, Robert
Morris, William
Morrison, Toni
```

```
Saint-Exupéry, Antoine de
St. Denis, Ruth
```

If two or more entries citing coauthors begin with the same name, alphabetize by the last names of the second authors listed.

```
Scholes, Robert, and Robert Kellogg
Scholes, Robert, and Eric S. Rabkin
```

If the author's name is unknown, alphabetize by the title, ignoring any initial *A*, *An*, or *The*. For example, the title *An Encyclopedia of the Latin-American Novel* would be alphabetized under *E* rather than *A*. An alphabetical listing makes it easy for the reader to find the entry corresponding to a citation in the text.

Other kinds of bibliographies may be arranged differently. An annotated list, a list of works consulted, or a list of selected readings for a historical study, for example, may be organized chronologically by publication date. Some bibliographies are divided into sections and the items alphabetized in each section. A list may be broken down into primary and secondary sources or into different research media (books, articles, recordings). Alternatively, it may be arranged by subject matter (literature and law, law in literature, law as literature), by period (classical utopia, Renaissance utopia), or by area (Egyptian mythology, Greek mythology, Norse mythology).

4.6. CITING BOOKS

4.6.1. The Basic Entry: A Book by a Single Author

One of the most common items in students' works-cited lists is the entry for a book by a single author. Such an entry characteristically has three main divisions:

```
Author's name. Title of the book. Publication
    information.
```

Here is an example:

```
Kaku, Michio. Hyperspace: A Scientific Odyssey through
    Parallel Universes, Time Warps, and the Tenth
    Dimension. New York: Oxford UP, 1994.
```

Author's Name

Reverse the author's name for alphabetizing, adding a comma after the last name (Porter, Katherine Anne). Put a period after the complete name.

    Kaku, Michio.

Apart from reversing the order, give the author's name as it appears on the title page. Never abbreviate a name given in full. If, for example, the title page lists the author as "Carleton Brown," do not enter the name as "Brown, C." But use initials if the title page does.

    Eliot, T. S.
    McLuhan, H. Marshall.

You may spell out a name abbreviated on the title page if you think the additional information would be helpful to readers. Put square brackets around the material you add.

    Hinton, S[usan] E[loise].
    Tolkien, J[ohn] R[onald] R[euel].

Similarly, you may give the real name of an author listed under a pseudonym, enclosing the added name in square brackets.

    Le Carré, John [David Cornwell].

In general, omit titles, affiliations, and degrees that precede or follow names.

ON TITLE PAGE	IN WORKS-CITED LIST
Anthony T. Boyle, PhD	Boyle, Anthony T.
Sister Jean Daniel	Daniel, Jean.
Gerard Manley Hopkins, SJ	Hopkins, Gerard Manley.
Lady Mary Wortley Montagu	Montagu, Mary Wortley.
Sir Philip Sidney	Sidney, Philip.
Saint Teresa de Jesús	Teresa de Jesús.

A suffix that is an essential part of the name—like *Jr.* or a roman numeral—appears after the given name, preceded by a comma.

    Rockefeller, John D., IV.
    Rust, Arthur George, Jr.

Title of the Book

In general, follow the recommendations for titles given in 2.6. State the full title of the book, including any subtitle. If the book has a subtitle, put a colon directly after the main title, unless the main title ends in a question mark, an exclamation point, or a dash. Place a period after the entire title (including any subtitle), unless it ends in another punctuation mark. Underline the entire title, including any colon, subtitle, and punctuation in the title, but do not underline the period that follows the title.

Kaku, Michio. <u>Hyperspace: A Scientific Odyssey through Parallel Universes, Time Warps, and the Tenth Dimension</u>.

Publication Information

In general, give the city of publication, publisher's name, and year of publication. Take these facts directly from the book, not from a source such as a bibliography or a library catalog. The publisher's name that appears on the title page is generally the name to cite. The name may be accompanied there by the city and date. Any publication information not available on the title page can usually be found on the copyright page (i.e., the reverse of the title page) or, particularly in books published outside the United States, on a page at the back of the book. Use a colon between the place of publication and the publisher, a comma between the publisher and the date, and a period after the date.

Kaku, Michio. <u>Hyperspace: A Scientific Odyssey through Parallel Universes, Time Warps, and the Tenth Dimension</u>. New York: Oxford UP, 1994.

If several cities are listed in the book, give only the first. For cities outside the United States, add an abbreviation of the country (or of the province for cities in Canada) if the name of the city may be ambiguous or unfamiliar to your reader (see 6.3 for abbreviations of geographic names).

Manchester, Eng.
Sherbrooke, PQ

Shorten the publisher's name, following the guidelines in 6.5. If the year of publication is not recorded on the title page, use the latest copyright date.

Here are some additional examples of the basic book entry:

```
Berlage, Gai Ingham. Women in Baseball: The Forgotten
     History. Westport: Greenwood, 1994.
Freedman, Richard R. What Do Unions Do? New York: Basic,
     1984.
Hinton, S[usan] E[loise]. Tex. New York: Delacorte, 1979.
Le Carré, John [David Cornwell]. The Russia House. New
     York: Knopf, 1989.
Tatar, Maria. Off with Their Heads! Fairy Tales and the
     Culture of Childhood. Princeton: Princeton
     UP, 1992.
Taves, Brian. The Romance of Adventure: The Genre of
     Historical Adventure Movies. Jackson: UP of
     Mississippi, 1993.
Townsend, Robert M. The Medieval Village Economy.
     Princeton: Princeton UP, 1993.
```

Sometimes additional information is required. This list shows most of the possible components of a book entry and the order in which they are normally arranged:

1. Author's name
2. Title of a part of the book (see esp. 4.6.7–9)
3. Title of the book
4. Name of the editor, translator, or compiler (see esp. 4.6.7 and 4.6.12–13)
5. Edition used (see 4.6.14)
6. Number(s) of the volume(s) used (see 4.6.15)
7. Name of the series (see 4.6.16)
8. Place of publication, name of the publisher, and date of publication
9. Page numbers (see esp. 4.6.7)
10. Supplementary bibliographic information and annotation (see esp. 4.6.13 and 4.6.15)

The rest of 4.6 explains how to cite these items.

4.6.2. An Anthology or a Compilation

To cite an anthology or a compilation (e.g., a bibliography) that was edited or compiled by someone whose name appears on the title page, begin your entry with the name of the editor or compiler, followed by a comma and the abbreviation *ed.* or *comp.* If the person named performed more than one function—serving, say, as editor and translator—give both roles in the order in which they appear on the title page.

> Lopate, Phillip, ed. <u>The Art of the Personal Essay: An Anthology from the Classical Era to the Present</u>. New York: Anchor-Doubleday, 1994.
>
> McRae, Murdo William, ed. <u>The Literature of Science: Perspectives on Popular Science Writing</u>. Athens: U of Georgia P, 1993.
>
> Nichols, Fred J., ed. and trans. <u>An Anthology of Neo-Latin Poetry</u>. New Haven: Yale UP, 1979.
>
> Rueschemeyer, Marilyn, ed. <u>Women in the Politics of Postcommunist Eastern Europe</u>. Armonk: Sharpe, 1994.
>
> Sevillano, Mando, comp. <u>The Hopi Way: Tales from a Vanishing Culture</u>. Flagstaff: Northland, 1986.
>
> Spafford, Peter, comp. and ed. <u>Interference: The Story of Czechoslovakia in the Words of Its Writers</u>. Cheltenham: New Clarion, 1992.

See also the sections on works in an anthology (4.6.7); introductions, prefaces, and similar parts of books (4.6.9); editions (4.6.12); and translations (4.6.13).

4.6.3. Two or More Books by the Same Author

To cite two or more books by the same author, give the name in the first entry only. Thereafter, in place of the name, type three hyphens, followed by a period and the title. The three hyphens stand for exactly the same name as in the preceding entry. If the person named edited, translated, or compiled the book, place a comma (not a period) after the three hyphens, and write the appropriate abbreviation (*ed.*, *trans.*, or *comp.*) before giving the title. If the same person served as, say, the editor of two or more works listed consecutively, the abbreviation *ed.* must be repeated with each entry. This sort of label does not affect the order in which entries appear; works listed under the same name are alphabetized by title.

> Borroff, Marie. <u>Language and the Past: Verbal Artistry in Frost, Stevens, and Moore</u>. Chicago: U of Chicago P, 1979.
>
> ---, trans. <u>Sir Gawain and the Green Knight</u>. New York: Norton, 1967.
>
> ---, ed. <u>Wallace Stevens: A Collection of Critical Essays</u>. Englewood Cliffs: Prentice, 1963.
>
> Frye, Northrop. <u>Anatomy of Criticism: Four Essays</u>. Princeton: Princeton UP, 1957.
>
> ---, ed. <u>Design for Learning: Reports Submitted to the Joint Committee of the Toronto Board of Education and the University of Toronto</u>. Toronto: U of Toronto P, 1962.
>
> ---. <u>The Double Vision: Language and Meaning in Religion</u>. Toronto: U of Toronto P, 1991.
>
> ---, ed. <u>Sound and Poetry</u>. New York: Columbia UP, 1957.

4.6.4. A Book by Two or More Authors

To cite a book by two or three authors, give their names in the same order as on the title page—not necessarily in alphabetical order. Reverse only the name of the first author, add a comma, and give the other name or names in normal form (Wellek, René, and Austin Warren). Place a period after the last name. Even if the authors have the same last name, state each name in full (Durant, Will, and Ariel Durant). If the persons listed on the title page are editors, translators, or compilers, place a comma (not a period) after the final name and add the appropriate abbreviation (*eds., trans.,* or *comps.* for "editors," "translators," or "compilers").

> Jakobson, Roman, and Linda R. Waugh. <u>The Sound Shape of Language</u>. Bloomington: Indiana UP, 1979.

Kerrigan, William, and Gordon Braden. <u>The Idea of the
    Renaissance</u>. Baltimore: Johns Hopkins UP, 1989.

Marquart, James W., Sheldon Ekland Olson, and Jonathan R.
    Sorensen. <u>The Rope, the Chair, and the Needle:
    Capital Punishment in Texas, 1923-1990</u>. Austin: U of
    Texas P, 1994.

Rabkin, Eric S., Martin H. Greenberg, and Joseph D.
    Olander, eds. <u>No Place Else: Explorations in Utopian
    and Dystopian Fiction</u>. Carbondale: Southern Illinois
    UP, 1983.

Welsch, Roger L., and Linda K. Welsch. <u>Cather's Kitchens:
    Foodways in Literature and Life</u>. Lincoln: U of
    Nebraska P, 1987.

If there are more than three authors, you may name only the first and
add *et al.* ("and others"), or you may give all names in full in the order
in which they appear on the title page.

Gilman, Sander, et al. <u>Hysteria beyond Freud</u>. Berkeley:
    U of California P, 1993.

Quirk, Randolph, et al. <u>A Comprehensive Grammar of the
    English Language</u>. London: Longman, 1985.

or

Gilman, Sander, Helen King, Roy Porter, George Rousseau,
    and Elaine Showalter. <u>Hysteria beyond Freud</u>.
    Berkeley: U of California P, 1993.

Quirk, Randolph, Sidney Greenbaum, Geoffrey Leech, and
    Jan Svartvik. <u>A Comprehensive Grammar of the
    English Language</u>. London: Longman, 1985.

If a single author cited in an entry is also the first of multiple authors
in the following entry, repeat the name in full; do not substitute three
hyphens. Repeat the name in full whenever you cite the same person
as part of a different authorship. The three hyphens are never used in
combination with persons' names.

Scholes, Robert. <u>Semiotics and Interpretation</u>. New
    Haven: Yale UP, 1982.

---. <u>Textual Power: Literary Theory and the Teaching of
   English</u>. New Haven: Yale UP, 1985.

Scholes, Robert, and Robert Kellogg. <u>The Nature of
   Narrative</u>. New York: Oxford UP, 1966.

Scholes, Robert, and Eric S. Rabkin. <u>Science Fiction:
   History, Science, Vision</u>. New York: Oxford UP, 1977.

Tannen, Deborah, ed. <u>Gender and Conversational
   Interaction</u>. New York: Oxford UP, 1993.

---. <u>You Just Don't Understand: Women and Men in
   Conversation</u>. New York: Morrow, 1990.

Tannen, Deborah, and Roy O. Freedle, eds. <u>Linguistics in
   Context: Connecting Observation and Understanding</u>.
   Norwood: Ablex, 1988.

Tannen, Deborah, and Muriel Saville-Troike, eds.
   <u>Perspectives on Silence</u>. Norwood: Ablex, 1985.

4.6.5. Two or More Books by the Same Authors

To cite two or more books by the same authors, give the names in the
first entry only. Thereafter, in place of the names, type three hyphens,
followed by a period and the title. The three hyphens stand for exactly
the same names as in the preceding entry.

Durant, Will, and Ariel Durant. <u>The Age of Voltaire</u>. New
   York: Simon, 1965.

---. <u>A Dual Autobiography</u>. New York: Simon, 1977.

Gilbert, Sandra M. <u>Blood Pressure</u>. New York: Norton,
   1989.

---. <u>Emily's Bread: Poems</u>. New York: Norton, 1984.

Gilbert, Sandra M., and Susan Gubar. <u>The Madwoman in the
   Attic: The Woman Writer and the Nineteenth-Century
   Literary Imagination</u>. New Haven: Yale UP, 1979.

---, eds. <u>The Norton Anthology of Literature by Women:
   The Tradition in English</u>. New York: Norton, 1985.

4.6.6. A Book by a Corporate Author

A corporate author may be a commission, an association, a committee, or any other group whose individual members are not identified on the title page. Cite the book by the corporate author, even if the corporate author is the publisher. (On citing government publications, see 4.6.21.)

American Medical Association. <u>The American Medical</u>
      <u>Association Encyclopedia of Medicine</u>. New York:
      Random, 1989.
National Research Council. <u>China and Global Change:</u>
      <u>Opportunities for Collaboration</u>. Washington: Natl.
      Acad., 1992.
Public Agenda Foundation. <u>The Health Care Crisis:</u>
      <u>Containing Costs, Expanding Coverage</u>. New York:
      McGraw, 1992.

4.6.7. A Work in an Anthology

If you are citing an essay, a short story, a poem, or another work that appears within an anthology or some other book collection, you need to add the following information to the basic book entry (4.6.1).

Author, title, and (if relevant) translator of the part of the book being cited. Begin the entry with the author and title of the piece, normally enclosing the title in quotation marks.

Allende, Isabel. "Toad's Mouth."

But if the work was originally published independently (as, e.g., autobiographies, plays, and novels generally are), underline its title instead (see the sample entries below for Douglass, Hansberry, and Sastre). Follow the title of the part of the book with a period. If the anthology contains the work of more than one translator, give the translator's name next, preceded by the abbreviation *Trans.* ("Translated by").

Allende, Isabel. "Toad's Mouth." Trans. Margaret Sayers
      Peden.

Then state the title of the anthology (underlined).

```
Allende, Isabel. "Toad's Mouth." Trans. Margaret Sayers
     Peden. A Hammock beneath the Mangoes: Stories from
     Latin America.
```

Name of the editor, translator, or compiler of the book being cited. If all the works in the collection have the same translator or if the book has an editor or compiler, write *Trans., Ed.,* or *Comp.* ("Translated by," "Edited by," or "Compiled by"), as appropriate, after the book title and give that person's name.

```
Allende, Isabel. "Toad's Mouth." Trans. Margaret Sayers
     Peden. A Hammock beneath the Mangoes: Stories from
     Latin America. Ed. Thomas Colchie.
```

If someone served in more than one role—say, as editor and translator—state the roles in the order in which they appear on the title page (e.g., "Ed. and trans."; see the entry below for Hanzlík). Similarly, if more than one person served in different roles, give the names in the order in which they appear on the title page: "Trans. Jessie Coulson. Ed. George Gibian."

Page numbers of the cited piece. Give the inclusive page numbers of the piece you are citing. Be sure to provide the page numbers for the entire piece, not just for the material you used. Inclusive page numbers, usually without any identifying abbreviation, follow the publication date and a period. (If the book has no page numbers, see 4.6.25.)

```
Allende, Isabel. "Toad's Mouth." Trans. Margaret Sayers
     Peden. A Hammock beneath the Mangoes: Stories from
     Latin America. Ed. Thomas Colchie. New York: Plume,
     1992. 83-88.
```

Here are some sample entries for works in anthologies:

```
Calvino, Italo. "Cybernetics and Ghosts." The Uses of
     Literature: Essays. Trans. Patrick Creagh. San
     Diego: Harcourt, 1982. 3-27.
Hansberry, Lorraine. A Raisin in the Sun. Black Theater:
     A Twentieth-Century Collection of the Work of Its
     Best Playwrights. Ed. Lindsay Patterson. New York:
     Dodd, 1971. 221-76.
```

Hanzlík, Josef. "Vengeance." Trans. Ewald Osers.
Interference: The Story of Czechoslovakia in the
Words of Its Writers. Comp. and ed. Peter Spafford.
Cheltenham: New Clarion, 1992. 54.

Sastre, Alfonso. Sad Are the Eyes of William Tell.
Trans. Leonard Pronko. The New Wave of Spanish
Drama. Ed. George Wellwarth. New York: New York UP,
1970. 165-321.

"A Witchcraft Story." The Hopi Way: Tales from a
Vanishing Culture. Comp. Mando Sevillano.
Flagstaff: Northland, 1986. 33-42.

Often the works in anthologies have been published before. If you
wish to inform your reader of the date when a previously published
piece other than a scholarly article first appeared, you may follow the
title of the piece with the year of original publication and a period.

Douglass, Frederick. Narrative of the Life of Frederick
Douglass, an American Slave, Written by Himself.
1845. Classic American Autobiographies. Ed. William
L. Andrews. New York: Mentor, 1992. 229-327.

Franklin, Benjamin. "Emigration to America." 1782. The
Faber Book of America. Ed. Christopher Ricks and
William L. Vance. Boston: Faber, 1992. 24-26.

To cite a previously published scholarly article in a collection, give
the complete data for the earlier publication and then add *Rpt. in*
("Reprinted in"), the title of the collection, and the new publication
facts. (On citing articles in periodicals, see 4.7.)

Frye, Northrop. "Literary and Linguistic Scholarship in
a Postliterate Age." PMLA 99 (1984): 990-95. Rpt.
in Myth and Metaphor: Selected Essays, 1974-88. Ed.
Robert D. Denham. Charlottesville: UP of Virginia,
1990. 18-27.

Roberts, Sheila. "A Confined World: A Rereading of
Pauline Smith." World Literature Written in English
24 (1984): 232-38. Rpt. in Twentieth-Century

> Literary Criticism. Ed. Dennis Poupard. Vol. 25.
>
> Detroit: Gale, 1988. 399-402.

If the article was originally published under a different title, first state the new title and publication facts, followed by *Rpt. of* ("Reprint of"), the original title, and the original publication facts.

> Lewis, C. S. "Viewpoints: C. S. Lewis." Twentieth-Century
>
> Interpretations of Sir Gawain and the Green Knight.
>
> Ed. Denton Fox. Englewood Cliffs: Prentice, 1968.
>
> 100-01. Rpt. of "The Anthropological Approach."
>
> English and Medieval Studies Presented to J. R. R.
>
> Tolkien on the Occasion of His Seventieth Birthday.
>
> Ed. Norman Davis and C. L. Wrenn. London: Allen,
>
> 1962. 219-23.

If you refer to more than one piece from the same collection, you may wish to cross-reference each citation to a single entry for the book (see 4.6.10). On citing articles in reference books, see 4.6.8. On citing introductions, prefaces, and the like, see 4.6.9. On citing a piece in a multivolume anthology, see 4.6.15.

4.6.8. An Article in a Reference Book

Treat an encyclopedia article or a dictionary entry as you would a piece in a collection (4.6.7), but do not cite the editor of the reference work. If the article is signed, give the author first (often articles in reference books are signed with initials identified elsewhere in the work); if it is unsigned, give the title first. If the encyclopedia or dictionary arranges articles alphabetically, you may omit volume and page numbers.

When citing familiar reference books, especially those that frequently appear in new editions, do not give full publication information. For such works, list only the edition (if stated) and the year of publication.

> "Azimuthal Equidistant Projection." Merriam-Webster's
>
> Collegiate Dictionary. 10th ed. 1993.
>
> "Ginsburg, Ruth Bader." Who's Who in America. 48th ed.
>
> 1994.
>
> "Mandarin." The Encyclopedia Americana. 1993 ed.

```
Mohanty, Jitendra M. "Indian Philosophy." The New
     Encyclopaedia Britannica: Macropaedia. 15th
     ed. 1987.
```

When citing less familiar reference books, however, especially those that have appeared in only one edition, give full publication information.

```
Brakeley, Theresa C. "Mourning Songs." Funk and Wagnalls
     Standard Dictionary of Folklore, Mythology, and
     Legend. Ed. Maria Leach and Jerome Fried. 2 vols.
     New York: Crowell, 1950.
Trainen, Isaac N., et al. "Religious Directives in
     Medical Ethics." Encyclopedia of Bioethics. Ed.
     Warren T. Reich. 4 vols. New York: Free, 1978.
```

4.6.9. An Introduction, a Preface, a Foreword, or an Afterword

To cite an introduction, a preface, a foreword, or an afterword, begin with the name of its author and then give the name of the part being cited, capitalized but neither underlined nor enclosed in quotation marks (*Introduction, Preface, Foreword, Afterword*). If the writer of the piece is different from the author of the complete work, cite the author of the work after its title, giving the full name, in normal order, preceded by the word *By*. If the writer of the piece is also the author of the complete work, use only the last name after *By*. Continue with full publication information and, finally, the inclusive page numbers.

```
Borges, Jorge Luis. Foreword. Selected Poems, 1923-1967.
     By Borges. Ed. Norman Thomas Di Giovanni. New York:
     Delta-Dell, 1973. xv-xvi.
Doctorow, E. L. Introduction. Sister Carrie. By Theodore
     Dreiser. New York: Bantam, 1982. v-xi.
Drabble, Margaret. Introduction. Middlemarch. By George
     Eliot. New York: Bantam, 1985. vii-xvii.
Elliott, Emory. Afterword. The Jungle. By Upton
     Sinclair. New York: Signet, 1990. 342-50.
Hamill, Pete. Introduction. The Brooklyn Reader: Thirty
     Writers Celebrate America's Favorite Borough. Ed.
```

> Andrea Wyatt Sexton and Alice Leccese Powers. New
> York: Harmony, 1994. xi-xiv.

Marsalis, Wynton. Foreword. <u>Beyond Category: The Life</u>
<u>and Genius of Duke Ellington</u>. By John Edward Hasse.
New York: Simon, 1993. 13-14.

4.6.10. Cross-References

To avoid unnecessary repetition in citing two or more works from the
same collection, you may create a complete entry for the collection
and cross-reference individual pieces to the entry. In a cross-reference,
state the author and the title of the piece, the last name of the editor of
the collection, and the inclusive page numbers. If the piece is a translation, add the name of the translator after the title, unless one person
translated the entire volume.

Hamill, Pete. Introduction. Sexton and Powers xi-xiv.

Mayakovsky, Vladimir. "Brooklyn Bridge." Trans. Max
Hayward and George Reavey. Sexton and Powers 136-41.

McCullers, Carson. "Brooklyn Is My Neighborhood." Sexton
and Powers 143-47.

Sexton, Andrea Wyatt, and Alice Leccese Powers, eds. <u>The</u>
<u>Brooklyn Reader: Thirty Writers Celebrate America's</u>
<u>Favorite Borough</u>. New York: Harmony, 1994.

Walcott, Derek. "A Letter from Brooklyn." Sexton and
Powers 264-65.

Whitman, Walt. "Crossing Brooklyn Ferry." Sexton and
Powers 267-74.

If you list two or more works under the editor's name, however, add
the title (or a shortened version of it) to the cross-reference.

Angelou, Maya. "Pickin Em Up and Layin Em Down." Baker,
<u>Norton</u> 276-78.

Baker, Russell, ed. <u>The Norton Book of Light Verse</u>. New
York: Norton, 1986.

---, ed. <u>Russell Baker's Book of American Humor</u>. New
York: Norton, 1993.

Hurston, Zora Neale. "Squinch Owl Story." Baker, <u>Russell</u>
     <u>Baker's Book</u> 458-59.

Lebowitz, Fran. "Manners." Baker, <u>Russell Baker's Book</u>
     556-59.

Lennon, John. "The Fat Budgie." Baker, <u>Norton</u> 357-58.

4.6.11. An Anonymous Book

If a book has no author's or editor's name on the title page, begin the
entry with the title. Do not use either *Anonymous* or *Anon.* Alphabetize the entry by the title, ignoring any initial *A*, *An*, or *The*. (Note in
the sample entries that *A Guide to Our Federal Lands* is alphabetized
under *G*.)

<u>Encyclopedia of Virginia</u>. New York: Somerset, 1993.

<u>A Guide to Our Federal Lands</u>. Washington: Natl.
     Geographic Soc., 1984.

<u>New York Public Library Student's Desk Reference</u>. New
     York: Prentice, 1993.

4.6.12. An Edition

Every published book is, in at least one sense, an edition; for example,
a book may be a first edition, a second edition, and so forth (see
4.6.14). Researchers also use the term *edition*, however, to denote a
work that was prepared for publication by someone other than the
author—by an editor. For example, a 1995 printing of Shakespeare's
Hamlet was obviously not prepared for publication by Shakespeare.
An editor selected a version of *Hamlet* from the various versions available, decided on any changes in spelling or punctuation, and perhaps
added explanatory notes or wrote an introduction. This 1995 version
of *Hamlet* would be called an "edition," and the editor's name would
most likely appear on the title page along with Shakespeare's.

   To cite an edition, begin with the author (or the title, for an anonymous work) if you refer primarily to the text itself; give the editor's
name, preceded by the abbreviation *Ed.* ("Edited by"), after the title. If
for clarity you wish to indicate the original date of publication, place
the year directly after the title (see the entry for Crane).

Crane, Stephen. <u>The Red Badge of Courage: An Episode of</u>
    <u>the American Civil War</u>. 1895. Ed. Fredson Bowers.
    Charlottesville: UP of Virginia, 1975.

Edgeworth, Maria. Castle Rackrent <u>and</u> Ennui. Ed. Marilyn
    Butler. London: Penguin, 1992.

<u>Octovian</u>. Ed. Frances McSparran. Early English Text Soc.
    289. London: Oxford UP, 1986.

Shakespeare, William. <u>Hamlet</u>. Ed. Barbara A. Mowat and
    Paul Werstine. New York: Washington Square-Pocket,
    1992.

Smith, Charlotte. <u>The Poems of Charlotte Smith</u>. Ed.
    Stuart Curran. New York: Oxford UP, 1993.

Twain, Mark. <u>Roughing It</u>. Ed. Harriet E. Smith and
    Edgar M. Branch. Berkeley: U of California P, 1993.

Wollstonecraft, Mary. <u>A Vindication of the Rights of</u>
    <u>Woman</u>. Ed. Carol H. Poston. New York: Norton, 1975.

If your citations are generally to the work of the editor (e.g., the introduction, the notes, or editorial decisions regarding the text), begin the
entry with the editor's name followed by a comma and the abbreviation *ed.* ("editor"), and give the author's name, preceded by the word
By, after the title.

Bowers, Fredson, ed. <u>The Red Badge of Courage: An</u>
    <u>Episode of the American Civil War</u>. By Stephen
    Crane. 1895. Charlottesville: UP of Virginia, 1975.

Consult 4.6.15 if you are citing more than one volume of a multivolume work or if the book is a part of a multivolume edition—say, *The
Works of Mark Twain*—and you wish to give supplementary information about the entire project.

4.6.13. A Translation

To cite a translation, state the author's name first if you refer primarily
to the work itself; give the translator's name, preceded by *Trans.* ("Translated by"), after the title. If the book has an editor as well as a translator,

give the names, with appropriate abbreviations, in the order in which they appear on the title page (see the sample entry for Dostoevsky).

> Dostoevsky, Feodor. <u>Crime and Punishment</u>. Trans. Jessie
>   Coulson. Ed. George Gibian. New York: Norton, 1964.
> Esquivel, Laura. <u>Like Water for Chocolate: A Novel in
>   Monthly Installments, with Recipes, Romances, and
>   Home Remedies</u>. Trans. Carol Christensen and Thomas
>   Christensen. New York: Doubleday, 1992.
> Murasaki Shikibu. <u>The Tale of Genji</u>. Trans. Edward G.
>   Seidensticker. New York: Knopf, 1976.

If your citations are mostly to the translator's comments or choice of wording, begin the bibliographic entry with the translator's name, followed by a comma and the abbreviation *trans.* ("translator"), and give the author's name, preceded by the word *By*, after the title. (On citing anthologies of translated works by different authors, see 4.6.7.)

> Coulson, Jessie, trans. <u>Crime and Punishment</u>. By Feodor
>   Dostoevsky. Ed. George Gibian. New York: Norton,
>   1964.

Although not required, some or all of the original publication facts may be added as supplementary information at the end of the entry.

> Grimal, Pierre. <u>Love in Ancient Rome</u>. Trans. Arthur
>   Train, Jr. Norman: U of Oklahoma P, 1986. Trans. of
>   <u>L'amour à Rome</u>. 1980.
> Levi, Primo. <u>Survival in Auschwitz: The Nazi Assault on
>   Humanity</u>. Trans. Stuart Woolf. New York: Collier-
>   Macmillan, 1987. Trans. of <u>Se questo è un uomo</u>.
>   Torino: Einaudi, 1958.

On citing a book in a language other than English, see 4.6.23.

4.6.14. A Book Published in a Second or Subsequent Edition

A book with no edition number or name on its title page is probably a first edition. Unless informed otherwise, readers assume that bibliographic entries refer to first editions. When you use a later edition of a work, identify the edition in your entry by number (*2nd ed., 3rd ed., 4th ed.*), by name (*Rev. ed.*, for "Revised edition"; *Abr. ed.*, for "Abridged edition"), or by year (*1995 ed.*)—whichever the title page indicates. The specification of edition comes after the name of the editor, translator, or compiler, if there is one, or otherwise after the title of the book. (On citing encyclopedias, dictionaries, and similar works revised regularly, see 4.6.8.)

Chaucer, Geoffrey. The Works of Geoffrey Chaucer. Ed.
    F. W. Robinson. 2nd ed. Boston: Houghton, 1957.

Feuer, Jane. The Hollywood Musical. 2nd ed. Bloomington:
    Indiana UP, 1993.

Hyde, Margaret O., and Elizabeth Held Forsyth. Suicide:
    The Hidden Epidemic. Rev. ed. New York: Watts, 1986.

Murasaki Shikibu. The Tale of Genji. Trans. Edward G.
    Seidensticker. Abr. ed. New York: Vintage-Random,
    1985.

Newcomb, Horace, ed. Television: The Critical View. 5th
    ed. New York: Oxford UP, 1994.

4.6.15. A Multivolume Work

If you are using two or more volumes of a multivolume work, cite the total number of volumes in the work ("5 vols."). This information comes after the title—or after any editor's name or identification of edition—and before the publication information. Specific references to volume and page numbers ("3: 212–13") belong in the text. (See ch. 5 for parenthetical documentation.)

Blanco, Richard L., ed. The American Revolution, 1775-
    1783: An Encyclopedia. 2 vols. Hamden:
    Garland, 1993.

Doyle, Arthur Conan. The Oxford Sherlock Holmes. Ed. Owen
    Dudley Edwards. 9 vols. New York: Oxford UP, 1993.

Lauter, Paul, et al., eds. The Heath Anthology of
    American Literature. 2nd ed. 2 vols. Lexington:
    Heath, 1994.

Sadie, Stanley, ed. The New Grove Dictionary of Music
and Musicians. 20 vols. London: Macmillan, 1980.

Schlesinger, Arthur M., gen. ed. History of U.S.
Political Parties. 4 vols. New York: Chelsea, 1973.

Weinberg, Bernard. A History of Literary Criticism in
the Italian Renaissance. 2 vols. Chicago: U of
Chicago P, 1961.

If the volumes of the work were published over a period of years,
give the inclusive dates at the end of the citation ("1952–70"). If the
work is still in progress, write *to date* after the number of volumes ("3
vols. to date") and leave a space after the hyphen that follows the
beginning date ("1982– ").

Boswell, James. The Life of Johnson. Ed. George
Birkbeck Hill and L. F. Powell. 6 vols. Oxford:
Clarendon, 1934-50.

Cassidy, Frederic, ed. Dictionary of American Regional
English. 2 vols. to date. Cambridge: Belknap-
Harvard UP, 1985- .

Churchill, Winston S. A History of the English-Speaking
Peoples. 4 vols. New York: Dodd, 1956-58.

Crane, Stephen. The University of Virginia Edition of
the Works of Stephen Crane. Ed. Fredson Bowers. 10
vols. Charlottesville: UP of Virginia, 1969-76.

Wellek, René. A History of Modern Criticism, 1750-1950.
8 vols. New Haven: Yale UP, 1955-92.

If you are using only one volume of a multivolume work, state the
number of the volume in the bibliographic entry ("Vol. 2") and give publication information for that volume alone; then you need give only
page numbers when you refer to that work in the text.

Doyle, Arthur Conan. The Oxford Sherlock Holmes. Ed. Owen
Dudley Edwards. Vol. 8. New York: Oxford UP, 1993.

Stowe, Harriet Beecher. "Sojourner Truth, the Libyan
Sibyl." 1863. The Heath Anthology of American
Literature. Ed. Paul Lauter et al. 2nd ed. Vol. 1.
Lexington: Heath, 1994. 2425-33.

```
Wellek, René. A History of Modern Criticism, 1750-1950.
     Vol. 5. New Haven: Yale UP, 1986.
```

Although not required, the complete number of volumes may be added as supplementary information at the end of the listing, along with other relevant publication facts, such as inclusive dates of publication if the volumes were published over a period of years (see the sample entry for Wellek).

```
Doyle, Arthur Conan. The Oxford Sherlock Holmes. Ed. Owen
     Dudley Edwards. Vol. 8. New York: Oxford UP, 1993.
     9 vols.
Stowe, Harriet Beecher. "Sojourner Truth, the Libyan
     Sibyl." 1863. The Heath Anthology of American
     Literature. Ed. Paul Lauter et al. 2nd ed. Vol. 1.
     Lexington: Heath, 1994. 2425-33. 2 vols.
Wellek, René. A History of Modern Criticism, 1750-1950.
     Vol. 5. New Haven: Yale UP, 1986. 8 vols. 1955-92.
```

If you are using only one volume of a multivolume work and the volume has an individual title, you may cite the book without reference to the other volumes in the work.

```
Churchill, Winston S. The Age of Revolution. New York:
     Dodd, 1957.
Durant, Will, and Ariel Durant. The Age of Voltaire. New
     York: Simon, 1965.
```

Although not required, supplementary information about the complete multivolume work may follow the basic citation: the volume number, preceded by *Vol.* and followed by the word *of*; the title of the complete work; the total number of volumes; and, if the work appeared over a period of years, the inclusive publication dates.

```
Churchill, Winston S. The Age of Revolution. New York:
     Dodd, 1957. Vol. 3 of A History of the English-
     Speaking Peoples. 4 vols. 1956-58.
Durant, Will, and Ariel Durant. The Age of Voltaire. New
     York: Simon, 1965. Vol. 9 of The Story of
     Civilization. 11 vols. 1935-75.
```

If the volume you are citing is part of a multivolume scholarly edition (see 4.6.12), you may similarly give supplementary information about the entire edition. Follow the publication information for the volume with the appropriate volume number, preceded by *Vol.* and followed by the word *of*; the title of the complete work; the name of the general editor of the multivolume edition, followed by a comma and *gen. ed.*; the total number of volumes; and the inclusive publication dates for the edition (see the entry for Howells). If the entire edition was edited by one person, state the editor's name after the title of the edition rather than after the title of the volume (see the entry for Crane).

```
Crane, Stephen. The Red Badge of Courage: An Episode of
     the American Civil War. 1895. Charlottesville: UP
     of Virginia, 1975. Vol. 2 of The University of
     Virginia Edition of the Works of Stephen Crane. Ed.
     Fredson Bowers. 10 vols. 1969-76.
Howells, W. D. Their Wedding Journey. Ed. John K. Reeves.
     Bloomington: Indiana UP, 1968. Vol. 5 of A Selected
     Edition of W. D. Howells. Edwin H. Cady, gen. ed.
     32 vols. 1968-83.
```

4.6.16. A Book in a Series

If the title page or the preceding page (the half-title page) indicates that the book you are citing is part of a series, include the series name, neither underlined nor enclosed in quotation marks, and the series number, followed by a period, before the publication information. Use common abbreviations for words in the series name (see 6.4), including *Ser.* if *Series* is part of the name.

```
Kamens, Edward, ed. Approaches to Teaching Murasaki
     Shikibu's The Tale of Genji. Approaches to Teaching
     World Lit. 47. New York: MLA, 1993.
Maravall, José Antonio. Culture of the Baroque: Analysis
     of a Historical Structure. Trans. Terry Cochran.
     Theory and History of Lit. 25. Minneapolis: U of
     Minnesota P, 1986.
```

Stewart, Joan Hinde. <u>Colette</u>. Twayne's World Authors
    Ser. 679. Boston: Twayne, 1983.

4.6.17. A Republished Book

To cite a republished book—for example, a paperback version of a
book originally published in a clothbound version—give the original
publication date, followed by a period, before the publication information for the book you are citing.

Atwood, Margaret. <u>Surfacing</u>. 1972. New York: Fawcett,
    1987.

Doctorow, E. L. <u>Welcome to Hard Times</u>. 1960. New York:
    Vintage-Random, 1988.

Douglas, Mary. <u>Purity and Danger: An Analysis of the
    Concepts of Pollution and Taboo</u>. 1966. London:
    Routledge, 1993.

Although not required, supplementary information pertaining to the
original publication may precede the original publication date.

Ishiguro, Kazuo. <u>The Remains of the Day</u>. London: Faber,
    1989. New York: Knopf, 1990.

New material added to the republication, such as an introduction,
should be cited after the original publication facts.

Dreiser, Theodore. <u>Sister Carrie</u>. 1900. Introd. E. L.
    Doctorow. New York: Bantam, 1982.

To cite a republished book that was originally issued under a different
title, first state the new title and publication facts, followed by *Rpt. of*
("Reprint of"), the original title, and the original date.

<u>The WPA Guide to 1930s New Jersey</u>. New Brunswick:
    Rutgers UP, 1986. Rpt. of <u>New Jersey: A Guide to
    Its Past and Present</u>. 1939.

4.6.18. A Publisher's Imprint

Publishers often group some of their books under imprints, or special names. Among Doubleday's many imprints, for example, have been Anchor Books, Crime Club, and Double D Western. If an imprint appears on a title page along with the publisher's name, state the imprint and follow it by a hyphen and the name of the publisher ("Anchor-Doubleday," "Collier-Macmillan," "Vintage-Random").

> Cassidy, Frederic, ed. <u>Dictionary of American Regional</u>
> <u>English</u>. 2 vols. to date. Cambridge: Belknap-
> Harvard UP, 1985- .
>
> Findlater, Mary, and Jane Findlater. <u>Crossriggs</u>. 1908.
> Introd. Paul Binding. New York: Virago-Penguin,
> 1986.
>
> Lopate, Phillip, ed. <u>The Art of the Personal Essay: An</u>
> <u>Anthology from the Classical Era to the Present</u>.
> New York: Anchor-Doubleday, 1994.

4.6.19. A Book with Multiple Publishers

If the title page lists two or more publishers—not just two or more offices of the same publisher—include all of them, in the order given, as part of the publication information, putting a semicolon after the name of each but the last.

> Duff, J. Wight. <u>A Literary History of Rome: From the</u>
> <u>Origins to the Close of the Golden Age</u>. Ed. A. M.
> Duff. 3rd ed. 1953. London: Benn; New York: Barnes,
> 1967.
>
> Wells, H. G. <u>The Time Machine</u>. 1895. London: Dent;
> Rutland: Tuttle, 1992.

4.6.20. A Pamphlet

Treat a pamphlet as you would a book.

Best Museums: New York City. New York: Trip Builder,
    1993.
Sugar, Bert Randolph, ed. Mecca 1911 Double-Folder
    Baseball Cards. Mineola: Dover, 1991.

4.6.21. A Government Publication

Government publications emanate from many sources and so present
special problems in bibliographic citation. In general, if you do not
know the writer of the document, cite as author the government agency
that issued it—that is, state the name of the government first, followed
by the name of the agency, using an abbreviation if the context makes
it clear. (But see below for citing a document whose author is known.)

California. Dept. of Industrial Relations.
United States. Cong. House.

If you are citing two or more works issued by the same government,
substitute three hyphens for the name in each entry after the first. If
you also cite more than one work by the same government agency, use
an additional three hyphens in place of the agency in the second entry
and each subsequent one.

United States. Cong. House.
---. ---. Senate.
---. Dept. of Health and Human Services.

The title of the publication, underlined, should follow immediately.
    In citing the *Congressional Record* (abbreviated *Cong. Rec.*), give
only the date and page numbers.

Cong. Rec. 7 Feb. 1973: 3831-51.

In citing other congressional documents, include such information as
the number and session of Congress, the house (*S* stands for Senate, *H*
and *HR* for House of Representatives), and the type and number of the
publication. Types of congressional publications include bills (S 33,
HR 77), resolutions (S. Res. 20, H. Res. 50), reports (S. Rept. 9, H. Rept.
142), and documents (S. Doc. 333, H. Doc. 222).
    The usual publication information comes next (i.e., place, publisher,
and date). Most federal publications, regardless of the branch of gov-

ernment issuing them, are published by the Government Printing Office (GPO), in Washington, DC; its British counterpart is Her (or His) Majesty's Stationery Office (HMSO), in London. Documents issued by the United Nations and most local governments, however, do not all emanate from a central office; give the publication information that appears on the title page.

Great Britain. Ministry of Agriculture, Fisheries, and
    Food. Radionuclide Levels in Food, Animals, and
    Agricultural Products: Post-Chernobyl Monitoring in
    England and Wales. London: HMSO, 1987.
New York State. Commission on the Adirondacks in the
    Twenty-First Century. The Adirondack Park in the
    Twenty-First Century. Albany: State of New York,
    1990.
---. Committee on State Prisons. Investigation of the
    New York State Prisons. 1883. New York: Arno, 1974.
United Nations. Consequences of Rapid Population Growth
    in Developing Countries. New York: Taylor, 1991.
---. Centre on Transnational Corporations. Foreign Direct
    Investment, the Service Sector, and International
    Banking. New York: United Nations, 1987.
---. Economic Commission for Africa. Industrial Growth
    in Africa. New York: United Nations, 1963.
United States. Cong. Joint Committee on the Investigation
    of the Pearl Harbor Attack. Hearings. 79th Cong.,
    1st and 2nd sess. 32 vols. Washington: GPO, 1946.
---. ---. Senate. Subcommittee on Constitutional
    Amendments of the Committee on the Judiciary.
    Hearings on the "Equal Rights" Amendment. 91st
    Cong., 2nd sess. S. Res. 61. Washington: GPO, 1970.
---. Dept. of Labor. Child Care: A Workforce Issue.
    Washington: GPO, 1988.
---. Dept. of State. The Global 2000 Report to the
    President: Entering the Twenty-First Century. 3
    vols. Washington: GPO, 1981.

If known, the name of the document's author may either begin the entry or, if the agency comes first, follow the title and the word *By*.

Washburne, E. B. <u>Memphis Riots and Massacres</u>. US 39th
      Cong., 2nd sess. H. Rept. 101. Washington: GPO,
      1866. New York: Arno, 1969.

or

United States. Cong. House. <u>Memphis Riots and Massacres</u>.
      By E. B. Washburne. 39th Cong., 2nd sess. H. Rept.
      101. Washington: GPO, 1866. New York: Arno, 1969.

4.6.22. The Published Proceedings of a Conference

Treat the published proceedings of a conference like a book, but add pertinent information about the conference (unless the book title includes such information).

Freed, Barbara F., ed. <u>Foreign Language Acquisition</u>
      <u>Research and the Classroom</u>. Proc. of Consortium for
      Language Teaching and Learning Conference, Oct.
      1989, U of Pennsylvania. Lexington: Heath, 1991.
Hall, Kira, Michael Meacham, and Richard Shapiro, eds.
      <u>Proceedings of the Fifteenth Annual Meeting of the</u>
      <u>Berkeley Linguistics Society, February 18-20, 1989:</u>
      <u>General Session and Parasession on Theoretical</u>
      <u>Issues in Language Reconstruction</u>. Berkeley:
      Berkeley Linguistics Soc., 1989.

Cite a presentation in the proceedings like a work in a collection of pieces by different authors (see 4.6.7).

Mann, Jill. "Chaucer and the 'Woman Question.'" <u>This</u>
      <u>Noble Craft: Proceedings of the Tenth Research</u>
      <u>Symposium of the Dutch and Belgian University</u>
      <u>Teachers of Old and Middle English and Historical</u>
      <u>Linguistics, Utrecht, 19-20 January 1989</u>. Ed. Erik
      Kooper. Amsterdam: Rodopi, 1991. 173-88.

4.6.23. A Book in a Language Other Than English

Cite a book published in a language other than English like any other
book. Give the author's name, title, and publication information
as they appear in the book. You may need to look in the colophon, at
the back of the book, for some or all of the publication information
found on the title or copyright page of English-language books. If it
seems necessary to clarify the title, provide a translation, in brackets:
"*Gengangere [Ghosts]*." Similarly, you may use brackets to give the
English name of a foreign city—"Wien [Vienna]"—or you may substitute the English name, depending on your reader's knowledge of the
language. Shorten the publisher's name appropriately (see 6.5). For
capitalization in languages other than English, see 2.8.

```
Bessière, Jean, ed. Mythologies de l'écriture: Champs
     critiques. Paris: PUF, 1990.
Dahlhaus, Carl. Musikästhetik. Köln: Gerig, 1967.
Eco, Umberto. Il nome della rosa. Milano: Bompiani, 1980.
Esquivel, Laura. Como agua para chocolate: Novelas de
     entregas mensuales, con recetas, amores y remedios
     caseros. Madrid: Mondadori, 1990.
Poche, Emanuel. Prazské Palace. Praha [Prague]: Odeon,
     1977.
```

4.6.24. A Book Published before 1900

When citing a book published before 1900, you may omit the name of
the publisher and use a comma, instead of a colon, after the place
of publication.

```
Brome, Richard. The Dramatic Works of Richard Brome.
     3 vols. London, 1873.
Dewey, John. The School and Society. Chicago, 1899.
Segni, Bernardo. Rettorica et poetica d'Aristotile.
     Firenze, 1586.
```

4.6.25. A Book without Stated Publication Information or Pagination

When a book does not indicate the publisher, the place or date of publication, or pagination, supply as much of the missing information as you can, using brackets to show that it did not come from the source.

```
New York: U of Gotham P, [1993].
```

If the date can only be approximated, put it after a *c.*, for *circa* 'around': "[c. 1993]." If you are uncertain about the accuracy of the information you supply, add a question mark: "[1993?]." Use the following abbreviations for information you cannot supply.

n.p.   No place of publication given
n.p.   No publisher given
n.d.   No date of publication given
n. pag.   No pagination given

Inserted before the colon, the abbreviation *n.p.* indicates *no place*; after the colon, it indicates *no publisher. N. pag.* explains the absence of page references in citations of the work.

NO PLACE

```
N.p.: U of Gotham P, 1993.
```

NO PUBLISHER

```
New York: n.p., 1993.
```

NO DATE

```
New York: U of Gotham P, n.d.
```

NO PAGINATION

```
New York: U of Gotham P, 1993. N. pag.
```

The examples above are hypothetical; the following ones are entries for actual books.

```
Bauer, Johann. Kafka und Prag. [Stuttgart]: Belser,
     [1971?].
Malachi, Zvi, ed. Proceedings of the International
     Conference on Literary and Linguistic Computing.
     [Tel Aviv]: [Fac. of Humanities, Tel Aviv U], n.d.
```

Michelangelo. The Sistine Chapel. New York: Wings, 1992.
    N. pag.
Photographic View Album of Cambridge. [England]: n.p.,
    n.d. N. pag.
Sendak, Maurice. Where the Wild Things Are. New York:
    Harper, 1963. N. pag.

4.6.26. An Unpublished Dissertation

Enclose the title of an unpublished dissertation in quotation marks; do
not underline it. Then write the descriptive label *Diss.*, and add the
name of the degree-granting university, followed by a comma and
the year.

Boyle, Anthony T. "The Epistemological Evolution of
    Renaissance Utopian Literature, 1516-1657." Diss.
    New York U, 1983.
Sakala, Carol. "Maternity Care Policy in the United
    States: Toward a More Rational and Effective
    System." Diss. Boston U, 1993.

For citing a dissertation abstract published in *Dissertation Abstracts*
or *Dissertation Abstracts International*, see 4.7.12. For documenting
other unpublished writing, see 4.10.13.

4.6.27. A Published Dissertation

Cite a published dissertation like a book, but add pertinent dissertation information before the publication facts. If the work was published by University Microfilms International (UMI), you may add the
order number as supplementary information.

Dietze, Rudolf F. Ralph Ellison: The Genesis of an
    Artist. Diss. U Erlangen-Nürnberg, 1982. Erlanger
    Beiträge zur Sprach- und Kunstwissenschaft 70.
    Nürnberg: Carl, 1982.
Valentine, Mary-Blair Truesdell. An Investigation of
    Gender-Based Leadership Styles of Male and Female

> Officers in the United States Army. Diss. George
> Mason U, 1993. Ann Arbor: UMI, 1993. 9316566.

4.7. CITING ARTICLES IN PERIODICALS

4.7.1. The Basic Entry: An Article in a Scholarly Journal with Continuous Pagination

A periodical is a publication that appears regularly at fixed intervals, such as a newspaper, a magazine, or a scholarly journal. Unlike newspapers and magazines, scholarly journals usually appear only about four times a year, and the issues present learned articles containing original research and original interpretations of data and texts. Such journals are intended not for general readers but for professionals and students. Since the research you do for your papers will inevitably lead you to consult scholarly journals, the entry for an article in a scholarly journal will be among the most common in the works-cited lists you compile.

The entry for an article in a periodical, like that for a book, has three main divisions:

> Author's name. "Title of the article." Publication
> information.

Here is an example:

> Scotto, Peter. "Censorship, Reading, and Interpretation:
> A Case Study from the Soviet Union." PMLA 109
> (1994): 61-70.

Author's Name

In general, follow the recommendations for citing names of authors of books (4.6.1). Take the author's name from the beginning or the end of the article. Reverse the name for alphabetizing, and put a period after it.

> Scotto, Peter.

Title of the Article

In general, follow the recommendations for titles given in 2.6. State the full title of the article, enclosed in quotation marks (not underlined). Unless the title has its own concluding punctuation (e.g., a question mark), put a period before the closing quotation mark.

```
Scotto, Peter. "Censorship, Reading, and Interpretation:
    A Case Study from the Soviet Union."
```

Publication Information

In general, after the title of the article, give the journal title (underlined), the volume number, the year of publication (in parentheses), a colon, the inclusive page numbers, and a period.

```
Scotto, Peter. "Censorship, Reading, and Interpretation:
    A Case Study from the Soviet Union." PMLA 109
    (1994): 61-70.
```

Take these facts directly from the journal, not from a source such as a bibliography. Publication information usually appears on the cover or title page of a journal. Omit any introductory article in the journal title (*William and Mary Quarterly*, not *The William and Mary Quarterly*). For newspaper titles, see 4.7.5.

In addition to the volume number, the journal's cover or title page may include an issue number ("Number 3") or a month or season before the year ("January 1995," "Fall 1994"). In general, the issues of a journal published in a single year compose one volume. Volumes are usually numbered in continuous sequence—each new volume is numbered one higher than its predecessor—while the numbering of issues starts over with 1 in each new volume. You may ignore the issue number and the month or season if the journal's pages are numbered continuously throughout each annual volume. In a journal with such pagination, if the first issue for a year ends on page 130, for instance, the second issue begins on page 131.

Most scholarly journals are paginated continuously throughout each annual volume. Then, at the end of the year, the issues in the volume are bound together and shelved in the library by year number. If you are looking for the article by Peter Scotto cited above, for example, which was published in 1994 in an issue of the scholarly journal *PMLA*, you will likely find it in your library in what appears to be a book with "*PMLA* 1994" printed on the spine. In that volume, you will find all the issues of *PMLA* published during 1994, and the pages of the volume will be continuous, from page 1 of the first issue through to the final page of the last issue published in the year. Suppose, then, that you wish to cite the article in your research paper. The title page of the issue containing the article includes this publication information: "Volume 109, Number 1, January 1994." But since *PMLA* is paged continuously by volume, you should omit the issue number and the month from your entry, for the reader will be able to find the source by knowing simply the volume number and the page numbers of the article.

Some scholarly journals do not use continuous pagination throughout the annual volume, however, and some use issue numbers alone without volume numbers; on citing articles in such journals, see 4.7.2–3. In addition, entries for newspapers and magazines do not require volume numbers (see 4.7.5–6). Your instructor or a librarian will help you if you are uncertain whether a periodical is a magazine or a scholarly journal. If any doubt remains, include the volume number. Do not precede the volume number with the word *volume* or the abbreviation *vol.*

The inclusive page numbers cited should encompass the complete article, not just the portion you used. (Specific page references appear parenthetically at appropriate places in your text; see ch. 5.) Follow the rules for writing inclusive numbers in 2.5.6. Write the page reference for the first page exactly as shown in the source ("198–232," "A32–34," "28/WETA–29," "TV-15–18," "lxii–lxv"). If an article is not printed on consecutive pages—if, for example, after beginning on page 6 it skips to page 10 and then to page 22—write only the first page number and a plus sign, leaving no intervening space: "6+." (See examples in 4.7.5–6.)

Here are some additional examples of the basic entry for an article in a scholarly journal with continuous pagination:

Craner, Paul M. "New Tool for an Ancient Art: The
    Computer and Music." <u>Computers and the Humanities</u>
    25 (1991): 303-13.

Fitzgerald, John. "The Misconceived Revolution: State and
    Society in China's Nationalist Revolution, 1923-26."
    <u>Journal of Asian Studies</u> 49 (1990): 323-43.

Flanigan, Beverly Olson. "Peer Tutoring and Second
    Language Acquisition in the Elementary School."
    Applied Linguistics 12 (1991): 141-58.
White, Sabina, and Andrew Winzelberg. "Laughter and
    Stress." Humor 5 (1992): 343-55.

Sometimes additional information is required in an entry. This list shows most of the possible components of an entry for an article in a periodical and the order in which they are normally arranged:

1. Author's name
2. Title of the article
3. Name of the periodical
4. Series number or name (if relevant; see 4.7.4)
5. Volume number (for a scholarly journal)
6. Issue number (if needed; see 4.7.2–3)
7. Date of publication
8. Page numbers
9. Supplementary information (see esp. 4.7.11)

The rest of 4.7 explains how to cite these items.

4.7.2. An Article in a Scholarly Journal That Pages Each Issue Separately

Some scholarly journals do not number pages continuously throughout an annual volume but begin each issue on page 1. For such journals, you must include the issue number to identify the source. Add a period and the issue number directly after the volume number, without any intervening space: "14.2" signifies volume 14, issue 2; "10.3–4," volume 10, issues 3 and 4 combined.

Barthelme, Frederick. "Architecture." Kansas Quarterly
    13.3-4 (1981): 77-80.
Baum, Rosalie Murphy. "Alcoholism and Family Abuse in
    Maggie and The Bluest Eye." Mosaic 19.3 (1986):
    91-105.
Hallin, Daniel C. "Sound Bite News: Television Coverage
    of Elections, 1968-1988." Journal of Communication
    42.2 (1992): 5-24.

4.7.3. An Article in a Scholarly Journal That Uses Only Issue Numbers

Some scholarly journals do not use volume numbers at all, numbering issues only. Treat the issue numbers of such journals as you would volume numbers.

> Bowering, George. "Baseball and the Canadian
>   Imagination." <u>Canadian Literature</u> 108 (1986):
>   115-24.
> Peters, Christoph. "The Image of Thomas More in
>   Twentieth-Century Plays: A Presentation of Five
>   More Dramas." <u>Moreana</u> 109 (1992): 23-46.

4.7.4. An Article in a Scholarly Journal with More Than One Series

Some scholarly journals have been published in more than one series. In citing a journal with numbered series, write the number (an arabic digit with the appropriate ordinal suffix: *2nd*, *3rd*, *4th*, etc.) and the abbreviation *ser.* between the journal title and the volume number (see the sample entry for Daniels). For a journal divided into a new series and an original series, indicate the series with *ns* or *os* before the volume number (see the entry for Gardinier).

> Daniels, John. "Indian Population of North America in
>   1492." <u>William and Mary Quarterly</u> 3rd ser. 49
>   (1992): 298-320.
> Gardinier, Suzanne. "Two Cities: On the <u>Iliad</u>." <u>Kenyon</u>
>   <u>Review</u> ns 14.2 (1992): 5-12.

4.7.5. An Article in a Newspaper

To cite a newspaper, give the name as it appears on the masthead but omit any introductory article (*New York Times*, not *The New York Times*). If the city of publication is not included in the name of a locally published newspaper, add the city in square brackets, not underlined, after the name: "*Star-Ledger* [Newark]." For nationally published newspapers (e.g., *USA Today*, *Wall Street Journal*, *Chronicle of Higher Education*), you need not add the city of publication. Next give the complete date—day, month, and year. Abbreviate the names of all months except May, June, and July (see 6.2). Do not give the volume and issue numbers even if they are listed. If an edition is named on the masthead, add a comma after the date and specify the edition (*natl. ed.*, *late ed.*). It is important to state the edition because different editions of the same issue of a newspaper contain different material. Follow the edition—or the date if there is no edition—with a colon and the page number or numbers. Here are examples illustrating how an article appeared in different sections of two editions of the *New York Times* on the same day:

```
Feder, Barnaby J. "For Job Seekers, a Toll-Free Gift of
     Expert Advice." New York Times 30 Dec. 1993, late
     ed.: D1+.

Feder, Barnaby J. "For Job Seekers, a Toll-Free Gift of
     Expert Advice." New York Times 30 Dec. 1993, natl.
     ed.: C1+.
```

If each section is paginated separately, indicate the appropriate section number or letter. Determining how to indicate a section can sometimes be complicated. The *New York Times*, for example, is currently divided in three distinct ways, depending on the day of the week, and each system calls for a different method of indicating section and page. On Monday through Friday, there are normally four sections, labeled *A*, *B*, *C*, and *D* and paginated separately, and a section letter is part of each page number: "A1," "B1," "C5," "D3." Whenever the pagination of a newspaper includes a section designation, give the first page number exactly as it appears.

DAILY *NEW YORK TIMES*

```
Manegold, Catherine S. "Becoming a Land of the Smoke-
     Free, Ban by Ban." New York Times 22 Mar. 1994,
     late ed.: A1+.
```

On Saturday, the *New York Times* is not divided into specific sections, and pagination is continuous from the first page to the last. There are no section designations to cite.

SATURDAY *NEW YORK TIMES*

Tagliabue, John. "Cleaned Last Judgment Unveiled." New
     York Times 9 Apr. 1994, late ed.: 13.

Finally, the Sunday edition contains several individually paged sections (covering the arts and entertainment, business, sports, travel, and so on) designated not by letters but by numbers ("Section 4," "Section 7"), which do not appear as parts of the page numbers. Whenever the section designation of a newspaper is not part of the pagination, put a comma after the date (or after the edition, if any) and add the abbreviation *sec.*, the appropriate letter or number, a colon, and the page number.

SUNDAY *NEW YORK TIMES*

Greeley, Andrew. "Today's Morality Play: The Sitcom."
     New York Times 17 May 1987, late ed., sec. 2: 1+.

Newspaper articles are often not printed on consecutive pages—for example, an article might begin on page 1, then skip to page 16. For such articles, write only the first page number and a plus sign, leaving no intervening space: "6+," "C3+."

Here are some additional examples from different newspapers:

Lederman, Douglas. "Athletic Merit vs. Academic Merit."
     Chronicle of Higher Education 30 Mar. 1994: A37-38.

Manning, Anita. "Curriculum Battles from Left and
     Right." USA Today 2 Mar. 1994: 5D.

Taylor, Paul. "Keyboard Grief: Coping with Computer-
     Caused Injuries." Globe and Mail [Toronto] 27 Dec.
     1993: A1+.

Trachtenberg, Jeffrey A. "What's in a Movie Soundtrack?
     Catchy Tunes and Big Business." Wall Street Journal
     1 Apr. 1994, eastern ed.: B1.

4.7.6. An Article in a Magazine

To cite a magazine published every week or every two weeks, give the complete date (beginning with the day and abbreviating the month), followed by a colon and the inclusive page numbers of the article. If the article is not printed on consecutive pages, write only the first page number and a plus sign, leaving no intervening space. Do not give the volume and issue numbers even if they are listed.

> Armstrong, Larry, Dori Jones Yang, and Alice Cuneo.
>
> "The Learning Revolution: Technology Is Reshaping
>
> Education--at Home and at School." <u>Business Week</u>
>
> 28 Feb. 1994: 80-88.
>
> Bazell, Robert. "Science and Society: Growth Industry."
>
> <u>New Republic</u> 15 Mar. 1993: 13-14.

To cite a magazine published every month or every two months, give the month or months and year. If the article is not printed on consecutive pages, write only the first page number and a plus sign, leaving no intervening space. Do not give the volume and issue numbers even if they are listed.

> Frank, Michael. "The Wild, Wild West." <u>Architectural</u>
>
> <u>Digest</u> June 1993: 180+.
>
> Marano, Hara Estroff. "Domestic Violence." <u>Psychology</u>
>
> <u>Today</u> Nov.-Dec. 1993: 48+.
>
> Murphy, Cullen. "Women and the Bible." <u>Atlantic Monthly</u>
>
> Aug. 1993: 39-64.
>
> Nimmons, David. "Sex and the Brain." <u>Discover</u> Mar.
>
> 1994: 64-71.
>
> Nixon, Will. "Are We Burying Ourselves in Junk Mail?"
>
> <u>E: Environmental Magazine</u> Nov.-Dec. 1993: 30+.

4.7.7. An Anonymous Article

If no author's name is given for the article you are citing, begin the entry with the title. Ignore any initial *A*, *An*, or *The* when you alphabetize the entry.

> "The Decade of the Spy." <u>Newsweek</u> 7 Mar. 1994: 26-27.
>
> "Dubious Venture." <u>Time</u> 3 Jan. 1994: 64-65.

4.7.8. An Editorial

If you are citing a signed editorial, begin with the author's name, give the title, and then add the descriptive label *Editorial*, neither underlined nor enclosed in quotation marks. Conclude with the appropriate publication information. If the editorial is unsigned, begin with the title and continue in the same way.

> "Death of a Writer." Editorial. New York Times 20 Apr.
> 1994, late ed.: A18.
> Zuckerman, Mortimer B. "Welcome to Communicopia."
> Editorial. US News and World Report 1 Nov. 1993:
> 116.

4.7.9. A Letter to the Editor

To identify a letter to the editor, add the descriptive label *Letter* after the name of the author, but do not underline the word or place it in quotation marks.

> Ozick, Cynthia. Letter. Partisan Review 57 (1990):
> 493-94.
> Safer, Morley. Letter. New York Times 31 Oct. 1993, late
> ed., sec. 2: 4.

Identify a published response to a letter as "Reply to letter of . . . ," adding the name of the writer of the initial letter. Do not underline this phrase or place it in quotation marks.

> Gray, Richard T. Reply to letter of Robert Frail. PMLA
> 109 (1994): 120-21.

4.7.10. A Review

To cite a review, give the reviewer's name and the title of the review (if there is one); then write *Rev. of* (neither underlined nor enclosed in quotation marks), the title of the work reviewed, a comma, the word *by*, and the name of the author. If the work of someone other than an author—say, an editor, a translator, or a director—is under review, use the appropriate abbreviation, such as *ed.*, *trans.*, or *dir.*, instead of *by*. For a review of a performance, add pertinent information about the production (see the sample entry for Dunning). If more than one work is under review, list titles and authors in the order given at the beginning of the review (see the entry for Bordewich). Conclude the entry with the name of the periodical and the rest of the publication information.

If the review is titled but unsigned, begin the entry with the title of the review and alphabetize by that title (see the entry for "The Cooling of an Admiration"). If the review is neither titled nor signed, begin the entry with *Rev. of* and alphabetize under the title of the work reviewed (see the entry for *Anthology of Danish Literature*).

Rev. of <u>Anthology of Danish Literature</u>, ed. F. J. Billeskov Jansen and P. M. Mitchell. <u>Times Literary Supplement</u> 7 July 1972: 785.

Bordewich, Fergus M. Rev. of <u>Once They Moved like the Wind: Cochise, Geronimo, and the Apache Wars</u>, by David Roberts, and <u>Brave Are My People: Indian Heroes Not Forgotten</u>, by Frank Waters. <u>Smithsonian</u> Mar. 1994: 125-31.

"The Cooling of an Admiration." Rev. of <u>Pound/Joyce: The Letters of Ezra Pound to James Joyce, with Pound's Essays on Joyce</u>, ed. Forrest Read. <u>Times Literary Supplement</u> 6 Mar. 1969: 239-40.

Crutchfield, Will. "Pure Italian." Rev. of <u>Verdi: A Biography</u>, by Mary Jane Phillips-Matz. <u>New Yorker</u> 31 Jan. 1994: 76-82.

Dunning, Jennifer. Rev. of <u>The River</u>, chor. Alvin Ailey. Dance Theater of Harlem. New York State Theater, New York. <u>New York Times</u> 17 Mar. 1994, late ed.: C18.

Kauffmann, Stanley. "A New Spielberg." Rev. of <u>Schindler's List</u>, dir. Steven Spielberg. <u>New Republic</u> 13 Dec. 1993: 30.

4.7.11. A Serialized Article

To cite a serialized article or a series of related articles published in more than one issue of a periodical, include all bibliographic information in one entry if each installment has the same author and title.

Gillespie, Gerald. "Novella, Nouvelle, Novelle, Short
Novel? A Review of Terms." <u>Neophilologus</u> 51 (1967):
117-27, 225-30.

Meserole, Harrison T., and James M. Rambeau. "Articles
on American Literature Appearing in Current
Periodicals." <u>American Literature</u> 52 (1981):
688-705; 53 (1981): 164-80, 348-59.

If the installments bear different titles, list each one separately. You may include a brief supplementary description at the end of the entry to indicate that the article is part of a series.

Dillon, Sam. "Special Education Absorbs School
Resources." <u>New York Times</u> 7 Apr. 1994, late ed.:
A1+. Pt. 2 of a series, A Class Apart: Special
Education in New York City, begun 6 Apr. 1994.

Richardson, Lynda. "Minority Students Languish in
Special Education System." <u>New York Times</u> 6 Apr.
1994, late ed.: A1+. Pt. 1 of a series, A Class
Apart: Special Education in New York City.

Winerip, Michael. "A Disabilities Program That 'Got out
of Hand.'" <u>New York Times</u> 8 Apr. 1994, late ed.:
A1+. Pt. 3 of a series, A Class Apart: Special
Education in New York City, begun 6 Apr. 1994.

4.7.12. An Abstract in an Abstracts Journal

An abstracts journal publishes summaries of journal articles and of other literature. If you are citing an abstract, begin the entry with the publication information for the original work. Then add the relevant information for the journal from which you derived the abstract—title (underlined), volume number, year (in parentheses), and either item number or page number, depending on how the journal presents its abstracts. Of the journals cited below, *Current Index to Journals in Education*, *Psychological Abstracts*, and *Sociological Abstracts* use item numbers; *Dissertation Abstracts* and *Dissertation Abstracts International* use page numbers. Precede an item number with the word *item*. If the title of the journal does not make clear that you are citing an abstract, add the word *Abstract*, neither underlined nor in quotation marks, immediately after the original publication information (see the sample entry for McCabe).

Dissertation Abstracts International (*DAI*) has a long and complex history that might affect the way you cite an abstract in it. Before volume 30 (1969), *Dissertation Abstracts International* was titled *Dissertation Abstracts* (*DA*). From volume 27 to volume 36, *DA* and *DAI* were paginated in two series: *A*, for humanities and social sciences, and *B*, for sciences and engineering. With volume 37, *DAI* added a third separately paginated section: *C*, for abstracts of European dissertations; in 1989, this section expanded its coverage to include institutions throughout the world. (For recommendations on citing dissertations themselves, see 4.6.26–27.)

Clinton, Jacqueline, and Sheryl T. Kelber. "Stress and
    Coping in Fathers of Newborns: Comparisons of
    Planned versus Unplanned Pregnancy." International
    Journal of Nursing Studies 30 (1993): 437-43.
    Psychological Abstracts 81 (1994): item 9291.
Gans, Eric L. "The Discovery of Illusion: Flaubert's
    Early Works, 1835-1837." Diss. Johns Hopkins U,
    1967. DA 27 (1967): 3046A.
McCabe, Donald L. "Faculty Responses to Academic
    Dishonesty: The Influence of Student Honor Codes."
    Research in Higher Education 34 (1993): 647-58.
    Abstract. Current Index to Journals in Education 26
    (1994): item EJ471017.
Sakala, Carol. "Maternity Care Policy in the United
    States: Toward a More Rational and Effective
    System." Diss. Boston U, 1993. DAI 54 (1993): 1360B.
Tamney, Joseph B., Stephen D. Johnson, and Ronald Burton.
    "The Abortion Controversy: Conflicting Beliefs and

Values in American Society." <u>Journal for the</u>
<u>Scientific Study of Religion</u> 31 (1992): 32-46.
<u>Sociological Abstracts</u> 40 (1992): item 92Z2448.

4.7.13. An Article in a Microform Collection of Articles

If you are citing an article that was provided by a reference source such as *Newsbank*, which selects periodical articles and makes them available on microfiche, begin the entry with the original publication information. Then add the relevant information concerning the microform from which you derived the article—title of source (underlined), volume number, year (in parentheses), and appropriate identifying numbers ("fiche 42, grids 5–6").

Chapman, Dan. "Panel Could Help Protect Children."
     <u>Winston-Salem Journal</u> 14 Jan. 1990: 14. <u>Newsbank:</u>
     <u>Welfare and Social Problems</u> 12 (1990): fiche 1,
     grids A8-11.

4.7.14. An Article Reprinted in a Loose-Leaf Collection of Articles

If you are citing a reprinted article that was provided by an information service such as the Social Issues Resources Series (SIRS), which selects articles from periodicals and publishes them in loose-leaf volumes, each dedicated to a specific topic, begin the entry with the original publication information. Then add the relevant information for the loose-leaf volume in which the article is reprinted, treating the volume like a book (see 4.6)—title (underlined), name of editor (if any), volume number (if any), city of publication, publisher, year of publication, and article number (preceded by the abbreviation *Art.*).

Edmondson, Brad. "AIDS and Aging." <u>American Demographics</u>
     Mar. 1990: 28+. <u>The AIDS Crisis</u>. Ed. Eleanor
     Goldstein. Vol. 2. Boca Raton: SIRS, 1991. Art. 24.

4.8. CITING CD-ROMS AND OTHER PORTABLE DATABASES

4.8.1. Introduction

Researchers can find a wealth of sources in electronic form, as well as in print. It is convenient to divide electronic publications into two types: portable databases and online databases. Portable databases are distributed on CD-ROMs (compact discs that can store large amounts of information), diskettes, and magnetic tapes. To be read, these media require a computer with the proper equipment. This section explains how to cite portable databases in the list of works cited; the following section, 4.9, deals with citing online databases.

Portable databases have the following characteristics in common with books and periodicals:

- Portable databases are created, manufactured, and issued by publishers as products that you can buy in a store and carry around with you.
- Publishers update these products by creating and issuing new editions, new versions, or new releases.
- The publishers may issue many identical copies of the same products.

Because of these similarities, entries in a works-cited list for CD-ROMs and other portable databases are much like those for printed sources (4.6–7). There are a few differences, however, the most important of which follow:

Publication medium. When you cite an electronic publication, it is important to state the medium of publication you used (e.g., CD-ROM, diskette, magnetic tape), for the cited material may be published in more than one format and may not be the same in each.

Vendor's name. Some information providers publish electronic versions of the data they compile, but many do not, choosing instead to lease the data to vendors to distribute in electronic form. For example, the Modern Language Association of America produces the contents of the *MLA International Bibliography*, but the vendor SilverPlatter distributes the CD-ROM version of the bibliography. It is necessary to state the vendor's name in your works-cited list because the information provider may have leased electronic versions of the data to more than one vendor, and the versions may not be identical. Major vendors include Information Access, SilverPlat-ter, UMI-Proquest, and Wilson. The vendor's name is usually made evident in the database—for example, on the title screen or above the menu of the database—and in the user's manual. If you are uncertain about a vendor, ask a librarian for the appropriate infor-mation. (See also the individual recommendations in this section if such information is unavailable to you.)

Date of electronic publication. Many portable database products are updated regularly (e.g., annually, quarterly). Updates add informa-tion and may also correct or otherwise alter information that previ-ously appeared in the database. Therefore, you may need to give two publication dates in your citation, just as you do for reprinted or republished books and articles (see, e.g., 4.6.17, 4.7.14). For example, if the database indicates that the material you are using was originally published in the *New York Times* on 13 April 1993, you must, of course, include that date in the citation. In addition, because the electronic version may differ from the printed version, you must also state the publication date of the database to let your reader know exactly what you read. For the date of electronic publi-cation, use the release date of the database. For some databases, this date includes a month and year; for others, just a year. State whichever is appropriate to the database you are consulting. The date usually appears on the title screen or above the menu of the database. If no release date is present, use the date at which the cov-erage of the database concludes. For example, given a database with the following menu, you would list October 1994 as the electronic publication date:

New York Times Jan. 1991–Dec. 1991
New York Times Jan. 1992–Dec. 1992
New York Times Jan. 1993–Dec. 1993
New York Times Jan. 1994–Oct. 1994

A useful and comprehensive reference work for electronic publica-tions is *Gale Directory of Databases*, volume 2 of which covers CD-ROMs, diskettes, magnetic tapes, and other database products offered in portable form; consult the most recent edition. This directory con-tains not only a detailed description of each product listed but also the name and address of the information provider or database producer as well as of the vendor or distributor of the product. A geographic index, a subject index, and a master index help you locate products and organizations in the directory.

Sections 4.8.2–6 recommend citation forms for publications on CD-ROMs, diskettes, and magnetic tapes. (On citing sound recordings on compact discs, see 4.10.2; on citing videodiscs, see 4.10.3.)

4.8.2. Material Accessed from a Periodically Published Database on CD-ROM

Numerous periodicals (newspapers, magazines, journals) and periodically published reference works, such as annual bibliographies and collections of abstracts, are published on CD-ROM as databases, or parts of databases, that are commonly used in library research (see 1.4.3 and app. A). Documents and information from such databases can be divided into two groups:

- Material that indicates publication information for a printed source or printed analogue
- Material that does not indicate a specific print counterpart

a. Material with Publication Information for a Printed Source or Printed Analogue

Many databases collect and present materials previously or simultaneously made available in print. If the electronic work you are using gives publication data for a printed source or printed analogue, begin your citation with this information. If the print version is a book or a pamphlet (see the sample entry for *Guidelines for Family Television Viewing*), follow the recommendations in 4.6; if the print version is an article in a periodical, follow the recommendations in 4.7. When given, information about the printed source or analogue normally appears at the beginning of the file accessed.

If a printed source or analogue is indicated for the material you are citing, your entry in the works-cited list should consist of the following items:

1. Name of the author (if given)
2. Publication information for the printed source or analogue (including title and date of print publication)
3. Title of the database (underlined)
4. Publication medium (*CD-ROM*)
5. Name of the vendor (if relevant)
6. Electronic publication date

Angier, Natalie. "Chemists Learn Why Vegetables Are Good
    for You." New York Times 13 Apr. 1993, late ed.: C1.
    New York Times Ondisc. CD-ROM. UMI-Proquest. Oct.
    1993.

Galloway, Stephen. "TV Takes the Fall in Violence Poll."
    Hollywood Reporter 23 July 1993: 16. Predicasts F
    and S Plus Text: United States. CD-ROM.
    SilverPlatter. Oct. 1993.

Guidelines for Family Television Viewing. Urbana: ERIC
    Clearinghouse on Elementary and Early Childhood
    Educ., 1990. ERIC. CD-ROM. SilverPlatter. June 1993.

Russo, Michelle Cash. "Recovering from Bibliographic
    Instruction Blahs." RQ: Reference Quarterly 32
    (1992): 178-83. Infotrac: Magazine Index Plus.
    CD-ROM. Information Access. Dec. 1993.

Stempel, Carl William. "Towards a Historical Sociology
    of Sport in the United States, 1825-1875." DAI 53
    (1993): 3374A. U of Oregon, 1992. Dissertation
    Abstracts Ondisc. CD-ROM. UMI-Proquest. Sept. 1993.

If you cannot find some of the information required—for example,
the vendor's name—cite what is available.

Angier, Natalie. "Chemists Learn Why Vegetables Are Good
    for You." New York Times 13 Apr. 1993, late ed.: C1.
    New York Times Ondisc. CD-ROM. Oct. 1993.

b. Material with No Printed Source or Printed Analogue Specified

If no printed source or printed analogue is indicated for the material
you are citing, your entry in the works-cited list should consist of the
following items:

1. Name of the author (if given)
2. Title of the material accessed (in quotation marks)
3. Date of the material (if given)
4. Title of the database (underlined)
5. Publication medium (*CD-ROM*)
6. Name of the vendor (if relevant)
7. Electronic publication date

Shearson Lehman Brothers, Inc. "Reebok: Company Report."
    29 July 1993. <u>General Business File</u>. CD-ROM.
    Information Access. Dec. 1993.

"Time Warner, Inc.: Sales Summary, 1988-1992."
    <u>Disclosure/Worldscope</u>. CD-ROM. W/D Partners. Oct.
    1993.

United States. Dept. of State. "Industrial Outlook for
    Petroleum and Natural Gas." 1992. <u>National Trade</u>
    <u>Data Bank</u>. CD-ROM. US Dept. of Commerce. Dec. 1993.

"U.S. Population by Age: Urban and Urbanized Areas."
    <u>1990 U.S. Census of Population and Housing</u>. CD-ROM.
    US Bureau of the Census. 1990.

If you cannot find some of the information required—for example, the vendor's name—cite what is available.

"Time Warner, Inc.: Sales Summary, 1988-1992."
    <u>Disclosure/Worldscope</u>. CD-ROM. Oct. 1993.

4.8.3. A Nonperiodical Publication on CD-ROM

Many CD-ROM publications are not published periodically but are issued as most books are—that is, a single time, without a plan to update or otherwise revise the work regularly. Cite a nonperiodical CD-ROM database product as you would a book, but add a description of the medium of publication. Since the information provider and the publisher are usually the same for CD-ROM databases that are not published periodically, no vendor's name appears. Your entry in the works-cited list should consist of the following items:

1. Name of the author (if given)
2. Title of the part of the work, if relevant (underlined or in quotation marks)
3. Title of the product (underlined)
4. Edition, release, or version (if relevant)
5. Publication medium (*CD-ROM*)
6. City of publication
7. Name of the publisher
8. Year of publication

The CIA World Factbook. CD-ROM. Minneapolis: Quanta,
     1992.

English Poetry Full-Text Database. Rel. 2. CD-ROM.
     Cambridge, Eng.: Chadwyck, 1993.

Orchestra. CD-ROM. Burbank: Warner New Media, 1992.

The Oxford English Dictionary. 2nd ed. CD-ROM. Oxford:
     Oxford UP, 1992.

Where in the World Is Carmen Sandiego? Deluxe ed. CD-ROM.
     Novato: Brøderbund, 1992.

If you cannot find some of the information required—for example,
the city and name of the publisher—cite what is available.

The CIA World Factbook. CD-ROM. 1992.

If you are citing only a part of the work, state which part. If the part
is a book, a play, a pamphlet, a painting, or a similar work, underline
the title (see 2.6.2); if it is a source like an article, an essay, a poem, or
a short story, enclose the title in quotation marks (see 2.6.3).

"Albatross." The Oxford English Dictionary. 2nd ed.
     CD-ROM. Oxford: Oxford UP, 1992.

American Heritage Dictionary. Microsoft Bookshelf. 1993
     ed. CD-ROM. Redmond: Microsoft, 1993.

"Brontë, Emily." Discovering Authors. Vers. 1.0. CD-ROM.
     Detroit: Gale, 1992.

Holbein, Hans. The Ambassadors. Microsoft Art Gallery:
     The Collection of the National Gallery, London.
     CD-ROM. Redmond: Microsoft, 1994.

"Oboe." Orchestra. CD-ROM. Burbank: Warner New Media,
     1992.

If publication information for a printed source or printed analogue
is indicated, begin the citation with that information.

Aristotle. The Complete Works of Aristotle: The Revised
     Oxford Translation. Ed. Jonathan Barnes. 2 vols.
     Princeton: Princeton UP, 1984. CD-ROM. Clayton:
     Intelex, 1994.

Coleridge, Samuel Taylor. "Dejection: An Ode." <u>The</u>
<u>Complete Poetical Works of Samuel Taylor Coleridge</u>.
Ed. Ernest Hartley Coleridge. Vol. 1. Oxford:
Clarendon, 1912. 362-68. <u>English Poetry Full-Text</u>
<u>Database</u>. Rel. 2. CD-ROM. Cambridge, Eng.:
Chadwyck, 1993.

Jacobson, Jodi L. "Holding Back the Sea." <u>Futurist</u>
Sept.-Oct. 1990: 20-27. <u>Earth Science</u>. Ed. Eleanor
Goldstein. 1991. Art. 25. <u>SIRS CD-ROM</u>. CD-ROM. Boca
Raton: SIRS, 1993.

4.8.4. A Publication on Diskette

Cite a diskette publication as you would a book, but add a description of the medium of publication. Your entry in the works-cited list should consist of the following items:

1. Name of the author (if given)
2. Title of the part of the work, if relevant (in quotation marks)
3. Title of the product (underlined)
4. Edition, release, or version (if relevant)
5. Publication medium (*Diskette*)
6. City of publication
7. Name of the publisher
8. Year of publication

<u>Alpha Four</u>. Vers. 3.0. Diskette. Burlington: Alpha, 1993.

"Ellison, Ralph." <u>Disclit: American Authors</u>. Diskette.
Boston: Hall, 1991.

Joyce, Michael. <u>Afternoon: A Story</u>. Diskette. Watertown:
Eastgate, 1987.

Lanham, Richard D. <u>The Electronic Word: Democracy,</u>
<u>Technology, and the Arts</u>. Diskette. Chicago: U of
Chicago P, 1993.

"Nuclear Medicine Technologist." <u>Guidance Information</u>
<u>System</u>. 17th ed. Diskette. Cambridge: Riverside-
Houghton, 1992.

```
Reinhold, Walter. Culture. Vers. 2.0. Diskette.
     Cranford: Cultural Resources, 1992.
Thiesmeyer, Elaine C., and John E. Thiesmeyer. Editor.
     Vers. 5.0. Diskette. New York: MLA, 1994.
```

If you cannot find some of the information required—for example, the city and name of the publisher—cite what is available.

```
Reinhold, Walter. Culture. Vers. 2.0. Diskette. 1992.
```

If publication information for a printed source or printed analogue is indicated, begin the citation with that information.

```
Coleridge, Samuel Taylor. "Dejection: An Ode." The
     Complete Poetical Works of Samuel Taylor Coleridge.
     Ed. Ernest Hartley Coleridge. Vol. 1. Oxford:
     Clarendon, 1912. 362-68. The Poetical Works of
     Samuel Taylor Coleridge. Diskette. Oxford: Oxford
     UP, 1993.
```

4.8.5. A Publication on Magnetic Tape

Cite a magnetic-tape publication as you would a book, but add a description of the medium of publication. Your entry in the works-cited list should consist of the following items:

1. Name of the author (if given)
2. Title of the part of the work, if relevant (in quotation marks)
3. Title of the product (underlined)
4. Edition, release, or version (if relevant)
5. Publication medium (*Magnetic tape*)
6. City of publication
7. Name of the publisher
8. Year of publication

```
"Agnes Scott College." Peterson's College Database.
     Magnetic tape. Princeton: Peterson's, 1992.
"Children's Television Workshop." Encyclopedia of
     Associations. Magnetic tape. Detroit: Gale, 1994.
English Poetry Full-Text Database. Rel. 2. Magnetic
     tape. Cambridge, Eng.: Chadwyck, 1993.
```

If you cannot find some of the information required—for example, the city and name of the publisher—cite what is available.

> "Children's Television Workshop." Encyclopedia of
> Associations. Magnetic tape. 1994.

If publication information for a printed source or printed analogue is indicated, begin the citation with that information.

> Coleridge, Samuel Taylor. "Dejection: An Ode." The
> Complete Poetical Works of Samuel Taylor Coleridge.
> Ed. Ernest Hartley Coleridge. Vol. 1. Oxford:
> Clarendon, 1912. 362-68. English Poetry Full-Text
> Database. Rel. 2. Magnetic tape. Cambridge, Eng.:
> Chadwyck, 1993.

4.8.6. A Work in More Than One Publication Medium

A number of electronic publications are issued as a package of materials in different publication media—for example, a CD-ROM and a diskette may make up one publication. Cite such a publication as you would a nonperiodical CD-ROM product, specifying the media that constitute the product.

> Franking, Holly. Negative Space: A Computerized Video
> Novel. Vers. 1.0. Diskette, videocassette. Prairie
> Village: Diskotech, 1990.
> Perseus 1.0: Interactive Sources and Studies on Ancient
> Greece. CD-ROM, videodisc. New Haven: Yale UP, 1992.

If you cannot find some of the information required—for example, the city and name of the publisher—cite what is available.

> Perseus 1.0: Interactive Sources and Studies on Ancient
> Greece. CD-ROM, videodisc. 1992.

4.9. CITING ONLINE DATABASES

4.9.1. Introduction

Online databases differ from CD-ROMs and other portable database products in a number of ways, including those that follow:

- Online databases are not portable or even tangible; you cannot buy them in a store or carry them around. You access material from them on a computer through a service or a telecommunications network.
- Online databases may be continually updated, corrected, and otherwise revised without notification to users. You cannot generally be sure whether material you consult online has changed since the last time you consulted it. Documents and data derived from an online database must therefore be considered unique.

Accordingly, citations of publications from online databases, like citations of publications on portable databases (4.8), require some elements that citations of printed sources do not:

Publication medium. Many databases online are also published in other formats and may not be exactly the same in each. You must therefore include the publication medium (*Online*) in your entry in the works-cited list.

Name of computer service or computer network. Online publications are accessed through a computer service—such as BRS, Dialog, Dow Jones News Retrieval, CompuServe, Nexis, OCLC, and Prodigy—or a computer network, such as the Internet. For your documentation to be complete, you have to state the name of the service or network that provided your source. (See also the individual recommendations in this section if such information is unavailable to you.)

Date of access. Since each online publication must be considered unique, you may need to indicate two dates in your citation, just as you do for reprinted or republished books and articles (see, e.g., 4.6.17, 4.7.14). For example, if the online database indicates that the material you are using was originally published in the *New York Times* on 13 April 1993, you must, of course, include that date in the citation. In addition, to acknowledge that what you are using may differ from not only the printed version but also any past or future online version, state the date when you accessed the material.

Sections 4.9.2–3 recommend citation forms for material accessed through a computer service and through a computer network. (To cite electronic mail and public online postings, see 4.10.7.)

4.9.2. Material Accessed through a Computer Service

A useful and comprehensive reference work for online publications available through computer services is *Gale Directory of Databases*, volume 1; consult the most recent edition. This directory contains not only a detailed description of each database listed but also the name and address of the information provider or database producer as well as of the online services that offer the database. A geographic index, a subject index, and a master index help you locate databases and organizations in the directory.

Documents and data from online databases available through computer services can be divided into two groups:

- Material that indicates publication information for a printed source or printed analogue
- Material that does not indicate a specific print counterpart

a. Material with Publication Information for a Printed Source or Printed Analogue

Many databases collect and present materials previously or simultaneously made available in print. If the electronic work you are using gives publication data for a printed source or printed analogue, begin your citation with this information. If the print version is a book or a pamphlet (see the sample entry for *Guidelines for Family Television Viewing*), follow the recommendations in 4.6; if the print version is an article in a periodical, follow the recommendations in 4.7. When given, information about the printed source or analogue normally appears at the beginning of the file accessed.

If a printed source or analogue is indicated for the material you are citing, your entry in the works-cited list should consist of the following items:

1. Name of the author (if given)
2. Publication information for the printed source or analogue (including title and date of print publication)
3. Title of the database (underlined)

4. Publication medium (*Online*)
5. Name of the computer service
6. Date of access

> Angier, Natalie. "Chemists Learn Why Vegetables Are Good
>   for You." <u>New York Times</u> 13 Apr. 1993, late ed.: C1.
>   <u>New York Times Online</u>. Online. Nexis. 10 Feb. 1994.
>
> Galloway, Stephen. "TV Takes the Fall in Violence Poll."
>   <u>Hollywood Reporter</u> 23 July 1993: 16. <u>PTS F and S</u>
>   <u>Indexes</u>. Online. Dialog. 14 Jan. 1994.
>
> <u>Guidelines for Family Television Viewing</u>. Urbana: ERIC
>   Clearinghouse on Elementary and Early Childhood
>   Educ., 1990. <u>ERIC</u>. Online. BRS. 22 Nov. 1993.
>
> Stempel, Carl William. "Towards a Historical Sociology
>   of Sport in the United States, 1825-1875." <u>DAI</u> 53
>   (1993): 3374A. U of Oregon, 1992. <u>Dissertation</u>
>   <u>Abstracts Online</u>. Online. OCLC Epic. 3 Dec. 1993.

If you cannot find some of the information required—for example, the name of the computer service—cite what is available.

> Angier, Natalie. "Chemists Learn Why Vegetables Are Good
>   for You." <u>New York Times</u> 13 Apr. 1993, late ed.: C1.
>   <u>New York Times Online</u>. Online. 10 Feb. 1994.

b. Material with No Printed Source or Printed Analogue Specified

If no specific printed source or printed analogue is indicated for the material you are citing, your entry in the works-cited list should consist of the following items:

1. Name of the author (if given)
2. Title of the material accessed (in quotation marks)
3. Date of the material (if given)
4. Title of the database (underlined)
5. Publication medium (*Online*)
6. Name of the computer service
7. Date of access

"Comex Gold Contracts: Quotes from 4 Nov. 1992 to Dec.
1994." <u>Dow Jones Futures and Index Quotes</u>. Online.
Dow Jones News Retrieval. 6 Nov. 1992.

"Foreign Weather: European Cities." <u>Accu-Data</u>. Online.
Dow Jones News Retrieval. 20 Aug. 1993.

Glicken, Morley D. "A Five-Step Plan to Renew Your
Creativity." <u>National Business Employment Weekly</u>.
Online. Dow Jones News Retrieval. 10 Nov. 1992.

"Middle Ages." <u>Academic American Encyclopedia</u>. Online.
Prodigy. 30 Mar. 1992.

"Time Warner, Inc.: Sales Summary, 1988-1992."
<u>Disclosure/Worldscope</u>. Online. Lexis. 4 Jan. 1994.

"U.S. Population by Age: Urban and Urbanized Areas."
<u>1990 U.S. Census of Population and Housing</u>. Online.
Human Resource Information Network. 3 May 1994.

If you cannot find some of the information required—for example,
the name of the computer service—cite what is available.

"Time Warner, Inc.: Sales Summary, 1988-1992."
<u>Disclosure/Worldscope</u>. Online. 4 Jan. 1994.

4.9.3. Material Accessed through a Computer Network

For guides to the numerous resources available on computer net-
works, consult the most recent editions of such books as Eric Braun,
The Internet Directory (New York: Fawcett); Harley Hahn and Rick
Stout, *The Internet Complete Reference* (Berkeley: Osborne-McGraw);
Edward T. L. Hardie and Vivian Neou, editors, *Internet Mailing Lists*
(Englewood Cliffs: SRI-Prentice); Richard J. Smith and Mark Gibbs,
Navigating the Internet (Indianapolis: Sams); and Ed Krol, *The Whole
Internet: User's Guide and Catalog* (Sebastopol: O'Reilly).

Among important online sources for writers of research papers are
these two categories:

- Electronic journals, electronic newsletters, and electronic conferences (e.g., moderated forums, such as discussion lists)
- Electronic texts

a. Material from Electronic Journals, Electronic Newsletters, and Electronic Conferences

A useful and comprehensive reference work for research and scholarly articles published directly in electronic form is Lisabeth A. King, Diane Kovacs, and others, *Directory of Electronic Journals, Newsletters, and Academic Discussion Lists*, edited by Ann Okerson (Washington: Assn. of Research Libs.); consult the most recent edition. This directory not only describes publications in detail but also tells how to subscribe to them and access information from them. For example, figure 11 shows the entry for the electronic journal *Bryn Mawr Classical Review*. An

Bryn Mawr Classical Review Timely and interesting reviews of current work in Greek and Roman studies. Responses to reviews and multiple reviews of the same book are encouraged. Reviewers are drawn from a wide range of institutions. In 1991 and 1992 approximately 130 individual titles were reviewed each year. Published in paper and in electronic versions with a numbering of issues in both forms that facilitates cross-checking.

ISSN:	1063-2948
Free:	yes
Price:	$15.00/year, paper
First issue:	11/90
Peer rev'd:	yes
Formats:	ASCII, hardcopy
Distribution:	Listserv, gopher
Periodicity:	irregular (averaging 150 items/year)
Subs/Access:	Email: `listserv@cc.brynmawr.edu`, SUBSCRIBE BMCR-L
	<your name>
	Gopher: `gopher.cic.net`
Back issues:	Gopher: `orion.lib.virginia.edu:70`
Contact:	James J. O'Donnell
	Bryn Mawr Commentaries, Inc.
	Thomas Library
	Bryn Mawr College
	Bryn Mawr, PA 19010
	Phone: 215-526-5384
	Fax: 215-898-0933 (attn: J. O'Donnell)
	`jod@ccat.sas.upenn.edu`
	Richard Hamilton, Co-Editor
	`rhamilto@cc.brynmawr.edu`
Submissions:	`jod@ccat.sas.upenn.edu` or `rhamilto@cc.brynmawr.edu`
URL:	gopher://`orion.lib.virginia.edu:70/11/alpha/bmcr`
Iss Agency:	Bryn Mawr College

Fig. 11. An entry for an electronic journal from the 1994 edition of *Directory of Electronic Journals, Newsletters, and Academic Discussion Lists* (72).

index of keywords, titles, and institutional affiliations helps you locate publications in the directory. (Much of the information in this directory also appears in the books cited at the beginning of this section.)

Your entry in the works-cited list for material from an electronic journal, electronic newsletter, or electronic conference document should be similar to one for an article in a print periodical (see 4.7), though there are a few necessary differences. The entry should consist of the following items:

1. Name of the author (if given)
2. Title of the article or document (in quotation marks)
3. Title of the journal, newsletter, or conference (underlined)
4. Volume number, issue number, or other identifying number
5. Year or date of publication (in parentheses)
6. Number of pages or paragraphs (if given) or *n. pag.* ("no pagination")
7. Publication medium (*Online*)
8. Name of the computer network
9. Date of access

```
Alston, Robin. "The Battle of the Books." Humanist
      7.0176 (10 Sept. 1993): 10 pp. Online. Internet.
      10 Oct. 1993.
Lindsay, Robert K. "Electronic Journals of Proposed
      Research." EJournal 1.1 (1991): n. pag. Online.
      Internet. 10 Apr. 1991.
Moulthrop, Stuart. "You Say You Want a Revolution?
      Hypertext and the Laws of Media." Postmodern Culture
      1.3 (1991): 53 pars. Online. BITNET. 10 Jan. 1993.
Readings, Bill. "Translatio and Comparative Literature:
      The Terror of European Humanism." Surfaces 1.11
      (Dec. 1991): 19 pp. Online. Internet. 2 Feb. 1992.
Steele, Ken. "Special Discounts on the New Variorum
      Shakespeare." Shaksper 2.124 (4 May 1991): n. pag.
      Online. BITNET. 1 June 1991.
```

At the end of the entry, you may add as supplementary information the electronic address you used to access the document; precede the address with the word *Available*. Your instructor may require this information.

Readings, Bill. "<u>Translatio</u> and Comparative Literature:
The Terror of European Humanism." <u>Surfaces</u> 1.11
(Dec. 1991): 19 pp. Online. Internet. 2 Feb. 1992.
Available FTP: harfang.cc.umontreal.ca.

b. An Electronic Text

A great variety of texts, such as literary works and historical documents, are available through computer networks. Projects like the Center for Electronic Texts in the Humanities (CETH, Rutgers Univ. and Princeton Univ.), the Catalogue of Projects in Electronic Text (CPET, Georgetown Univ.), the Electronic Text Center and On-line Archive of Electronic Texts (Univ. of Virginia), the Internet Wiretap Online Library, the Machine-Assisted Realization of the Virtual Electronic Library (MARVEL, Lib. of Congress), and the Oxford Text Archive provide information about and access to electronic texts. The books cited at the beginning of this section describe texts available on computer networks and explain access procedures. For example, figure 12 shows the entry for the Oxford Text Archive that appears in Eric Braun's *The Internet Directory*.

If you plan to study an electronic text of a literary or historical work, remember that not all texts are equally reliable or authoritative (see 1.6 and 4.6.12 for discussions of scholarly editions). Be sure to use a text that states the title, editor, and date of the edition serving as its source. Ask your instructor for advice if you have any questions about the reliability of an electronic text.

The Oxford Text Archive (OTA)

As of July 1993, the Oxford Text Archive contained 1,336 titles in 28 languages. Most of these are scholarly articles; this is an important resource for the humanities. A complete index of the texts, as well as a few of the texts themselves, is available by anonymous FTP. The others are available by written agreement on magnetic tape, floppy disks, or over the Internet.

i archive@ox.ac.uk
Access: FTP black.ox.ac.uk in /ota/
Includes: Marvell, Edgar Rice Burroughs, Conrad, Darwin, Dickens, Arthur Conan Doyle, Henry James, London, Melville, Milton, Orczy, Bram Stoker, Trollope, Mark Twain, H.G. Wells, and more, as well as dictionaries and a number of U.S. historical documents.

Fig. 12. An entry for an electronic-text archive from the 1994 edition of *The Internet Directory* (564).

Your citation of an electronic text should contain the following items:

1. Name of the author (if any)
2. Title of the text (underlined)
3. Publication information for the printed source
4. Publication medium (*Online*)
5. Name of the repository of the electronic text (e.g., Oxford Text Archive)
6. Name of the computer network
7. Date of access

```
Hardy, Thomas. Far from the Madding Crowd. Ed. Ronald
        Blythe. Harmondsworth: Penguin, 1978. Online.
        Oxford Text Archive. Internet. 24 Jan. 1994.

Octovian. Ed. Frances McSparran. Early English Text Soc.
        289. London: Oxford UP, 1986. Online. U of Virginia
        Lib. Internet. 6 Apr. 1994.

Shakespeare, William. Hamlet. The Works of William
        Shakespeare. Ed. Arthur H. Bullen. Stratford Town
        Ed. Stratford-on-Avon: Shakespeare Head, 1911.
        Online. Dartmouth Coll. Lib. Internet. 26 Dec. 1992.

United States. General Accounting Office. Drug-Exposed
        Infants: Report to the Chairman, Committee on
        Finance, U.S. Senate. 6 Nov. 1992. Online. U of
        Minnesota Lib. Internet. 1 May 1993.
```

At the end of the entry, you may add as supplementary information the electronic address you used to access the document; precede the address with the word *Available*. Your instructor may require this information.

```
Octovian. Ed. Frances McSparran. Early English Text
        Soc. 289. London: Oxford UP, 1986. Online. U of
        Virginia Lib. Internet. 6 Apr. 1994. Available FTP:
        etext.virginia.edu.
```

4.10. CITING OTHER SOURCES

4.10.1. A Television or Radio Program

The information in an entry for a television or radio program usually appears in the following order:

1. Title of the episode or segment, if appropriate (in quotation marks)
2. Title of the program (underlined)
3. Title of the series, if any (neither underlined nor in quotation marks)
4. Name of the network
5. Call letters and city of the local station (if any)
6. Broadcast date

For example, *Middlemarch* is the name of a six-episode program in the series Masterpiece Theatre. Use a comma between the call letters and the city ("KETC, St. Louis"). A period follows each of the other items. For the inclusion of other information that may be pertinent (e.g., performers, director, narrator, number of episodes), see the sample entries.

Elektra. By Richard Strauss. Perf. Eva Marton and Leonie
    Rysanek. Cond. Leonard Slatkin. Lyric Opera of
    Chicago. Nuveen-Lyric Opera of Chicago Radio
    Network. WFMT, Chicago. 5 June 1993.

"Frankenstein: The Making of the Monster." Great Books.
    Narr. Donald Sutherland. Writ. Eugenie Vink. Dir.
    Jonathan Ward. Learning Channel. 8 Sept. 1993.

"Frederick Douglass." Civil War Journal. Narr. Danny
    Glover. Dir. Craig Haffner. Arts and Entertainment
    Network. 6 Apr. 1993.

Into the Woods. By Stephen Sondheim. Dir. James Lapine.
    Perf. Bernadette Peters and Joanna Gleason. American
    Playhouse. PBS. WNET, New York. 3 Mar. 1991.

Middlemarch. By George Eliot. Adapt. Andrew Davies.
    Dir. Anthony Pope. Perf. Juliet Aubrey and Patrick
    Malahide. 6 episodes. Masterpiece Theatre. Introd.
    Russell Baker. PBS. WGBH, Boston. 10 Apr.-15 May
    1994.

The Secret of Life. Narr. David Suzuki. 8 episodes. PBS.
WETA, Washington. 26-29 Sept. 1993.

"Shakespearean Putdowns." Narr. Robert Siegel and Linda
Wertheimer. All Things Considered. Natl. Public
Radio. WNYC, New York. 6 Apr. 1994.

"Yes . . . but Is It Art?" Narr. Morley Safer. Sixty
Minutes. CBS. WCBS, New York. 19 Sept. 1993.

If your reference is primarily to the work of a particular individual,
cite that person's name before the title.

Davies, Andrew, adapt. Middlemarch. By George Eliot.
Dir. Anthony Pope. Perf. Juliet Aubrey and Patrick
Malahide. 6 episodes. Masterpiece Theatre. Introd.
Russell Baker. PBS. WGBH, Boston. 10 Apr.-15 May
1994.

Welles, Orson, dir. The War of the Worlds. By H. G.
Wells. Adapt. Howard Koch. Mercury Theatre on the
Air. CBS Radio. WCBS, New York. 30 Oct. 1938.

See 4.10.8 for interviews on television and radio programs; see also
4.10.2–3 for recordings and 4.10.4 for performances.

4.10.2. A Sound Recording

In an entry for a commercially available recording, which person is
cited first (e.g., the composer, conductor, or performer) depends on
the desired emphasis. List the title of the recording (or the titles of the
works included), the artist or artists, the manufacturer ("Capitol"), and
the year of issue (if the year is unknown, write *n.d.*). Place a comma
between the manufacturer and the date; periods follow the other
items. If you are not using a compact disc, indicate the medium, neither underlined nor enclosed in quotation marks, before the manufacturer's name: *Audiocassette* (see the sample entry for Marsalis),
Audiotape (reel-to-reel tape), or *LP* (long-playing record; see the entry
for Ellington).

In general, underline titles of recordings (*Romances for Saxophone*),
but do not underline or enclose in quotation marks the titles of musical compositions identified only by form, number, and key (see the

entry for Norrington). You may wish to indicate, in addition to the
year of issue, the date of recording (see the entry for Ellington).

Bartoli, Cecilia. If You Love Me: Eighteenth-Century
Italian Songs. London, 1992.

Ellington, Duke, cond. Duke Ellington Orchestra. First
Carnegie Hall Concert. Rec. 23 Jan. 1943. LP.
Prestige, 1977.

Gabriel, Peter. Passion: Music for The Last Temptation
of Christ, a Film by Martin Scorsese. Geffen, 1989.

Holiday, Billie. The Essence of Billie Holiday.
Columbia, 1991.

Joplin, Scott. Treemonisha. Perf. Carmen Balthrop, Betty
Allen, and Curtis Rayam. Houston Grand Opera Orch.
and Chorus. Cond. Gunther Schuller. Deutsche
Grammophon, 1976.

Marsalis, Branford. Romances for Saxophone. English
Chamber Orch. Cond. Andrew Litton. Audiocassette.
CBS, 1986.

Norrington, Roger, cond. Symphony no. 1 in C and
Symphony no. 6 in F. By Ludwig van Beethoven.
London Classical Players. EMI, 1988.

Simon, Paul. The Rhythm of the Saints. Warner Bros.,
1990.

Sondheim, Stephen. Into the Woods. Orch. Jonathan Tunick.
Perf. Bernadette Peters and Joanna Gleason. Cond.
Paul Gemignani. RCA Victor, 1987.

Sting, narr. Peter and the Wolf, op. 67. By Sergei
Prokofiev. Chamber Orch. of Europe. Cond. Claudio
Abbado. Deutsche Grammophon, 1990.

If you are citing a specific song, place the title of the song in quotation marks.

Bartoli, Cecilia. "Caro mio ben." By Giuseppe Giordani.
If You Love Me: Eighteenth-Century Italian Songs.
London, 1992.

Gabriel, Peter. "A Different Drum." Perf. Gabriel,
    Shankar, and Youssou N'Dour. <u>Passion: Music for</u> The
    Last Temptation of Christ<u>, a Film by Martin</u>
    <u>Scorsese</u>. Geffen, 1989.

Holiday, Billie. "God Bless the Child." Rec. 9 May 1941.
    <u>The Essence of Billie Holiday</u>. Columbia, 1991.

Simon, Paul, and Milton Nascimento. "Spirit Voices." <u>The</u>
    <u>Rhythm of the Saints</u>. Warner Bros., 1990.

Treat a spoken-word recording as you would a musical recording.
Begin with the speaker, the writer, or the production director, depending on the desired emphasis. You may add the original publication date of the work immediately after the title.

Burnett, Frances Hodgson. <u>The Secret Garden</u>. 1911. Read
    by Helena Bonham Carter. Audiocassette. Penguin-
    High Bridge, 1993.

Scott, George C., narr. <u>World War II</u>. Audiocassette.
    Carmichael, 1990.

Shakespeare, William. <u>Othello</u>. Perf. Laurence Olivier,
    Maggie Smith, Frank Finley, and Derek Jacobi. Dir.
    John Dexter. LP. RCA Victor, 1964.

Welles, Orson, dir. <u>The War of the Worlds</u>. By H. G.
    Wells. Adapt. Howard Koch. Mercury Theatre on the
    Air. Rec. 30 Oct. 1938. LP. Evolution, 1969.

Do not underline or enclose in quotation marks the title of a private or archival recording or tape. Include the date recorded (if known) and the location and identifying number of the recording.

Wilgus, D. K. Southern Folk Tales. Rec. 23-25 Mar. 1965.
    Audiotape. U of California, Los Angeles, Archives
    of Folklore. B.76.82.

In citing the libretto, the booklet, the liner notes, or other material accompanying a recording, give the author's name, the title of the material (if any), and a description of the material ("Libretto"). Then provide the usual bibliographic information for a recording.

Colette. Libretto. <u>L'enfant et les sortilèges</u>. Music by
Maurice Ravel. Orch. National Bordeaux-Aquitaine.
Cond. Alain Lombard. Valois, 1993.

Lawrence, Vera Brodsky. "Scott Joplin and <u>Treemonisha</u>."
Booklet. <u>Treemonisha</u>. By Scott Joplin. Deutsche
Grammophon, 1976.

Lewiston, David. Liner notes. <u>The Balinese Gamelan:</u>
<u>Music from the Morning of the World</u>. LP. Nonesuch,
n.d.

4.10.3. A Film or Video Recording

A film entry usually begins with the title, underlined, and includes
the director, the distributor, and the year. You may include other data
that seem pertinent—such as the names of the writer, performers, and
producer—between the title and the distributor.

<u>It's a Wonderful Life</u>. Dir. Frank Capra. Perf. James
Stewart, Donna Reed, Lionel Barrymore, and Thomas
Mitchell. RKO, 1946.

<u>Like Water for Chocolate</u> [<u>Como agua para chocolate</u>].
Screenplay by Laura Esquivel. Dir. Alfonso Arau.
Perf. Lumi Cavazos, Marco Lombardi, and Regina
Torne. Miramax, 1993.

If you are citing the contribution of a particular individual, begin with
that person's name.

Chaplin, Charles, dir. <u>Modern Times</u>. Perf. Chaplin and
Paulette Goddard. United Artists, 1936.

Jhabvala, Ruth Prawer, adapt. <u>A Room with a View</u>. By
E. M. Forster. Dir. James Ivory. Prod. Ismail
Merchant. Perf. Maggie Smith, Denholm Eliot, Helena
Bonham Carter, and Daniel Day-Lewis. Cinecom Intl.
Films, 1985.

Mifune, Toshiro, perf. <u>Rashomon</u>. Dir. Akira Kurosawa.
Daiei, 1950.

Rota, Nino, composer. <u>Juliet of the Spirits</u> [<u>Giulietta</u>
     <u>degli spiriti</u>]. Dir. Federico Fellini. Perf.
     Giulietta Masina. Rizzoli, 1965.

Cite a videocassette, videodisc, slide program, or filmstrip like a
film, but include the original release date (if relevant) and the
medium, neither underlined nor enclosed in quotation marks, before
the name of the distributor.

<u>Alcohol Use and Its Medical Consequences: A Comprehensive</u>
     <u>Teaching Program for Biomedical Education</u>. Prod.
     Project Cork, Dartmouth Medical School. Slide
     program. Milner-Fenwick, 1982.
<u>Un ballo in maschera</u>. By Giuseppe Verdi. Perf. Luciano
     Pavarotti and Aprile Millo. Metropolitan Opera
     Orch. and Chorus. Cond. James Levine. Videocassette.
     Deutsche Grammophon, 1991.
Hitchcock, Alfred, dir. <u>Rebecca</u>. Perf. Joan Fontaine,
     Laurence Olivier, and Judith Anderson. 1940.
     Videodisc. Voyager, 1990.
<u>It's a Wonderful Life</u>. Dir. Frank Capra. Perf. James
     Stewart, Donna Reed, Lionel Barrymore, and Thomas
     Mitchell. 1946. Videocassette. Republic, 1988.
<u>Looking at Our Earth: A Visual Dictionary</u>. Sound
     filmstrip. Natl. Geographic Educ. Services, 1992.
<u>Medicine at the Crossroads</u>. Prod. 13/WNET and BBC TV.
     Videocassette. PBS Video, 1993.
Mifune, Toshiro, perf. <u>Rashomon</u>. Dir. Akira Kurosawa.
     1950. Videocassette. Embassy, 1986.
Renoir, Jean, dir. <u>Grand Illusion</u> [<u>La grande illusion</u>].
     Perf. Jean Gabin and Erich von Stroheim. 1938.
     Videodisc. Voyager, 1987.

4.10.4. A Performance

An entry for a performance (play, opera, ballet, concert) usually begins
with the title, contains facts similar to those given for a film (see

4.10.3), and concludes with the site of the performance (usually the theater and city, separated by a comma and followed by a period) and the date of the performance.

Hamlet. By William Shakespeare. Dir. John Gielgud. Perf.
    Richard Burton. Shubert Theatre, Boston. 4 Mar.
    1964.

Medea. By Euripides. Trans. Alistair Elliot. Dir.
    Jonathan Kent. Perf. Diana Rigg. Longacre Theatre,
    New York. 7 Apr. 1994.

The River. Chor. Alvin Ailey. Dance Theater of Harlem.
    New York State Theater, New York. 15 Mar. 1994.

I vespri siciliani. By Giuseppe Verdi. Dir. Christopher
    Alden. Cond. Charles Mackerras. Perf. Carol Vaness,
    Chris Merritt, James Morris, and Timothy Noble. San
    Francisco Opera. War Memorial House, San Francisco.
    10 Sept. 1993.

If you are citing the contribution of a particular individual or group, begin with the appropriate name.

Ars Musica Antiqua. In Praise of Women: Music by Women
    Composers from the Twelfth through the Eighteenth
    Centuries. Concert. Scotch Plains Public Lib., NJ.
    5 Apr. 1994.

Freni, Mirella, soprano. Adriana Lecouvreur. By Francesco
    Cilèa. Cond. Roberto Abbado. Metropolitan Opera.
    Metropolitan Opera House, New York. 19 Mar. 1994.

Joplin, Scott. Treemonisha. Dir. Frank Corsaro. Cond.
    Gunther Schuller. Perf. Carmen Balthrop, Betty
    Allen, and Curtis Rayam. Houston Grand Opera.
    Miller Theatre, Houston. 18 May 1975.

Rigg, Diana, perf. Medea. By Euripides. Trans. Alistair
    Elliot. Dir. Jonathan Kent. Longacre Theatre, New
    York. 7 Apr. 1994.

For television and radio broadcasts of performances, see 4.10.1; for sound recordings of performances, see 4.10.2; for video recordings of performances, see 4.10.3.

4.10.5. A Musical Composition

To cite a musical composition, begin with the composer's name. Underline the title of an opera, a ballet, or a piece of instrumental music identified by name (*Symphonie fantastique*), but do not underline or enclose in quotation marks an instrumental composition identified only by form, number, and key.

```
Beethoven, Ludwig van. Symphony no. 8 in F, op. 93.

Berlioz, Hector. Symphonie fantastique, op. 14.

Wagner, Richard. Götterdämmerung.
```

Treat a published score, however, like a book. Give the title, underlined, as it appears on the title page, and capitalize the abbreviations *no.* and *op.*

```
Beethoven, Ludwig van. Symphony No. 8 in F, Op. 93. New
     York: Dover, 1989.
```

If you wish to indicate when a musical composition was written, add the date immediately after the title.

```
Beethoven, Ludwig van. Symphony No. 8 in F, Op. 93.
     1812. New York: Dover, 1989.
```

See 4.10.2 for sound recordings of musical compositions, 4.10.1 for television and radio programs of music, and 4.10.4 for performances of music.

4.10.6. A Work of Art

To cite a work of art, state the artist's name first. In general, underline the title of a painting or sculpture. Name the institution that houses the work (e.g., a museum) or, for a work in a private collection, the individual who owns it, and follow the name by a comma and the city.

Bearden, Romare. <u>The Street</u>. Private collection of Mrs.
    Robert M. Benjamin, New York.

Bernini, Gianlorenzo. <u>Ecstasy of St. Teresa</u>. Santa Maria
    della Vittoria, Rome.

Rembrandt van Rijn. <u>Aristotle Contemplating the Bust of
    Homer</u>. Metropolitan Museum of Art, New York.

If you use a photograph of the work, indicate not only the institution
or private owner and the city but also the complete publication information for the source in which the photograph appears, including the
page, slide, figure, or plate number, whichever is relevant.

Cassatt, Mary. <u>Mother and Child</u>. Wichita Art Museum,
    Wichita. <u>American Painting: 1560-1913</u>. By John
    Pearce. New York: McGraw, 1964. Slide 22.

El Greco. <u>Burial of Count Orgaz</u>. San Tomé, Toledo.
    <u>Renaissance Perspectives in Literature and the
    Visual Arts</u>. By Murray Roston. Princeton: Princeton
    UP, 1987. 274.

If you wish to indicate when a work of art was created, add the date
immediately after the title.

Cassatt, Mary. <u>Mother and Child</u>. 1890. Wichita Art
    Museum, Wichita. <u>American Painting: 1560-1913</u>. By
    John Pearce. New York: McGraw, 1964. Slide 22.

4.10.7. A Letter, a Memo, an E-Mail Communication, or a Public Online Posting

As bibliographic entries, letters fall into three general categories:
- Published letters
- Unpublished letters in archives
- Letters received by the researcher

Treat a published letter like a work in a collection (see 4.6.7), adding
the date of the letter and the number (if the editor assigned one).

Woolf, Virginia. "To T. S. Eliot." 28 July 1920. Letter
    1138 of <u>The Letters of Virginia Woolf</u>. Ed. Nigel

```
Nicolson and Joanne Trautmann. Vol. 2. New York:
    Harcourt, 1976. 437-38.
```

If you use more than one letter from a published collection, however, provide a single entry for the entire work and cite the letters individually in the text, following the form recommended for cross-references in works-cited lists (see 4.6.10).

In citing an unpublished letter, follow the guidelines for manuscripts and typescripts (see 4.10.13).

```
Benton, Thomas Hart. Letter to Charles Fremont. 22 June
    1847. John Charles Fremont Papers. Southwest Museum
    Lib., Los Angeles.
```

Cite a letter that you received as follows:

```
Morrison, Toni. Letter to the author. 17 May 1992.
```

Treat memos and electronic mail similarly: give the name of the writer of the document, a description of the document that includes the recipient (e.g., "E-mail to the author"), and the date of the document. Any title of the document should be enclosed in quotation marks and placed immediately after the document writer's name.

```
Danford, Tom. "Monday Greetings." E-mail to Terry Craig.
    13 Sept. 1993.
Lancashire, Ian. E-mail to the author. 1 Mar. 1994.
Moore, Bill. Memo to assessment liaisons, State Board
    for Community and Technical Colls., Olympia, WA.
    29 May 1992.
```

You might find information that seems reliable and useful among the public postings on electronic networks—bulletin boards, commercial online services, or Usenet (a collection of mostly unmoderated "newsgroups" accessible on the Internet). To cite a public online posting, follow the author's name and the title of the document with the date when the material was posted. Then give the description *Online posting*; the name or names of the location where you found the posting (e.g., the newsgroup or forum); and the name of the network (e.g., Usenet). Conclude with the date of access.

Ernandes, Ken. "STS-64 Rev 138 Vector." 18 Sept. 1994.

    Online posting. Space Flight Forum, Space Shuttle

    Section. CompuServe. 28 Sept. 1994.

Shaumann, Thomas Michael. "Re: Technical German."

    5 Aug. 1994. Online posting. Newsgroup

    comp.edu.languages.natural. Usenet. 7 Sept. 1994.

4.10.8. An Interview

For purposes of documentation, there are three kinds of interviews:

- Published or recorded interviews
- Interviews broadcast on television or radio
- Interviews conducted by the researcher

Begin with the name of the person interviewed. If the interview is part of a publication, recording, or program, enclose the title of the interview, if any, in quotation marks; if the interview was published independently, underline the title. If the interview is untitled, use the descriptive label *Interview*, neither underlined nor enclosed in quotation marks. The interviewer's name may be added if known and pertinent to your paper (see the sample entries for Blackmun and Updike). Conclude with the appropriate bibliographic information.

Blackmun, Harry. Interview with Ted Koppel and Nina

    Totenberg. <u>Nightline</u>. ABC. WABC, New York. 5 Apr.

    1994.

Fellini, Federico. "The Long Interview." <u>Juliet of the</u>

    <u>Spirits</u>. Ed. Tullio Kezich. Trans. Howard

    Greenfield. New York: Ballantine, 1966. 17-64.

Gordimer, Nadine. Interview. <u>New York Times</u> 10 Oct. 1991,

    late ed.: C25.

Lansbury, Angela. Interview. <u>Off-Camera: Conversations</u>

    <u>with the Makers of Prime-Time Television</u>. By Richard

    Levinson and William Link. New York: Plume-NAL,

    1986. 72-86.

Updike, John. Interview with Scott Simon. <u>Weekend</u>

    <u>Edition</u>. Natl. Public Radio. WBUR, Boston. 2 Apr.

    1994.

```
Wolfe, Tom. Interview. The Wrong Stuff: American
     Architecture. Dir. Tom Bettag. Videocassette.
     Carousel, 1983.
```

To cite an interview that you conducted, give the name of the person interviewed, the kind of interview (*Personal interview, Telephone interview*), and the date.

```
Pei, I. M. Personal interview. 22 July 1993.
Poussaint, Alvin F. Telephone interview. 10 Dec. 1990.
```

4.10.9. A Map or Chart

In general, treat a map or chart like an anonymous book (4.6.11), but add the appropriate descriptive label (*Map, Chart*).

```
The First Aid Card. Chart. N.p.: Papertech, 1988.
Washington, DC. Map. Chicago: Rand, 1992.
```

For guidance on how to cite such sources as dioramas, flash cards, games, globes, kits, and models, see Eugene B. Fleischer, *A Style Manual for Citing Microform and Nonprint Media* (Chicago: ALA, 1978).

4.10.10. A Cartoon

To cite a cartoon, state the cartoonist's name; the title of the cartoon (if any), in quotation marks; and the descriptive label *Cartoon*, neither underlined nor enclosed in quotation marks. Conclude with the usual publication information.

```
Chast, Roz. Cartoon. New Yorker 11 Apr. 1994: 58.
Trudeau, Garry. "Doonesbury." Cartoon. Star-Ledger
     [Newark] 3 Jan. 1994: 24.
```

4.10.11. An Advertisement

To cite an advertisement, state the name of the product, company, or institution that is the subject of the advertisement, followed by the descriptive label *Advertisement*, neither underlined nor enclosed in quotation marks. Conclude with the usual publication information.

    Chanel for Men. Advertisement. GQ Dec. 1993: 125-26.
    Delta Airlines. Advertisement. CNN. 12 July 1994.

4.10.12. A Lecture, a Speech, or an Address

In a citation of an oral presentation, give the speaker's name; the title of the presentation (if known), in quotation marks; the meeting and the sponsoring organization (if applicable); the location; and the date. If there is no title, use an appropriate descriptive label (*Address, Lecture, Keynote speech, Reading*), neither underlined nor enclosed in quotation marks.

    Atwood, Margaret. "Silencing the Scream." Boundaries of
        the Imagination Forum. MLA Convention. Royal York
        Hotel, Toronto. 29 Dec. 1993.
    Hyman, Earle. Reading of Shakespeare's Othello. Symphony
        Space, New York. 28 Mar. 1994.
    Terkel, Studs. Address. Conf. on Coll. Composition and
        Communication Convention. Palmer House, Chicago.
        22 Mar. 1990.

4.10.13. A Manuscript or Typescript

To cite a manuscript or a typescript, state the author, the title or a description of the material (e.g., *Notebook*), the form of the material (*ms.* for a manuscript, *ts.* for a typescript), and any identifying number assigned to it. Give the name and location of any library or other research institution housing the material.

    Chaucer, Geoffrey. The Canterbury Tales. Harley ms. 7334.
        British Library, London.
    Octovian. Ms. 91. Dean and Chapter Lib., Lincoln, Eng.
    Salviati, Lionardo. Poetica d'Aristotile parafrasata e
        comentata. Ms. 2.2.11. Biblioteca Nazionale
        Centrale, Firenze.

```
Smith, Sonia. "Shakespeare's Dark Lady Revisited."
    Unpublished essay, 1993.
Twain, Mark. Notebook 32, ts. Mark Twain Papers. U of
    California, Berkeley.
```

4.10.14. A Legal Source

The citation of legal documents and law cases may be complicated. If your paper requires many such references, consult the most recent edition of *A Uniform System of Citation* (Cambridge: Harvard Law Rev. Assn.), an indispensable guide in this field.

In general, do not underline or enclose in quotation marks the titles of laws, acts, and similar documents in either the text or the list of works cited (Declaration of Independence, Constitution of the United States, Taft-Hartley Act). Such titles are usually abbreviated, and the works are cited by sections, with the years added if relevant. Although lawyers and legal scholars adopt many abbreviations in their citations, use only familiar abbreviations when writing for a more general audience (see ch. 6).

```
21 US Code. Sec. 1401a. 1988.
US Const. Art. 1, sec.1.
```

Note that references to the United States Code, which is often abbreviated *USC*, begin with the title number; in the above USC entry, for example, title 21 refers to laws concerned with food and drugs. Alphabetize USC entries under *United States Code* even if you use the abbreviation. When including more than one reference to the code, list the individual entries in numerical order.

If you are citing an act, state the name of the act, its Public Law number, the date it was enacted, and its Statutes at Large cataloging number. Use the abbreviations *Pub. L.* for Public Law and *Stat.* for Statutes at Large.

```
Pesticide Monitoring Improvements Act of 1988. Pub. L.
    100-418. 23 Aug. 1988. Stat. 102.1412.
```

Names of law cases are similarly abbreviated ("Brown v. Board of Ed.," for the case of Oliver Brown versus the Board of Education of Topeka, Kansas), but the first important word of each party's name is always spelled out. Names of cases, unlike those of laws, are underlined in the text but not in bibliographic entries. In citing a case, include, in addition to the names of the first plaintiff and the first defendant, the volume, name (not underlined), and page (in that order) of the law report cited; the name of the court that decided the case; and the year of the decision. Once again, considerable abbreviation is the norm. The following citation, for example, refers to page 755 of volume 148 of the *United States Patent Quarterly*, dealing with the case of Stevens against the National Broadcasting Company, which was decided by the California Superior Court in 1966.

```
Stevens v. National Broadcasting Co. 148 USPQ 755. CA
    Super. Ct. 1966.
```

5 Documentation: Citing Sources in the Text

5.1. PARENTHETICAL DOCUMENTATION AND THE LIST OF WORKS CITED

The list of works cited at the end of your research paper plays an important role in your acknowledgment of sources (see ch. 4), but the list does not in itself provide sufficiently detailed and precise documentation. You must indicate to your readers not only what works you used in writing the paper but also exactly what you derived from each source and exactly where in the work you found the material. The most practical way to supply this information is to insert a brief parenthetical acknowledgment in your paper wherever you incorporate another's words, facts, or ideas. Usually the author's last name and a page reference are enough to identify the source and the specific location from which you borrowed material.

> Medieval Europe was a place both of "raids, pillages,
> slavery, and extortion" and of "traveling merchants,
> monetary exchange, towns if not cities, and active
> markets in grain" (Townsend 10).

The parenthetical reference "(Townsend 10)" indicates that the quotations come from page 10 of a work by Townsend. Given the author's last name, your readers can find complete publication information for the source in the alphabetically arranged list of works cited that follows the text of your paper.

> Townsend, Robert M. The Medieval Village Economy.
>   Princeton: Princeton UP, 1993.

The sample references in 5.4 offer recommendations for documenting many other kinds of sources.

5.2. INFORMATION REQUIRED IN PARENTHETICAL DOCUMENTATION

In determining the information needed to document sources accurately, keep the following guidelines in mind.

References in the text must clearly point to specific sources in the list of works cited. The information in your parenthetical references in the text must match the corresponding information in the entries in your list of works cited. For a typical works-cited-list entry, which begins with the name of the author (or editor, translator, or narrator), the parenthetical reference begins with the same name. When the list contains only one work by the author cited, you need give only the author's last name to identify the work: "(Patterson 183–85)." If your list contains more than one author with the same last name, you must add the first initial—"(A. Patterson 183–85)" and "(L. Patterson 230)"—or, if the initial is shared too, the full first name. If two or three names begin the entry, give the last name of each person listed: "(Rabkin, Greenberg, and Olander vii)." If the work has more than three authors, follow the form in the bibliographic entry: either give the first author's last name followed by *et al.*, without any intervening punctuation—"(Lauter et al. 2425–33)"—or give all the last names. If there is a corporate author, use its name, shortened or in full (see 5.4.5). If the work is listed by title, use the title, shortened or in full (see 5.4.4). If the list contains more than one work by the author, add the cited title, shortened or in full, after the author's last name (see 5.4.6).

Identify the location of the borrowed information as specifically as possible. Give the relevant page number or numbers in the parenthetical reference (see esp. 5.4.2) or, if you cite from more than one volume of a multivolume work, the volume and page numbers (see 5.4.3). In a reference to a literary work, it is helpful to give information other than, or in addition to, the page number—for example, the chapter, book, or stanza number or the numbers of the act, scene, and line (see 5.4.8). You may omit page numbers when citing complete works (see 5.4.1), as well as articles in works arranged alphabetically (like encyclopedias) and, of course, unpaginated sources (see esp. 5.4.4). A page reference is similarly unnecessary if, for example, you use a passage from a one-page work.

5.3. READABILITY

Keep parenthetical references as brief—and as few—as clarity and accuracy permit. Give only the information needed to identify a source, and do not add a parenthetical reference unnecessarily. Identify sources by author and, if necessary, title; do not use abbreviations such as *ed.*, *trans.*, and *comp.* after the name. If you are citing an entire work, for example, rather than a specific part of it, the author's name in the text may be the only documentation required. The statement "Booth has devoted an entire book to the subject" needs no parenthetical documentation if the list of works cited includes only one work by Booth. If, for the reader's convenience, you wished to name the book in your text, you could recast the sentence: "Booth has devoted an entire book, *The Rhetoric of Fiction*, to the subject."

Remember that there is a direct relation between what you integrate into your text and what you place in parentheses. If, for example, you include an author's name in a sentence, you need not repeat the name in the parenthetical page citation that follows, provided that the reference is clearly to the work of the author you mention. The paired sentences below illustrate alternative ways of identifying authors. Note that sometimes one version is more concise than the other.

AUTHOR'S NAME IN TEXT

Tannen has argued this point (178-85).

AUTHOR'S NAME IN REFERENCE

This point has already been argued (Tannen 178-85).

AUTHORS' NAMES IN TEXT

Others, like Kerrigan and Braden (210-15), hold the opposite point of view.

AUTHORS' NAMES IN REFERENCE

Others hold the opposite point of view (e.g., Kerrigan and Braden 210-15).

AUTHOR'S NAME IN TEXT

Only Daiches has seen this relation (2: 776-77).

AUTHOR'S NAME IN REFERENCE

Only one scholar has seen this relation (Daiches 2: 776-77).

AUTHOR'S NAME IN TEXT

It may be true, as Robertson maintains, that "in the
appreciation of medieval art the attitude of the
observer is of primary importance . . ." (136).

AUTHOR'S NAME IN REFERENCE

It may be true that "in the appreciation of medieval
art the attitude of the observer is of primary
importance . . ." (Robertson 136).

To avoid interrupting the flow of your writing, place the parenthetical reference where a pause would naturally occur (preferably at the
end of a sentence), as near as possible to the material documented. The
parenthetical reference precedes the punctuation mark that concludes
the sentence, clause, or phrase containing the borrowed material.

In his <u>Autobiography</u>, Benjamin Franklin states that he
prepared a list of thirteen virtues (135-37).

A reference directly after a quotation follows the closing quotation mark.

In the late Renaissance, Machiavelli contended that human
beings were by nature "ungrateful" and "mutable" (1240),
and Montaigne thought them "miserable and puny" (1343).

If the quotation, whether of poetry or prose, is set off from the text (see
2.7.2–4), type a space after the concluding punctuation mark of the
quotation and insert the parenthetical reference.

John K. Mahon adds a further insight to our understanding
of the War of 1812:

> Financing the war was very difficult at the
> time. Baring Brothers, a banking firm of the
> enemy country, handled routine accounts for the
> United States overseas, but the firm would take
> on no loans. The loans were in the end absorbed
> by wealthy Americans at great hazard--also, as
> it turned out, at great profit to them. (385)

```
Elizabeth Bishop's "In the Waiting Room" is rich in
evocative detail:
        It was winter. It got dark
        early. The waiting room
        was full of grown-up people,
        arctics and overcoats,
        lamps and magazines. (6-10)
```

For guidelines on citing literary works, see 5.4.8.

If you need to document several sources for a statement, you may cite them in a note to avoid unduly disrupting the text (see 5.5). If you quote more than once from the same page within a single paragraph—and no quotation from another source intervenes—you may give a single parenthetical reference after the last quotation.

5.4. SAMPLE REFERENCES

Each of the following sections concludes with a list of the works cited in the examples. Note that the lists for the first five sections (5.4.1–5) do not include more than one work by the same author. On citing two or more works by an author, see 5.4.6.

5.4.1. Citing an Entire Work

If you wish to cite an entire work rather than part of the work, it is usually preferable to include the author's name in the text instead of in a parenthetical reference.

```
But Peter Scotto has offered another view.

McRae's The Literature of Science includes many examples
of this trend.

Natalie Angier reported on research showing that
ingredients in fruit and vegetables work "to retard the
bodily breakdown that results in cancer and other
chronic diseases."
```

Kurosawa's <u>Rashomon</u> was one of the first Japanese films
to attract a Western audience.

Margaret Atwood's remarks drew an enthusiastic response.

Stempel has tried to develop a "historical sociology" of
sport in nineteenth-century America.

I vividly recall Diana Rigg's interpretation of Medea.

Michael Joyce was among the first to write fiction in
hypertext.

Gilbert and Gubar broke new ground on the subject.

Lauter and his coeditors have provided a useful
anthology of American literature.

Scholars received news about a new edition of
Shakespeare through Steele's notice in the electronic
discussion list known as <u>Shaksper</u>.

Works Cited

Angier, Natalie. "Chemists Learn Why Vegetables Are Good
for You." <u>New York Times</u> 13 Apr. 1993, late ed.: C1.
<u>New York Times Online</u>. Online. Nexis. 10 Feb. 1994.

Atwood, Margaret. "Silencing the Scream." Boundaries of
the Imagination Forum. MLA Convention. Royal York
Hotel, Toronto. 29 Dec. 1993.

Gilbert, Sandra M., and Susan Gubar. <u>The Madwoman in the
Attic: The Woman Writer and the Nineteenth-Century
Literary Imagination</u>. New Haven: Yale UP, 1979.

Joyce, Michael. <u>Afternoon: A Story</u>. Diskette. Watertown:
Eastgate, 1987.

Kurosawa, Akira, dir. <u>Rashomon</u>. Perf. Toshiro Mifune.
Daiei, 1950.

Lauter, Paul, et al., eds. <u>The Heath Anthology of
American Literature</u>. 2nd ed. 2 vols. Lexington:
Heath, 1994.

McRae, Murdo William, ed. <u>The Literature of Science:</u>
<u>Perspectives on Popular Science Writing</u>. Athens:
U of Georgia P, 1993.

Rigg, Diana, perf. <u>Medea</u>. By Euripides. Trans. Alistair
Elliot. Dir. Jonathan Kent. Longacre Theatre, New
York. 7 Apr. 1994.

Scotto, Peter. "Censorship, Reading, and Interpretation:
A Case Study from the Soviet Union." <u>PMLA</u> 109
(1994): 61-70.

Steele, Ken. "Special Discounts on the New Variorum
Shakespeare." <u>Shaksper</u> 2.124 (4 May 1991): n. pag.
Online. BITNET. 1 June 1991.

Stempel, Carl William. "Towards a Historical Sociology
of Sport in the United States, 1825-1875." <u>DAI</u> 53
(1993): 3374A. U of Oregon, 1992. <u>Dissertation</u>
<u>Abstracts Ondisc</u>. CD-ROM. UMI-Proquest. Sept. 1993.

5.4.2. Citing Part of an Article or of a Book

If you quote, paraphrase, or otherwise use a specific passage in a book
or article, give the relevant page number or numbers. When the author's
name is in the text, give only the page reference in parentheses, but if
the context does not clearly identify the author, add the author's last
name before the page reference. Leave a space between them, but do
not insert punctuation or the word *page* or *pages* or the abbreviation *p.*
or *pp.* If you used only one volume of a multivolume work and
included the volume number in the bibliographic entry, you need give
only page numbers in the reference (see the Lauter et al. example), but
if you used more than one volume of the work, you must cite both volume and page numbers (see 5.4.3). If your source uses paragraph numbers rather than page numbers—as, for example, some electronic
journals do—give the relevant number or numbers preceded by the
abbreviation *par.* or *pars.*; if the author's name begins such a citation,
place a comma after the name (see the Moulthrop example).

Brian Taves suggests some interesting conclusions
regarding the philosophy and politics of the adventure
film (153-54, 171).

Repetitive strain injury, or RSI, is reported to be "the fastest-growing occupational hazard of the computer age" (Taylor A1).

Another engaging passage is the opening of Isabel Allende's story "Toad's Mouth" (83).

Hypertext, as one theorist puts it, is "all about connection, linkage, and affiliation" (Moulthrop, par. 19).

The anthology by Lauter and his coeditors contains Stowe's "Sojourner Truth, the Libyan Sibyl" (2425-33).

"The study of comparative literature," Bill Readings writes, "takes off from the idea of humanity" (6).

In Hansberry's play A Raisin in the Sun, the rejection of Lindner's tempting offer permits Walter's family to pursue the new life they had long dreamed about (274-75).

Although writings describing utopia have always seemed to take place far from the everyday world, in fact "all utopian fiction whirls contemporary actors through a costume dance no place else but here" (Rabkin, Greenberg, and Olander vii).

Between the 1960s and the 1990s, television coverage of presidential elections changed dramatically (Hallin 5).

Among intentional spoonerisms, the "punlike metathesis of distinctive features may serve to weld together words etymologically unrelated but close in their sound and meaning" (Jakobson and Waugh 304).

Works Cited

Allende, Isabel. "Toad's Mouth." Trans. Margaret Sayers Peden. A Hammock beneath the Mangoes: Stories from Latin America. Ed. Thomas Colchie. New York: Plume, 1992. 83-88.

Hallin, Daniel C. "Sound Bite News: Television Coverage of Elections, 1968-1988." Journal of Communication 42.2 (1992): 5-24.

Hansberry, Lorraine. A Raisin in the Sun. Black Theater: A Twentieth-Century Collection of the Work of Its Best Playwrights. Ed. Lindsay Patterson. New York: Dodd, 1971. 221-76.

Jakobson, Roman, and Linda R. Waugh. The Sound Shape of Language. Bloomington: Indiana UP, 1979.

Lauter, Paul, et al., eds. The Heath Anthology of American Literature. 2nd ed. Vol. 1. Lexington: Heath, 1994.

Moulthrop, Stuart. "You Say You Want a Revolution? Hypertext and the Laws of Media." Postmodern Culture 1.3 (1991): 53 pars. Online. BITNET. 10 Jan. 1993.

Rabkin, Eric S., Martin H. Greenberg, and Joseph D. Olander. Preface. No Place Else: Explorations in Utopian and Dystopian Fiction. Ed. Rabkin, Greenberg, and Olander. Carbondale: Southern Illinois UP, 1983. vii-ix.

Readings, Bill. "Translatio and Comparative Literature: The Terror of European Humanism." Surfaces 1.11 (Dec. 1991): 19 pp. Online. Internet. 2 Feb. 1992.

Taves, Brian. The Romance of Adventure: The Genre of Historical Adventure Movies. Jackson: UP of Mississippi, 1993.

Taylor, Paul. "Keyboard Grief: Coping with Computer-Caused Injuries." Globe and Mail [Toronto] 27 Dec. 1993: A1+.

5.4.3. Citing Volume and Page Numbers of a Multivolume Work

When citing a volume number as well as a page reference for a multi-volume work, separate the two by a colon and a space: "(Wellek 2: 1–10)." Use neither the words *volume* and *page* nor their abbreviations. The functions of the numbers in such a citation are understood. If, however, you wish to refer parenthetically to an entire volume of a multivolume work, there is no need to cite pages. Place a comma after the author's name and include the abbreviation *vol.*: "(Wellek, vol. 2)." If you integrate such a reference into a sentence, spell out *volume*: "In volume 2, Wellek deals with. . . ."

In the middle of a multivolume history of modern
literary criticism, René Wellek admits, "An evolutionary
history of criticism must fail. I have come to this
resigned conclusion" (5: xxii).

The anthology by Lauter and his coeditors contains both
Stowe's "Sojourner Truth, the Libyan Sibyl" (1: 2425-33)
and Gilman's "The Yellow Wall-Paper" (2: 800-12).

Between the years 1945 and 1972, the political-party
system in the United States underwent profound changes
(Schlesinger, vol. 4).

Works Cited

Lauter, Paul, et al., eds. The Heath Anthology of
     American Literature. 2nd ed. 2 vols. Lexington:
     Heath, 1994.

Schlesinger, Arthur M., Jr., gen. ed. History of U.S.
     Political Parties. 4 vols. New York: Chelsea, 1973.

Wellek, René. A History of Modern Criticism, 1750-1950.
     8 vols. New Haven: Yale UP, 1955-92.

5.4.4. Citing a Work Listed by Title

In a parenthetical reference to a work alphabetized by title in the list of works cited, the full title (if brief) or a shortened version precedes the page number or numbers. When abbreviating the title, begin with the word by which it is alphabetized. Do not, for example, shorten *Glossary of Terms Used in Heraldry* to *Heraldry*, since this abbreviation would lead your reader to look for the bibliographic entry under *H* rather than *G*.

The word <u>albatross</u>, apparently derived from <u>alcatras</u>, the Spanish and Portuguese name for the pelican, first appears in the English language in the eighteenth century ("Albatross").

A document from the Educational Resources Information Center (ERIC) addresses problems associated with excessive television viewing and provides suggestions to help parents guide their children's television habits (<u>Guidelines</u>).

Even <u>Sixty Minutes</u> launched an attack on modern art, in a segment entitled "Yes . . . but Is It Art?"

The nine grades of mandarins were "distinguished by the color of the button on the hats of office" ("Mandarin").

<u>Perseus 1.0</u> revolutionized the way scholars conduct research on ancient civilizations.

A <u>New York Times</u> editorial called Ralph Ellison "a writer of universal reach" ("Death").

The classical Greek tragedy <u>Medea</u>, one of the most successful Broadway plays of the 1990s, made a lasting impression on me.

Works Cited

"Albatross." <u>The Oxford English Dictionary</u>. 2nd ed.
    CD-ROM. Oxford: Oxford UP, 1992.
"Death of a Writer." Editorial. <u>New York Times</u> 20 Apr.
    1994, late ed.: A18.
<u>Guidelines for Family Television Viewing</u>. Urbana: ERIC
    Clearinghouse on Elementary and Early Childhood
    Educ., 1990. <u>ERIC</u>. Online. BRS. 22 Nov. 1993.
"Mandarin." <u>The Encyclopedia Americana</u>. 1993 ed.
<u>Medea</u>. By Euripides. Trans. Alistair Elliot. Dir.
    Jonathan Kent. Perf. Diana Rigg. Longacre Theatre,
    New York. 7 Apr. 1994.

Perseus 1.0: Interactive Sources and Studies on Ancient
    Greece. CD-ROM, videodisc. New Haven: Yale UP, 1992.
"Yes . . . but Is It Art?" Narr. Morley Safer. Sixty
    Minutes. CBS. WCBS, New York. 19 Sept. 1993.

5.4.5. Citing a Work by a Corporate Author

To cite a work listed by a corporate author, you may use the author's
name followed by a page reference: "(United Nations, Economic Commission for Africa 79–86)." It is better, however, to include a long
name in the text, so that the reading is not interrupted with an
extended parenthetical reference.

In 1963 the United Nations Economic Commission for Africa
predicted that Africa would evolve into an advanced
industrial economy within fifty years (1-2, 4-6).

According to a study sponsored by the National Research
Council, the population of China is increasing by more
than fifteen million annually (15).

By 1992 it was apparent that the American health care
system, though impressive in many ways, needed "to be
fixed and perhaps radically modified" (Public Agenda
Foundation 4).

Works Cited

National Research Council. China and Global Change:
    Opportunities for Collaboration. Washington: Natl.
    Acad., 1992.
Public Agenda Foundation. The Health Care Crisis:
    Containing Costs, Expanding Coverage. New York:
    McGraw, 1992.
United Nations. Economic Commission for Africa.
    Industrial Growth in Africa. New York: United
    Nations, 1963.

5.4.6. Citing Two or More Works by the Same Author or Authors

In a parenthetical reference to one of two or more works by the same author, put a comma after the author's last name and add the title of the work (if brief) or a shortened version and the relevant page reference: "(Frye, *Double Vision* 85)," "(Durant and Durant, *Age* 214–48)." If you state the author's name in the text, give only the title and page reference in parentheses: "(*Double Vision* 85)," "(*Age* 214–48)." If you include both the author's name and the title in the text, indicate only the pertinent page number or numbers in parentheses: "(85)," "(214–48)."

> For Northrop Frye, one's death is not a unique experience, for "every moment we have lived through we have also died out of into another order" (Double Vision 85).
>
> In The Age of Voltaire, the Durants portray eighteenth-century England as a minor force in the world of music and art (214-48).
>
> Dreiser's universe, according to E. L. Doctorow, "is composed of merchants, workers, club-men, managers, actors, salesmen, doormen, cops, derelicts--a Balzacian population unified by the rules of commerce and the ideals of property and social position" (Introduction ix).
>
> Shakespeare's King Lear has been called a "comedy of the grotesque" (Frye, Anatomy 237).
>
> To Will and Ariel Durant, creative men and women make "history forgivable by enriching our heritage and our lives" (Dual Autobiography 406).
>
> The brief but dramatic conclusion of chapter 13 of Doctorow's Welcome to Hard Times constitutes the climax of the novel (206-09).

Works Cited

Doctorow, E. L. Introduction. Sister Carrie. By Theodore
     Dreiser. New York: Bantam, 1982. v-xi.
---. Welcome to Hard Times. 1960. New York: Vintage-
     Random, 1988.

Durant, Will, and Ariel Durant. <u>The Age of Voltaire</u>. New
    York: Simon, 1965. Vol. 9 of <u>The Story of</u>
    <u>Civilization</u>. 11 vols. 1933-75.

---. <u>A Dual Autobiography</u>. New York: Simon, 1977.

Frye, Northrop. <u>Anatomy of Criticism: Four Essays</u>.
    Princeton: Princeton UP, 1957.

---. <u>The Double Vision: Language and Meaning in Religion</u>.
    Toronto: U of Toronto P, 1991.

5.4.7. Citing Indirect Sources

Whenever you can, take material from the original source, not a
secondhand one. Sometimes, however, only an indirect source is
available—for example, someone's published account of another's
spoken remarks. If what you quote or paraphrase is itself a quotation,
put the abbreviation *qtd. in* ("quoted in") before the indirect source
you cite in your parenthetical reference. (You may document the original source in a note; see 5.5.1.)

Samuel Johnson admitted that Edmund Burke was an
"extraordinary man" (qtd. in Boswell 2: 450).

The commentary of the sixteenth-century literary scholars
Bernardo Segni and Lionardo Salviati shows them to be
less than faithful followers of Aristotle (qtd. in
Weinberg 1: 405, 616-17).

Works Cited

Boswell, James. <u>The Life of Johnson</u>. Ed. George Birkbeck
    Hill and L. F. Powell. 6 vols. Oxford: Clarendon,
    1934-50.

Weinberg, Bernard. <u>A History of Literary Criticism in</u>
    <u>the Italian Renaissance</u>. 2 vols. Chicago: U of
    Chicago P, 1961.

5.4.8. Citing Literary Works

In a reference to a classic prose work, such as a novel or play, that is available in several editions, it is helpful to provide more information than just a page number from the edition used; a chapter number, for example, would help readers to locate a quotation in any copy of a novel. In such a reference, give the page number first, add a semicolon, and then give other identifying information, using appropriate abbreviations: "(130; ch. 9)," "(271; bk. 4, ch. 2)."

> Raskolnikov first appears in <u>Crime and Punishment</u> as a man contemplating a terrible act but frightened of meeting his talkative landlady on the stairs (Dostoevsky 1; pt. 1, ch. 1).

> In <u>A Vindication of the Rights of Woman</u>, Mary Wollstonecraft recollects many "women who, not led by degrees to proper studies, and not permitted to choose for themselves, have indeed been overgrown children" (185; ch. 13, sec. 2).

> In one version of the William Tell story, the son urges the reluctant father to shoot the arrow (Sastre 315; sc. 6).

In citing classic verse plays and poems, omit page numbers altogether and cite by division (act, scene, canto, book, part) and line, with periods separating the various numbers—for example, "*Iliad* 9.19" refers to book 9, line 19, of Homer's *Iliad*. If you are citing only line numbers, do not use the abbreviation *l.* or *ll.*, which can be confused with numerals. Instead, initially use the word *line* or *lines* and then, having established that the numbers designate lines, give the numbers alone.

In general, use arabic numerals rather than roman numerals for division and page numbers. Although you must use roman numerals when citing pages of a preface or other section that are so numbered, designate volumes, parts, books, and chapters with arabic numerals even if your source does not. Some instructors prefer roman numerals, however, for citations of acts and scenes in plays (*King Lear* IV.i), but if your instructor does not recommend this practice, use arabic numerals (*King Lear* 4.1). On numbers, see 2.5.

When included in parenthetical references, the titles of the books of the Bible and of famous literary works are often abbreviated (1 Chron. 21.8, Rev. 21.3, *Oth.* 4.2.7–13, *FQ* 3.3.53.3). The most widely used and accepted abbreviations for such titles are listed in 6.7. Follow prevailing practices, as indicated by your sources, for other abbreviations (*Troilus* for Chaucer's *Troilus and Criseyde*, "Nightingale" for Keats's "Ode to a Nightingale," etc.).

> Like the bard who made the Ballad of Sir Patrick Spence, Coleridge sees the "new-moon winter bright" with the "old Moon in her lap, foretelling / The coming on of rain and squally blast" ("Dejection" 1.9, 13-14).

> The Dean and Chapter Library manuscript version of Octovian, as edited by Frances McSparran, has a more formal ending than other versions do: "And thus endis Octouean, / That in his tym was a doghety man . . ." (1629-30).

> Shakespeare's Hamlet seems resolute when he declares, "The play's the thing / Wherein I'll catch the conscience of the King" (2.2.633-34).

> Chaucer's purpose is "The double sorwe of Troilus to tellen, / That was the kyng Priamus sone of Troye" (Troilus 1.1-2).

Works Cited

Chaucer, Geoffrey. Troilus and Criseyde. The Works of
      Geoffrey Chaucer. Ed. F. N. Robinson. 2nd ed.
      Boston: Houghton, 1957. 385-479.
Coleridge, Samuel Taylor. "Dejection: An Ode." The
      Complete Works of Samuel Taylor Coleridge. Ed.
      Ernest Hartley Coleridge. Vol. 1. Oxford: Clarendon,
      1912. 362-68. English Poetry Full-Text Database.
      Rel. 2. CD-ROM. Cambridge, Eng.: Chadwyck, 1993.
Dostoevsky, Feodor. Crime and Punishment. Trans. Jessie
      Coulson. Ed. George Gibian. New York: Norton, 1964.

Octovian. Ed. Frances McSparran. Early English Text Soc.
　　289. London: Oxford UP, 1986. Online. U of Virginia
　　Lib. Internet. 6 Apr. 1994.

Sastre, Alfonso. Sad Are the Eyes of William Tell.
　　Trans. Leonard Pronko. The New Wave Spanish Drama.
　　Ed. George Wellwarth. New York: New York UP, 1970.
　　165-321.

Shakespeare, William. Hamlet. Ed. Barbara A. Mowat and
　　Paul Werstine. New York: Washington Square-Pocket,
　　1992.

Wollstonecraft, Mary. A Vindication of the Rights of
　　Woman. Ed. Carol H. Poston. New York: Norton, 1975.

5.4.9. Citing More Than One Work in a Single Parenthetical Reference

If you wish to include two or more works in a single parenthetical reference, cite each work as you normally would in a reference, and use semicolons to separate the citations.

(Kaku 42; McRae 101-33)

(National Research Council 25-35; Fitzgerald 330-43)

(Rabkin, Greenberg, and Olander vii; Boyle 96-125)

(Craner 308-11; Moulthrop, pars. 39-53)

(Gilbert and Gubar, Madwoman 1-25; Murphy 39-52)

(Gilbert and Gubar, Norton; Manning)

(Guidelines; Hallin 18-24)

(Lauter et al., vol. 1; Crane)

Keep in mind, however, that a long parenthetical reference such as the following example may prove intrusive and disconcerting to your reader:

(Taylor A1; Moulthrop, pars. 39-53; Armstrong, Yang, and
Cuneo 80-82; Craner 308-11; Kaku 42; Frank; Alston 1-5)

To avoid an excessive disruption, cite multiple sources in a note rather than in parentheses in the text (see 5.5.2).

Works Cited

Alston, Robin. "The Battle of the Books." Humanist
7.0176 (10 Sept. 1993): 10 pp. Online. Internet.
10 Oct. 1993.

Armstrong, Larry, Dori Jones Yang, and Alice Cuneo. "The
Learning Revolution: Technology Is Reshaping
Education--at Home and at School." Business Week
28 Feb. 1994: 80-88.

Boyle, Anthony T. "The Epistemological Evolution of
Renaissance Utopian Literature, 1516-1657." Diss.
New York U, 1983.

Crane, Stephen. The Red Badge of Courage: An Episode of
the American Civil War. 1895. Ed. Fredson Bowers.
Charlottesville: UP of Virginia, 1975.

Craner, Paul M. "New Tool for an Ancient Art: The
Computer and Music." Computers and the Humanities
25 (1991): 303-13.

Fitzgerald, John. "The Misconceived Revolution: State and
Society in China's Nationalist Revolution, 1923-26."
Journal of Asian Studies 49 (1990): 323-43.

Frank, Holly. Negative Space: A Computerized Video Novel.
Vers. 1.0. Diskette, videocassette. Prairie Village:
Diskotech, 1990.

Gilbert, Sandra M., and Susan Gubar. The Madwoman in the
Attic: The Woman Writer and the Nineteenth-Century
Literary Imagination. New Haven: Yale UP, 1979.

---, eds. The Norton Anthology of Literature by Women:
The Tradition in English. New York: Norton, 1985.

Guidelines for Family Television Viewing. Urbana: ERIC
Clearinghouse on Elementary and Early Childhood
Educ., 1990. ERIC. CD-ROM. SilverPlatter. Oct. 1993.

Hallin, Daniel C. "Sound Bite News: Television Coverage
of Elections, 1968-1988." Journal of Communication
42.2 (1992): 5-24.

Kaku, Michio. Hyperspace: A Scientific Odyssey through
    Parallel Universes, Time Warps, and the Tenth
    Dimension. New York: Oxford UP, 1994.

Lauter, Paul, et al., eds. The Heath Anthology of
    American Literature. 2nd ed. 2 vols. Lexington:
    Heath, 1994.

Manning, Anita. "Curriculum Battles from Left and Right."
    USA Today 2 Mar. 1994: 5D.

McRae, Murdo William, ed. The Literature of Science:
    Perspectives on Popular Science Writing. Athens:
    U of Georgia P, 1993.

Moulthrop, Stuart. "You Say You Want a Revolution?
    Hypertext and the Laws of Media." Postmodern Culture
    1.3 (1991): 53 pars. Online. BITNET. 10 Jan. 1993.

Murphy, Cullen. "Women and the Bible." Atlantic Monthly
    Aug. 1993: 39-64.

National Research Council. China and Global Change:
    Opportunities for Collaboration. Washington: Natl.
    Acad., 1992.

Rabkin, Eric S., Martin H. Greenberg, and Joseph D.
    Olander. Preface. No Place Else: Explorations in
    Utopian and Dystopian Fiction. Ed. Rabkin,
    Greenberg, and Olander. Carbondale: Southern
    Illinois UP, 1983. vii-ix.

Taylor, Paul. "Keyboard Grief: Coping with Computer-
    Caused Injuries." Globe and Mail [Toronto] 27 Dec.
    1993: A1+.

5.5. USING NOTES WITH PARENTHETICAL DOCUMENTATION

Two kinds of notes may be used with parenthetical documentation:

- Content notes offering the reader comment, explanation, or information that the text cannot accommodate

- Bibliographic notes containing either several sources or evaluative comments on sources

In providing this sort of supplementary information, place a superscript arabic numeral at the appropriate place in the text and write the note after a matching numeral either at the end of the text (as an endnote) or at the bottom of the page (as a footnote). See the examples in 5.5.1–2. For more information on using notes for documentation, see appendix B.

5.5.1. Content Notes

In your notes, avoid lengthy discussions that divert the reader's attention from the primary text. In general, comments that you cannot fit into the text should be omitted unless they provide essential justification or clarification of what you have written. You may use a note, for example, to give full publication facts for an original source for which you cite an indirect source and perhaps to explain why you worked from secondary material.

The commentary of the sixteenth-century literary scholars Bernardo Segni and Lionardo Salviati shows them to be less than faithful followers of Aristotle.[1]

Note

[1] Examples are conveniently available in Weinberg. See Segni, Rettorica et poetica d'Aristotile (Firenze, 1549) 281, qtd. in Weinberg 1: 405, and Salviati, Poetica d'Aristotile parafrasata e comentata, ms. 2.2.11, Biblioteca Nazionale Centrale, Firenze, 140v, qtd. in Weinberg 1: 616-17.

Work Cited

Weinberg, Bernard. A History of Literary Criticism in the Italian Renaissance. 2 vols. Chicago: U of Chicago P, 1961.

5.5.2. Bibliographic Notes

Use notes for evaluative comments on sources and for references containing numerous citations.

Many observers conclude that health care in the United States is inadequate.[1]

Technological advancements have brought advantages and joys as well as unexpected problems.[2]

Notes

[1] For strong points of view on different aspects of the issue, see Public Agenda Foundation 1-10 and Sakala 151-88.

[2] For a sampling of materials that reflect the full spectrum of experiences made possible by recent technological changes, see Taylor A1; Moulthrop, pars. 39-53; Armstrong, Yang, and Cuneo 80-82; Craner 308-11; Kaku 42; Frank; and Alston 1-5.

Works Cited

Alston, Robin. "The Battle of the Books." Humanist 7.0176 (10 Sept. 1993): 10 pp. Online. Internet. 10 Oct. 1993.

Armstrong, Larry, Dori Jones Yang, and Alice Cuneo. "The Learning Revolution: Technology Is Reshaping Education--at Home and at School." Business Week 28 Feb. 1994: 80-88.

Craner, Paul M. "New Tool for an Ancient Art: The Computer and Music." Computers and the Humanities 25 (1991): 303-13.

Frank, Holly. Negative Space: A Computerized Video Novel. Vers. 1.0. Diskette, videocassette. Prairie Village: Diskotech, 1990.

Kaku, Michio. Hyperspace: A Scientific Odyssey through Parallel Universes, Time Warps, and the Tenth Dimension. New York: Oxford UP, 1994.

Moulthrop, Stuart. "You Say You Want a Revolution?
     Hypertext and the Laws of Media." <u>Postmodern Culture</u>
     1.3 (1991): 53 pars. Online. BITNET. 10 Jan. 1993.
Public Agenda Foundation. <u>The Health Care Crisis:</u>
     <u>Containing Costs, Expanding Coverage</u>. New York:
     McGraw, 1992.
Sakala, Carol. "Maternity Care Policy in the United
     States: Toward a More Rational and Effective
     System." Diss. Boston U, 1993.
Taylor, Paul. "Keyboard Grief: Coping with Computer-
     Caused Injuries." <u>Globe and Mail</u> [Toronto] 27 Dec.
     1993: A1+.

6 Abbreviations

6.1. INTRODUCTION

Abbreviations are used regularly in the list of works cited and in tables but rarely in the text of a research paper (except within parentheses). In choosing abbreviations, keep your audience in mind. While economy of space is important, clarity is more so. Spell out a term if the abbreviation may puzzle your readers.

When abbreviating, always use accepted forms. In appropriate contexts, you may abbreviate the names of days, months, and other measurements of time (see 6.2); the names of states and countries (see 6.3); terms and reference words common in scholarship (see 6.4); publishers' names (see 6.5); and the titles of well-known literary and religious works (see 6.7).

The trend in abbreviation is to use neither periods after letters nor spaces between letters, especially for abbreviations made up of all capital letters.

```
BC                    PhD              S
NJ                    CD-ROM           US
```

The chief exception to this trend continues to be the initials used for personal names: a period and a space ordinarily follow each initial.

```
J. R. R. Tolkien
```

Most abbreviations that end in lowercase letters are followed by periods.

```
assn.                 fig.             Mex.
Eng.                  introd.          prod.
```

In most abbreviations made up of lowercase letters that each represent a word, a period follows each letter, but no space intervenes between letters.

```
a.m.                  i.e.
e.g.                  n.p.
```

But there are numerous exceptions.

```
mph                   os
ns                    rpm
```

6.2. TIME DESIGNATIONS

Spell out the names of months in the text but abbreviate them in the list of works cited, except for May, June, and July. Whereas words denoting units of time are also spelled out in the text (*second*, *minute*, *week*, *month*, *year*, *century*), some time designations are used only in abbreviated form (*a.m.*, *p.m.*, *AD*, *BC*, *BCE*, *CE*).

AD	after the birth of Christ (from the Latin *anno Domini* 'in the year of the Lord'; used before numerals: "AD 14")
a.m.	before noon (from the Latin *ante meridiem*)
Apr.	April
Aug.	August
BC	before Christ (used after numerals: "19 BC")
BCE	before the common era
CE	common era
cent.	century
Dec.	December
Feb.	February
Fri.	Friday
hr.	hour
Jan.	January
Mar.	March
min.	minute
mo.	month
Mon.	Monday
Nov.	November
Oct.	October
p.m.	after noon (from the Latin *post meridiem*)
Sat.	Saturday
sec.	second
Sep., Sept.	September
Sun.	Sunday
Thurs.	Thursday
Tues.	Tuesday
Wed.	Wednesday
wk.	week
yr.	year

6.3. GEOGRAPHIC NAMES

Spell out the names of states, territories, and possessions of the United States in the text, except usually in addresses and sometimes in parentheses. Likewise, spell out in the text the names of countries, with a few exceptions (e.g., USSR). In documentation, however, abbreviate the names of states, provinces, and countries.

AB	Alberta
Afr.	Africa
AK	Alaska
AL	Alabama
Alb.	Albania
Ant.	Antarctica
AR	Arkansas
Arg.	Argentina
Arm.	Armenia
AS	American Samoa
Aus.	Austria
Austral.	Australia
AZ	Arizona
BC	British Columbia
Belg.	Belgium
Braz.	Brazil
Bulg.	Bulgaria
CA	California
Can.	Canada
CO	Colorado
CT	Connecticut
CZ	Canal Zone
DC	District of Columbia
DE	Delaware
Den.	Denmark
Ecua.	Ecuador
Eng.	England
Eur.	Europe
FL	Florida
Fr.	France
GA	Georgia
Ger.	Germany

Gr.	Greece
Gt. Brit.	Great Britain
GU	Guam
HI	Hawaii
Hung.	Hungary
IA	Iowa
ID	Idaho
IL	Illinois
IN	Indiana
Ire.	Ireland
Isr.	Israel
It.	Italy
Jap.	Japan
KS	Kansas
KY	Kentucky
LA	Louisiana
LB	Labrador
Leb.	Lebanon
MA	Massachusetts
MB	Manitoba
MD	Maryland
ME	Maine
Mex.	Mexico
MI	Michigan
MN	Minnesota
MO	Missouri
MS	Mississippi
MT	Montana
NB	New Brunswick
NC	North Carolina
ND	North Dakota
NE	Nebraska
Neth.	Netherlands
NF	Newfoundland
NH	New Hampshire
NJ	New Jersey
NM	New Mexico
No. Amer.	North America
Norw.	Norway
NS	Nova Scotia
NT	Northwest Territories

NV	Nevada
NY	New York
NZ	New Zealand
OH	Ohio
OK	Oklahoma
ON	Ontario
OR	Oregon
PA	Pennsylvania
Pan.	Panama
PE	Prince Edward Island
Pol.	Poland
Port.	Portugal
PQ	Quebec (Province de Québec)
PR	Puerto Rico
PRC	People's Republic of China
RI	Rhode Island
Russ.	Russia
SC	South Carolina
Scot.	Scotland
SD	South Dakota
SK	Saskatchewan
So. Amer.	South America
Sp.	Spain
Swed.	Sweden
Switz.	Switzerland
TN	Tennessee
Turk.	Turkey
TX	Texas
UK	United Kingdom
US, USA	United States, United States of America
USSR	Union of Soviet Socialist Republics
UT	Utah
VA	Virginia
VI	Virgin Islands
VT	Vermont
WA	Washington
WI	Wisconsin
WV	West Virginia
WY	Wyoming
YT	Yukon Territory

6.4. COMMON SCHOLARLY ABBREVIATIONS

The following list includes abbreviations commonly used in humanities research studies in English. Abbreviations within parentheses are alternative but not recommended forms. Most of the abbreviations listed would replace the spelled forms only in parentheses, tables, and documentation.

abbr.	abbreviation, abbreviated
abr.	abridgment, abridged
acad.	academy
adapt.	adapter, adaptation, adapted by
adj.	adjective
adv.	adverb
Amer.	America, American
app.	appendix
arch.	archaic
art.	article
assn.	association
assoc.	associate, associated
attrib.	attributed to
aux.	auxiliary
b.	born
BA	bachelor of arts
bib.	biblical
bibliog.	bibliographer, bibliography, bibliographic
biog.	biographer, biography, biographical
BITNET	Because It's Time Network
bk.	book
BM	British Museum, London (now British Library)
BS	bachelor of science
bull.	bulletin
©	copyright ("© 1995")
c. (ca.)	circa, *or* around (used with approximate dates: "c. 1796")
CD	compact disc
CD-ROM	compact disc read-only memory
cf.	compare (not "see"; from the Latin *confer*)
ch. (chap.)	chapter
chor.	choreographer, choreographed by

col.	column
coll.	college
colloq.	colloquial
comp.	compiler, compiled by
cond.	conductor, conducted by
conf.	conference
Cong.	Congress
Cong. Rec.	*Congressional Record*
conj.	conjunction
Const.	Constitution
cont.	contents; continued
(contd.)	continued
d.	died
DA	doctor of arts
DA, DAI	*Dissertation Abstracts, Dissertation Abstracts International*
DAB	*Dictionary of American Biography*
dept.	department
dev.	development, developed by
dir.	director, directed by
diss.	dissertation
dist.	district
distr.	distributor, distributed by
div.	division
DNB	*Dictionary of National Biography*
doc.	document
ed.	editor, edition, edited by
EdD	doctor of education
educ.	education, educational
e.g.	for example (from the Latin *exempli gratia*; rarely capitalized; set off by commas, unless preceded by a different punctuation mark)
e-mail	electronic mail
enl.	enlarged (as in "rev. and enl. ed.")
esp.	especially
et al.	and others (from the Latin *et alii, et aliae*)
etc.	and so forth (from the Latin *et cetera*; like most abbreviations, not appropriate in text)
ex.	example
fac.	faculty
fig.	figure

fl.	flourished, *or* reached greatest development or influence (from the Latin *floruit*; used before dates of historical figures when birth and death dates are not known)
fr.	from
front.	frontispiece
FTP	File Transfer Protocol
fut.	future
fwd.	foreword, foreword by
gen.	general (as in "gen. ed.")
govt.	government
GPO	Government Printing Office, Washington, DC
H. Doc.	House Document
hist.	historian, history, historical
HMSO	Her (His) Majesty's Stationery Office, London
HR	House of Representatives
H. Rept.	House of Representatives Report
H. Res.	House of Representatives Resolution
i.e.	that is (from the Latin *id est*; rarely capitalized; set off by commas, unless preceded by a different punctuation mark)
illus.	illustrator, illustration, illustrated by
inc.	including; incorporated
infin.	infinitive
inst.	institute, institution
intl.	international
introd.	introduction, introduced by
irreg.	irregular
JD	doctor of law (from the Latin *juris doctor*)
jour.	journal
Jr.	Junior
l., ll.	line, lines (avoided in favor of *line* and *lines* or, if clear, numbers only)
lang.	language
LC	Library of Congress
leg.	legal
legis.	legislator, legislation, legislature, legislative
lib.	library
lit.	literally; literature, literary
LLB	bachelor of laws (from the Latin *legum baccalaureus*)

LLD	doctor of laws (from the Latin *legum doctor*)
LP	long-playing phonograph record
ltd.	limited
MA	master of arts
mag.	magazine
MD	doctor of medicine (from the Latin *medicinae doctor*)
misc.	miscellaneous
mod.	modern
MS	master of science
ms., mss.	manuscript, manuscripts (as in "Bodleian ms. Tanner 43")
n, nn	note, notes (used immediately after the number of the page containing the text of the note or notes: "56n," "56n3," "56nn3–5")
n.	noun
narr.	narrator, narrated by
natl.	national
NB	take notice (from the Latin *nota bene*; always capitalized)
n.d.	no date of publication
NED	*A New English Dictionary* (cf. *OED*)
no.	number (cf. *numb.*)
nonstand.	nonstandard
n.p.	no place of publication; no publisher
n. pag.	no pagination
ns	new series
NS	New Style (calendar designation)
numb.	numbered
obj.	object, objective
obs.	obsolete
OED	*The Oxford English Dictionary* (formerly *A New English Dictionary* [*NED*])
op.	opus (work)
orch.	orchestra (also Italian *orchestra*, French *orchestre*, etc.), orchestrated by
orig.	original, originally
os	old series; original series
OS	Old Style (calendar designation)
P	Press (used in documentation; see *UP*)

p., pp.	page, pages (omitted before page numbers unless necessary for clarity)
par.	paragraph
part.	participle
perf.	performer, performed by
PhD	doctor of philosophy (from the Latin *philosophiae doctor*)
philol.	philological
philos.	philosophical
pl.	plate; plural
poss.	possessive
pref.	preface, preface by
prep.	preposition
pres.	present
proc.	proceedings
prod.	producer, produced by
pron.	pronoun
pronunc.	pronunciation
PS	postscript
pseud.	pseudonym
pt.	part
pub. (publ.)	publisher, publication, published by
Pub. L.	Public Law
qtd.	quoted
r.	reigned
rec.	record, recorded
reg.	registered; regular
rel.	release
rept.	report, reported by
res.	resolution
resp.	respectively
rev.	review, reviewed by; revision, revised by (spell out *review* where *rev.* might be ambiguous)
rpm	revolutions per minute (used in reference to recordings)
rpt.	reprint, reprinted by
S	Senate
sc.	scene (omitted when act and scene numbers are used together: "*King Lear* 4.1")
S. Doc.	Senate Document
sec. (sect.)	section

ser.	series
sess.	session
sic	thus in the source (in square brackets as an editorial interpolation, otherwise in parentheses; not followed by an exclamation point)
sing.	singular
soc.	society
Sr.	Senior
S. Rept.	Senate Report
S. Res.	Senate Resolution
st.	stanza
St., Sts. (S, SS)	Saint, Saints
Stat.	Statutes at Large
subj.	subject, subjective; subjunctive
substand.	substandard
supp.	supplement
syn.	synonym
trans. (tr.)	transitive; translator, translation, translated by
ts., tss.	typescript, typescripts (cf. *ms.*)
U	University (also Spanish *Universidad*, Italian *Università*, German *Universität*, French *Université*, etc.; used in documentation; see *UP*)
UP	University Press (used in documentation: "Columbia UP")
usu.	usually
var.	variant
vb.	verb
vers.	version
vol.	volume
vs. (v.)	versus (*v.* preferred in titles of legal cases)
writ.	writer, written by

6.5. PUBLISHERS' NAMES

In the list of works cited, shortened forms of publishers' names immediately follow the cities of publication, enabling the reader to locate books or to acquire more information about them. Since publications like *Books in Print*, *Literary Market Place*, and *International Literary Market Place* list publishers' addresses, you need give only enough information so that your reader can look up the publishers in one of these sources. It is usually sufficient, for example, to give "Harcourt" as the publisher's name even if the title page shows "Harcourt Brace" or one of the earlier names of that firm (Harcourt, Brace; Harcourt, Brace, and World; Harcourt Brace Jovanovich). If you are preparing a bibliographic study, however, or if publication history is important to your paper, give the publisher's name in full.

In shortening publishers' names, keep in mind the following points:

- Omit articles (*A, An, The*), business abbreviations (*Co., Corp., Inc., Ltd.*), and descriptive words (*Books, House, Press, Publishers*). When citing a university press, however, always add the abbreviation *P* (Ohio State UP) because the university itself may publish independently of its press (Ohio State U).
- If the publisher's name includes the name of one person (Harry N. Abrams, W. W. Norton, John Wiley), cite the surname alone (Abrams, Norton, Wiley). If the publisher's name includes the names of more than one person, cite only the first of the surnames (Bobbs, Dodd, Faber, Farrar, Funk, Grosset, Harcourt, Harper, Houghton, McGraw, Prentice, Simon).
- Use standard abbreviations whenever possible (*Acad., Assn., Soc., UP*).
- If the publisher's name is commonly abbreviated with capital initial letters and if the abbreviation is likely to be familiar to your audience, use the abbreviation as the publisher's name (GPO, MLA, UMI). If your readers are not likely to know the abbreviation, shorten the name according to the general guidelines given above (Mod. Lang. Assn.).

Following are examples of how various types of publishers' names are shortened:

Acad. for Educ. Dev.	Academy for Educational Development, Inc.
ALA	American Library Association
Basic	Basic Books
CAL	Center for Applied Linguistics
Cambridge UP	Cambridge University Press
Eastgate	Eastgate Systems
Einaudi	Giulio Einaudi Editore
ERIC	Educational Resources Information Center
Farrar	Farrar, Straus and Giroux, Inc.

Feminist	The Feminist Press at the City University of New York
Gale	Gale Research, Inc.
Gerig	Gerig Verlag
GPO	Government Printing Office
Harper	Harper and Row, Publishers, Inc.; HarperCollins Publishers, Inc.
Harvard Law Rev. Assn.	Harvard Law Review Association
HMSO	Her (His) Majesty's Stationery Office
Houghton	Houghton Mifflin Co.
Knopf	Alfred A. Knopf, Inc.
Larousse	Librairie Larousse
Little	Little, Brown and Company, Inc.
Macmillan	Macmillan Publishing Co., Inc.
McGraw	McGraw-Hill, Inc.
MIT P	The MIT Press
MLA	The Modern Language Association of America
NCTE	The National Council of Teachers of English
NEA	The National Education Association
Norton	W. W. Norton and Co., Inc.
PUF	Presses Universitaires de France
Random	Random House, Inc.
Scribner's	Charles Scribner's Sons
Simon	Simon and Schuster, Inc.
SIRS	Social Issues Resources Series
State U of New York P	State University of New York Press
St. Martin's	St. Martin's Press, Inc.
UMI	University Microfilms International
U of Chicago P	University of Chicago Press
UP of Mississippi	University Press of Mississippi

6.6. SYMBOLS AND ABBREVIATIONS USED IN PROOFREADING AND CORRECTION

6.6.1. Selected Proofreading Symbols

Proofreaders use the symbols below when correcting typeset material. Many instructors also use them in marking student papers.

    ꜚ   add an apostrophe or a single quotation mark
    C   close up (basket‿ball)
    ⋏   add a comma
    ℓ   delete
    ∧   insert
    ¶   begin a new paragraph
 No¶   do not begin a new paragraph
    ⊙   add a period
  ꝏ   add double quotation marks
   #   add space
  ∿   transpose elements (usually with *tr* in margin) (thier)

6.6.2. Common Correction Symbols and Abbreviations

‖	lack of parallelism
ab	faulty abbreviation
adj	improper use of adjective
adv	improper use of adverb
agr	faulty agreement
amb	ambiguous expression or construction
awk	awkward expression or construction
cap	faulty capitalization
d	faulty diction
dgl	dangling construction
frag	fragment
lc	use lowercase
num	error in use of numbers
p	faulty punctuation
ref	unclear pronoun reference
rep	unnecessary repetition
r-o	run-on sentence

sp	error in spelling
ss	faulty sentence structure
t	wrong tense of verb
tr	transpose elements
vb	wrong verb form
wdy	wordy writing

6.7. TITLES OF LITERARY AND RELIGIOUS WORKS

In documentation, you may abbreviate the titles of works and parts of works. It is usually best to introduce an abbreviation in parentheses immediately after the first use of the full title in the text: "In *All's Well That Ends Well* (*AWW*), Shakespeare. . . ." Abbreviating titles is appropriate, for example, if you repeatedly cite a variety of works by the same author. In such a discussion, abbreviations make for more concise parenthetical documentation—"(*AWW* 3.2.100–29)," "(*MM* 4.3.93–101)"—than the usual shortened titles would: "(*All's Well* 3.2.100–29)," "(*Measure* 4.3.93–101)." For works not on the following lists, you may use the abbreviations you find in your sources, or you may devise simple, unambiguous abbreviations of your own.

6.7.1. Bible

The following abbreviations and spelled forms are commonly used for parts of the Bible (Bib.).

Old Testament (OT)

Gen.	Genesis
Exod.	Exodus
Lev.	Leviticus
Num.	Numbers
Deut.	Deuteronomy
Josh.	Joshua
Judg.	Judges
Ruth	Ruth
1 Sam.	1 Samuel

2 Sam.	2 Samuel
1 Kings	1 Kings
2 Kings	2 Kings
1 Chron.	1 Chronicles
2 Chron.	2 Chronicles
Ezra	Ezra
Neh.	Nehemiah
Esth.	Esther
Job	Job
Ps.	Psalms
Prov.	Proverbs
Eccles.	Ecclesiastes
Song Sol. (also Cant.)	Song of Solomon (also Canticles)
Isa.	Isaiah
Jer.	Jeremiah
Lam.	Lamentations
Ezek.	Ezekiel
Dan.	Daniel
Hos.	Hosea
Joel	Joel
Amos	Amos
Obad.	Obadiah
Jon.	Jonah
Mic.	Micah
Nah.	Nahum
Hab.	Habakkuk
Zeph.	Zephaniah
Hag.	Haggai
Zech.	Zechariah
Mal.	Malachi

Selected Apocryphal and Deuterocanonical Works

1 Esd.	1 Esdras
2 Esd.	2 Esdras
Tob.	Tobit
Jth.	Judith
Esth. (Apocr.)	Esther (Apocrypha)
Wisd. Sol. (also Wisd.)	Wisdom of Solomon (also Wisdom)
Ecclus. (also Sir.)	Ecclesiasticus (also Sirach)
Bar.	Baruch
Song 3 Childr.	Song of the Three Children

Sus.	Susanna
Bel and Dr.	Bel and the Dragon
Pr. Man.	Prayer of Manasseh
1 Macc.	1 Maccabees
2 Macc.	2 Maccabees

New Testament (NT)

Matt.	Matthew
Mark	Mark
Luke	Luke
John	John
Acts	Acts
Rom.	Romans
1 Cor.	1 Corinthians
2 Cor.	2 Corinthians
Gal.	Galatians
Eph.	Ephesians
Phil.	Philippians
Col.	Colossians
1 Thess.	1 Thessalonians
2 Thess.	2 Thessalonians
1 Tim.	1 Timothy
2 Tim.	2 Timothy
Tit.	Titus
Philem.	Philemon
Heb.	Hebrews
Jas.	James
1 Pet.	1 Peter
2 Pet.	2 Peter
1 John	1 John
2 John	2 John
3 John	3 John
Jude	Jude
Rev. (also Apoc.)	Revelation (also Apocalypse)

Selected Apocryphal Works

G. Thom.	Gospel of Thomas
G. Heb.	Gospel of the Hebrews
G. Pet.	Gospel of Peter

6.7.2. Shakespeare

Ado	*Much Ado about Nothing*
Ant.	*Antony and Cleopatra*
AWW	*All's Well That Ends Well*
AYL	*As You Like It*
Cor.	*Coriolanus*
Cym.	*Cymbeline*
Err.	*The Comedy of Errors*
F1	First Folio ed. (1623)
F2	Second Folio ed. (1632)
Ham.	*Hamlet*
1H4	*Henry IV, Part 1*
2H4	*Henry IV, Part 2*
H5	*Henry V*
1H6	*Henry VI, Part 1*
2H6	*Henry VI, Part 2*
3H6	*Henry VI, Part 3*
H8	*Henry VIII*
JC	*Julius Caesar*
Jn.	*King John*
LC	*A Lover's Complaint*
LLL	*Love's Labour's Lost*
Lr.	*King Lear*
Luc.	*The Rape of Lucrece*
Mac.	*Macbeth*
MM	*Measure for Measure*
MND	*A Midsummer Night's Dream*
MV	*The Merchant of Venice*
Oth.	*Othello*
Per.	*Pericles*
PhT	*The Phoenix and the Turtle*
PP	*The Passionate Pilgrim*
Q	Quarto ed.
R2	*Richard II*
R3	*Richard III*
Rom.	*Romeo and Juliet*
Shr.	*The Taming of the Shrew*
Son.	*Sonnets*
TGV	*The Two Gentlemen of Verona*
Tim.	*Timon of Athens*

Tit.	*Titus Andronicus*
Tmp.	*The Tempest*
TN	*Twelfth Night*
TNK	*The Two Noble Kinsmen*
Tro.	*Troilus and Cressida*
Ven.	*Venus and Adonis*
Wiv.	*The Merry Wives of Windsor*
WT	*The Winter's Tale*

6.7.3. Chaucer

CkT	The Cook's Tale
ClT	The Clerk's Tale
CT	*The Canterbury Tales*
CYT	The Canon's Yeoman's Tale
FranT	The Franklin's Tale
FrT	The Friar's Tale
GP	The General Prologue
KnT	The Knight's Tale
ManT	The Manciple's Tale
Mel	The Tale of Melibee
MerT	The Merchant's Tale
MilT	The Miller's Tale
MkT	The Monk's Tale
MLT	The Man of Law's Tale
NPT	The Nun's Priest's Tale
PardT	The Pardoner's Tale
ParsT	The Parson's Tale
PhyT	The Physician's Tale
PrT	The Prioress's Tale
Ret	Chaucer's Retraction
RvT	The Reeve's Tale
ShT	The Shipman's Tale
SNT	The Second Nun's Tale
SqT	The Squire's Tale
SumT	The Summoner's Tale
Th	The Tale of Sir Thopas
WBT	The Wife of Bath's Tale

6.7.4. Other Literary Works

Aen.	Vergil, *Aeneid*
Ag.	Aeschylus, *Agamemnon*
Ant.	Sophocles, *Antigone*
Bac.	Euripides, *Bacchae*
Beo.	*Beowulf*
Can.	Voltaire, *Candide*
Dec.	Boccaccio, *Decameron*
DJ	Byron, *Don Juan*
DQ	Cervantes, *Don Quixote*
Eum.	Aeschylus, *Eumenides*
FQ	Spenser, *The Faerie Queene*
Gil.	*Epic of Gilgamesh*
GT	Swift, *Gulliver's Travels*
Hept.	Marguerite de Navarre, *Heptaméron*
Hip.	Euripides, *Hippolytus*
Il.	Homer, *Iliad*
Inf.	Dante, *Inferno*
LB	Wordsworth, *Lyrical Ballads*
Lys.	Aristophanes, *Lysistrata*
MD	Melville, *Moby-Dick*
Med.	Euripides, *Medea*
Mis.	Molière, *Le misanthrope*
Nib.	*Nibelungenlied*
Od.	Homer, *Odyssey*
OR	Sophocles, *Oedipus Rex* (also called *Oedipus Tyrannus* [*OT*])
Or.	Aeschylus, *Oresteia*
OT	Sophocles, *Oedipus Tyrannus* (also called *Oedipus Rex* [*OR*])
Par.	Dante, *Paradiso*
PL	Milton, *Paradise Lost*
Prel.	Wordsworth, *The Prelude*
Purg.	Dante, *Purgatorio*
Rep.	Plato, *Republic*
SA	Milton, *Samson Agonistes*
SGGK	*Sir Gawain and the Green Knight*
Sym.	Plato, *Symposium*
Tar.	Molière, *Tartuffe*

Appendix A:
Selected Reference
Works by Field

A.1. Anthropology

A.2. Art

A.3. Biology

A.4. Business

A.5. Chemistry

A.6. Computer Science

A.7. Education

A.8. Environmental Sciences

A.9. Geography

A.10. Geology

A.11. History

A.12. Language and Literature

A.13. Law

A.14. Mathematics

A.15. Medicine

A.16. Music

A.17. Philosophy

A.18. Physics

A.19. Psychology

A.20. Religion

A.21. Science and Technology

A.22. Sociology

Each of the sections below is divided into two parts. The first contains titles of indexes, abstracts collections, annual bibliographies, and other such periodically published reference works; the availability of online and CD-ROM versions is indicated when relevant. The second part of each section contains titles of dictionaries, encyclopedias, and similar reference works.

A.1. ANTHROPOLOGY

Abstracts in Anthropology. Farmingdale: Baywood, 1970– .

Encyclopedia of Anthropology. Ed. David E. Hunter and Phillip Whitten. New York: Harper, 1976.

A.2. ART

Art Index. New York: Wilson, 1929– . Available online and on CD-ROM.
Avery Index to Architectural Periodicals. 2nd ed. Boston: Hall, 1973– . Available online and on CD-ROM.
BHA: Bibliography of the History of Art / Bibliographie d'histoire de l'art. Vandoeuvre-lès-Nancy: Centre National de la Recherche Scientifique; Santa Monica: Getty Art History Information Program, 1991– . Available online as *Art Literature International.*

Encyclopedia of World Art. 17 vols. New York: McGraw, 1959–87.
McGraw-Hill Dictionary of Art. Ed. Bernard S. Myers. 5 vols. New York: McGraw, 1969.
The Oxford Dictionary of Art. Ed. Ian Chilvers and Harold Osborne. New York: Oxford UP, 1988.

A.3. BIOLOGY

Biological Abstracts. Philadelphia: Biological Abstracts, 1926– . Available online (as part of *Biosis Previews*) and on CD-ROM.
Biological and Agricultural Index. New York: Wilson, 1964– . Available online and on CD-ROM.

Chambers Biology Dictionary. Ed. Peter Walker. 4th ed. New York: Cambridge UP, 1989.

Encyclopedia of Bioethics. Ed. Warren T. Reich. 5 vols. 2nd ed. New York: Macmillan, 1994.

Encyclopedia of Human Biology. Ed. Renato Dulbecco. 8 vols. San Diego: Harcourt, 1991.

Henderson's Dictionary of Biological Terms. Ed. Eleanor Lawrence. 10th ed. New York: Wiley, 1989.

A.4. BUSINESS

ABI/Inform. Ann Arbor: UMI, 1971– . Available online and on CD-ROM.

Business Periodicals Index. New York: Wilson, 1958– . Available online and on CD-ROM.

PAIS. New York: Public Affairs Information Service, 1972– . Available online and on CD-ROM.

Predicasts F and S Indexes. Cleveland: Predicasts, 1968– . Available online and on CD-ROM.

Dictionary of Business and Economics. Ed. Christine Ammer and Dean Ammer. Rev. ed. New York: Free, 1984.

The HarperCollins Dictionary of Economics. Ed. Christopher Pass. New York: Harper, 1991.

McGraw-Hill Encyclopedia of Economics. Ed. Douglas Greenwald. 2nd ed. New York: McGraw, 1993.

The MIT Dictionary of Modern Economics. Ed. David Pearce. 4th ed. Cambridge: MIT P, 1992.

A.5. CHEMISTRY

Chemical Abstracts. Washington: Amer. Chemical Soc., 1907– . Available online as *CA Search.*

Guide to Basic Information Sources in Chemistry. Ed. Arthur Antony. New York: Wiley, 1979.

Hawley's Condensed Chemical Dictionary. Ed. Richard J. Lewis. 12th ed. New York: Van Nostrand, 1993.

Lange's Handbook of Chemistry. Ed. John A. Dean. 14th ed. New York: McGraw, 1992.

Van Nostrand Reinhold Encyclopedia of Chemistry. Ed. Douglas M. Considine. 4th ed. New York: Van Nostrand, 1984.

A.6. COMPUTER SCIENCE

ACM Guide to Computing Literature. New York: Assn. for Computing Machinery, 1977– . Available online and on CD-ROM as part of *MathSci.*

Computer Abstracts. London: Technical Information, 1957– .

Computer Literature Index. Phoenix: Applied Computer Research, 1980– .

———

Dictionary of Computing. Ed. Valerie Illingsworth. 3rd ed. Oxford: Oxford UP, 1990.

Macmillan Encyclopedia of Computers. Ed. Gary Bitter. 2 vols. New York: Macmillan, 1992.

A.7. EDUCATION

CIJE: Current Index to Journals in Education. Phoenix: Oryx, 1969– . Available online and on CD-ROM as part of *ERIC.*

Education Index. New York: Wilson, 1929– . Available online and on CD-ROM.

Resources in Education. Washington: GPO, 1967– . Available online and on CD-ROM as part of *ERIC.*

———

Dictionary of Education. Ed. Carter V. Good. 3rd ed. New York: McGraw, 1973.

The Encyclopedia of Education. Ed. Lee C. Deighton. 10 vols. New York: Free, 1971.

Encyclopedia of Educational Research. Ed. Marvin C. Alkin. 6th ed. 4 vols. New York: Macmillan, 1992.

World Education Encyclopedia. Ed. George T. Kurian. 3 vols. New York: Facts on File, 1988.

A.8. ENVIRONMENTAL SCIENCES

Ecology Abstracts. Bethesda: Cambridge Scientific Abstracts, 1975– .
Available online as part of *CSA Life Sciences Collection*.

Environment Abstracts. New York: Environment Information Center,
1971– . Available online and on CD-ROM as *Enviroline*.

Environmental Periodicals Bibliography. Santa Barbara: Environmental Studies Inst., 1972– . Available online (as *Environmental Bibliography*) and on CD-ROM.

Environment Index. New York: Environment Information Center,
1971– .

Pollution Abstracts. Bethesda: Cambridge Scientific Abstracts, 1970– .
Available online.

---

*Encyclopedia of Community Planning and Environmental Manage-
ment*. Ed. Marilyn Schultz and Vivian Kasen. New York: Facts on
File, 1983.

Grzimek's Encyclopedia of Ecology. Ed. Bernhard Grzimek. New York:
Van Nostrand, 1977.

*McGraw-Hill Encyclopedia of Environmental Science and Engineer-
ing*. Ed. Sybil Parker. 3rd ed. New York: McGraw, 1993.

A.9. GEOGRAPHY

Geographical Abstracts. Norwich, Eng.: Geo Abstracts, 1972– . Available online as part of *Geobase*.

Encyclopedia of Geographic Information Sources. Ed. Jennifer Moss-
man. 4th ed. 2 vols. Detroit: Gale, 1986.

Geography and Cartography: A Reference Handbook. Ed. Clara B.
Lock. Hamden: Linnet, 1976.

Longman Dictionary of Geography. Ed. Audrey N. Clark. London:
Longman, 1986.

Modern Geography: An Encyclopedic Survey. Ed. Gary S. Dunbar. New
York: Garland, 1991.

A.10. GEOLOGY

Bibliography and Index of Geology. Alexandria: Amer. Geological Inst., 1933– . Available online and on CD-ROM as part of *GeoRef.*

Challinor's Dictionary of Geology. 6th ed. New York: Oxford UP, 1986.
The Encyclopedia of Field and General Geology. Ed. Charles W. Finkl. New York: Van Nostrand, 1988.
Geologic Reference Sources. Ed. Dederick C. Ward, Marjorie W. Wheeler, and Robert A. Bier. Metuchen: Scarecrow, 1981.
McGraw-Hill Encyclopedia of the Geological Sciences. Ed. Sybil Parker. 2nd ed. New York: McGraw, 1988.

A.11. HISTORY

America: History and Life. Santa Barbara: ABC-Clio, 1964– . Available online and on CD-ROM.
Historical Abstracts. Santa Barbara: ABC-Clio, 1955– . Available online and on CD-ROM.

Dictionary of American History. Rev. ed. 8 vols. New York: Scribner's, 1976.
Encyclopedia of American History. Ed. Richard B. Morris. 6th ed. New York: Harper, 1982.
An Encyclopedia of World History. Ed. William L. Langer. 5th ed. Boston: Houghton, 1972.

A.12. LANGUAGE AND LITERATURE

L'année philologique: Bibliographie critique et analytique de l'antiquité gréco-latine. Paris: Belles Lettres, 1924– .
Bibliographie linguistique / Linguistic Bibliography. Dordrecht: Kluwer, 1949– .
LLBA: Linguistics and Language Behavior Abstracts. San Diego: Sociological Abstracts, 1974– . Available online and on CD-ROM.
MLA International Bibliography. New York: MLA, 1921– . Available online and on CD-ROM.

The Cambridge Encyclopedia of Language. Ed. David Crystal. New York: Cambridge UP, 1987.

The Cambridge Guide to Literature in English. Ed. Ian Ousby. 2nd ed. Cambridge: Cambridge UP, 1994.

The Cambridge Guide to World Theatre. Ed. Martin Banham. Cambridge: Cambridge UP, 1988.

An Encyclopaedia of Language. Ed. N. E. Collinge. New York: Routledge, 1990.

International Encyclopedia of Linguistics. Ed. William Bright. 4 vols. New York: Oxford UP, 1992.

Literary Research Guide. By James L. Harner. 2nd ed. New York: MLA, 1993.

The New Princeton Encyclopedia of Poetry and Poetics. Ed. Alex Preminger and T. V. F. Brogan. Princeton: Princeton UP, 1993.

The Oxford Classical Dictionary. Ed. N. G. L. Hammond and H. H. Scullard. 2nd ed. Oxford: Clarendon, 1970.

The Oxford Companion to American Literature. Ed. James D. Hart. 5th ed. New York: Oxford UP, 1983.

The Oxford Companion to Canadian Literature. Ed. William Toye. New York: Oxford UP, 1983.

The Oxford Companion to Classical Literature. Ed. M. C. Howatson. 2nd ed. New York: Oxford UP, 1989.

The Oxford Companion to English Literature. Ed. Margaret Drabble. 5th ed. New York: Oxford UP, 1985.

A.13. LAW

Criminal Justice Abstracts. Monsey: Willow Tree, 1977– . Available online and on CD-ROM.

Criminal Justice Periodical Index. Ann Arbor: UMI, 1975– . Available online.

Index to Legal Periodicals. New York: Wilson, 1908– . Available online and on CD-ROM.

Black's Law Dictionary. 6th ed. Saint Paul: West, 1990.

A Dictionary of Modern Legal Usage. Ed. Bryan A. Garner. 2nd ed. New York: Oxford UP, 1991.

Encyclopedia of Crime and Justice. Ed. Sanford H. Kadish. 4 vols. New York: Free, 1983.

A.14. MATHEMATICS

Mathematical Reviews. Providence: Amer. Mathematical Soc., 1940– .
  Available online and on CD-ROM as part of *MathSci.*

————————

Encyclopedic Dictionary of Mathematics. Ed. Kiyosi Itô. 2nd ed. 4 vols.
  Cambridge: MIT P, 1987.
The Prentice-Hall Encyclopedia of Mathematics. Englewood Cliffs:
  Prentice, 1982.

A.15. MEDICINE

Cumulative Index to Nursing and Allied Health Literature. Glendale:
  CINAHL Information Services, 1977– . Available online and on CD-
  ROM as *Nursing and Allied Health Database.*
Index Medicus. Bethesda: US National Lib. of Medicine, 1960– . Avail-
  able online and on CD-ROM as part of *Medline.*

————————

The American Medical Association Encyclopedia of Medicine. Ed.
  Charles B. Clayman. New York: Random, 1989.
Dorland's Illustrated Medical Dictionary. 27th ed. Philadelphia: Saun-
  ders, 1988.
Stedman's Medical Dictionary. 25th ed. Baltimore: Williams, 1990.

A.16. MUSIC

Musical Literature International. New York: Intl. RILM Center, 1967– .
  Available online and on CD-ROM.
The Music Index. Detroit: Information Coordinators, 1949– . Available
  on CD-ROM.

————————

The New Grove Dictionary of American Music. Ed. H. Wiley Hitchcock
  and Stanley Sadie. 4 vols. London: Macmillan, 1986.
The New Grove Dictionary of Music and Musicians. Ed. Stanley Sadie.
  20 vols. New York: Macmillan, 1980.
The New Harvard Dictionary of Music. Ed. Don M. Randel. Cambridge:
  Harvard UP, 1986.

The New Oxford Companion to Music. Ed. Denis Arnold. 2 vols. 1983. Oxford: Oxford UP, 1990.

A.17. PHILOSOPHY

The Philosopher's Index. Bowling Green: Bowling Green State U, 1967– . Available online and on CD-ROM.

Encyclopedia of Ethics. Ed. Lawrence C. Becker and Charlotte B. Becker. 2 vols. New York: Garland, 1992.

The Encyclopedia of Philosophy. Ed. Paul Edwards. 8 vols. New York: Free, 1967.

The HarperCollins Dictionary of Philosophy. Ed. Peter A. Angeles. 2nd ed. New York: Harper, 1992.

A.18. PHYSICS

Physics Abstracts. Surrey: Inst. of Electrical Engineers, 1898– . Available online and on CD-ROM as part of *Inspec.*

The Encyclopedia of Physics. Ed. Robert M. Besançon. 3rd ed. New York: Van Nostrand, 1985.

Encyclopedia of Physics. Ed. Rita G. Lerner and George L. Trigg. 2nd ed. New York: VCH, 1991.

McGraw-Hill Encyclopedia of Physics. Ed. Sybil Parker. 2nd ed. New York: McGraw, 1993.

A.19. PSYCHOLOGY

Psychological Abstracts. Washington: Amer. Psychological Assn., 1927– . Available online as *PsycInfo* and on CD-ROM as *PsycLit.*

Encyclopedia of Psychology. Ed. Raymond J. Corsini. 2nd ed. 4 vols. New York: Wiley, 1994.

The International Dictionary of Psychology. Ed. Stuart Sutherland. New York: Continuum, 1989.

A.20. RELIGION

Religion Index. Chicago: Amer. Theological Lib. Assn., 1977– . Available online and on CD-ROM.

The Anchor Bible Dictionary. Ed. David Noel Freedman et al. 6 vols. New York: Doubleday, 1992.

The Dictionary of Bible and Religion. Ed. William H. Gentz. Nashville: Abingdon, 1986.

The Encyclopedia of Religion. Ed. Mircea Eliade. 16 vols. New York: Macmillan, 1987.

The International Standard Bible Encyclopedia. Ed. Geoffrey W. Bromiley et al. 4 vols. Grand Rapids: Eerdsmans, 1979–88.

A.21. SCIENCE AND TECHNOLOGY

Applied Science and Technology Index. New York: Wilson, 1958– . Available online and on CD-ROM.

Engineering Index. New York: Engineering Information, 1906– . Available online and on CD-ROM as part of *Compendex.*

General Science Index. New York: Wilson, 1978– . Available online and on CD-ROM.

Science Citation Index. Philadelphia: Inst. for Scientific Information, 1945– . Available online and on CD-ROM as part of *SciSearch.*

Hammond Barnhart Dictionary of Science. Ed. Robert Barnhart. Maplewood: Hammond, 1986.

McGraw-Hill Encyclopedia of Engineering. Ed. Sybil Parker. 2nd ed. New York: McGraw, 1993.

McGraw-Hill Encyclopedia of Science and Technology. 7th ed. 20 vols. New York: McGraw, 1992.

A.22. SOCIOLOGY

Sociological Abstracts. San Diego: Sociological Abstracts, 1953– . Available online and on CD-ROM.

Encyclopedia of Sociology. Ed. Edgar F. Borgatta and Marie L. Borgatta. 4 vols. New York: Macmillan, 1992.

The HarperCollins Dictionary of Sociology. Ed. David Jary and Julia Jary. New York: Harper, 1991.

Appendix B:
Other Systems
of Documentation

This appendix describes three documentation systems other than the MLA system. The appendix ends with a selected list of specialized style manuals.

B.1. ENDNOTES AND FOOTNOTES

Some scholars in the fields of art, dance, history, music, religion, theater, and theology use endnotes or footnotes to document sources.

B.1.1. Documentation Notes versus the List of Works Cited and Parenthetical References

If you use notes for documentation, you may not need a list of works cited or a bibliography. (Check your instructor's preference.) The first note referring to a source includes the publication information found in a bibliographic entry—the author's name, the title, and the publication facts—as well as the page reference identifying the portion of the source you refer to at that point in the text. (Subsequent references to the work require less information; see B.1.10.) A bibliographic entry for a work published as part of a book or periodical usually ends with the inclusive page numbers for the entire work cited, but a documentation note, in contrast, ends with the page number or numbers only of the portion you refer to. Note form differs slightly from bibliographic form in other ways (see B.1.3), and note numbers replace parenthetical references at the points in the text where citations are necessary (see B.1.2). Documentation notes appear either at the end of the text, as endnotes, or at the bottoms of relevant pages, as footnotes (see B.1.4).

B.1.2. Note Numbers

Number notes consecutively, starting from 1, throughout a research paper, except for any notes accompanying special material, such as a figure or a table (see 3.7). Do not number them by page or designate them by asterisks or other symbols. Format note numbers as superior, or superscript, arabic numerals (i.e., raised slightly above the line, like this[1]), without periods, parentheses, or slashes. The numbers follow punctuation marks, except dashes. In general, to avoid interrupting the continuity of the text, place a note number, like a parenthetical reference, at the end of the sentence, clause, or phrase containing the material quoted or referred to.

B.1.3. Note Form versus Bibliographic Form

With some exceptions, documentation notes and bibliographic entries provide the same information but differ in form.

Bibliographic Form

A bibliographic entry has three main divisions, each followed by a period: the author's name reversed for alphabetizing, the title, and the publication data.

```
Tannen, Deborah. You Just Don't Understand: Women and
     Men in Conversation. New York: Morrow, 1990.
```

Note Form

A documentation note has four main divisions: the author's name in normal order, followed by a comma; the title; the publication data in parentheses; and a page reference. There is a period only at the end.

```
1 Deborah Tannen, You Just Don't Understand: Women
and Men in Conversation (New York: Morrow, 1990) 52.
```

B.1.4. Endnotes versus Footnotes

In research papers, make all notes endnotes, unless you are instructed otherwise. As their name implies, endnotes appear after the text, starting on a new page numbered in sequence with the preceding page. Center the title *Notes* one inch from the top, double-space, indent one-half inch (or five spaces, if you are using a typewriter) from the left margin, and add the note number, without punctuation, slightly above the line. Type a space and then the reference. If the note extends to two or more lines, begin subsequent lines at the left margin. Type the notes consecutively, double-spaced, and number all pages.

Footnotes appear at the bottoms of pages, beginning four lines (two double spaces) below the text. Single-space footnotes, but double-space between them. When a note continues on the following page, add a solid line across the new page two lines (one double space) below the last line of the text and continue the note two lines (one double space) below the solid line. Footnotes for the new page immediately follow the note continued from the previous page, after a double space.

B.1.5. Sample First Note References: Books

For additional information on citing the following types of sources, consult the related sections on bibliographic entries, indicated in parentheses after the headings.

a. A Book by a Single Author (4.6.1)

[1] Michio Kaku, <u>Hyperspace: A Scientific Odyssey through Parallel Universes, Time Warps, and the Tenth Dimension</u> (New York: Oxford UP, 1994) 32.

b. An Anthology or a Compilation (4.6.2)

[2] Fred J. Nichols, ed. and trans., <u>An Anthology of Neo-Latin Poetry</u> (New Haven: Yale UP, 1979).

c. A Book by Two or More Authors (4.6.4)

[3] James W. Marquart, Sheldon Ekland Olson, and Jonathan R. Sorensen, <u>The Rope, the Chair, and the Needle: Capital Punishment in Texas, 1923-1990</u> (Austin: U of Texas P, 1994) 52-57.

d. A Book by a Corporate Author (4.6.6)

[4] Public Agenda Foundation, <u>The Health Care Crisis: Containing Costs, Expanding Coverage</u> (New York: McGraw, 1992) 69.

e. A Work in an Anthology (4.6.7)

[5] Isabel Allende, "Toad's Mouth," trans. Margaret Sayers Peden, <u>A Hammock beneath the Mangoes: Stories from Latin America</u>, ed. Thomas Colchie (New York: Plume, 1992) 83.

f. An Article in a Reference Book (4.6.8)

[6] "Mandarin," The Encyclopedia Americana, 1993 ed.

g. An Introduction, a Preface, a Foreword, or an Afterword (4.6.9)

[7] Emory Elliott, afterword, The Jungle, by Upton
Sinclair (New York: Signet, 1990) 348-50.

h. An Anonymous Book (4.6.11)

[8] A Guide to Our Federal Lands (Washington: Natl.
Geographic Soc., 1984) 241-47.

i. An Edition (4.6.12)

[9] Charlotte Smith, The Poems of Charlotte Smith, ed.
Stuart Curran (New York: Oxford UP, 1993) 121.

[10] Fredson Bowers, ed., The Red Badge of Courage: An
Episode of the American Civil War, by Stephen Crane
(Charlottesville: UP of Virginia, 1975).

j. A Translation (4.6.13)

[11] Laura Esquivel, Like Water for Chocolate: A Novel
in Monthly Installments, with Recipes, Romances, and Home
Remedies, trans. Carol Christensen and Thomas Christensen
(New York: Doubleday, 1992) 1-5.

k. A Book Published in a Second or Subsequent Edition (4.6.14)

[12] Geoffrey Chaucer, The Works of Geoffrey Chaucer,
ed. F. W. Robinson, 2nd ed. (Boston: Houghton, 1957) 545.

l. A Multivolume Work (4.6.15)

[13] Paul Lauter et al., eds., The Heath Anthology of
American Literature, 2nd ed., 2 vols. (Lexington: Heath,
1994).

[14] Arthur Conan Doyle, The Oxford Sherlock Holmes,
ed. Owen Dudley Edwards, vol. 8 (New York: Oxford UP,
1993).

[15] René Wellek, <u>A History of Modern Criticism, 1750-1950</u>, vol. 5 (New Haven: Yale UP, 1986) 322-26.

m. A Book in a Series (4.6.16)

[16] Joan Hinde Stewart, <u>Colette</u>, Twayne's World Authors Ser. 679 (Boston: Twayne, 1983) 62.

n. A Republished Book (4.6.17)

[17] Margaret Atwood, <u>Surfacing</u> (1972; New York: Fawcett, 1987) 209-12.

o. A Publisher's Imprint (4.6.18)

[18] Mary Findlater and Jane Findlater, <u>Crossriggs</u>, introd. Paul Binding (New York: Virago-Penguin, 1986) 206.

p. A Book with Multiple Publishers (4.6.19)

[19] J. Wight Duff, <u>A Literary History of Rome: From the Origins to the Close of the Golden Age</u>, ed. A. M. Duff, 3rd ed. (1953; London: Benn; New York: Barnes, 1967) 88.

q. A Pamphlet (4.6.20)

[20] <u>Best Museums: New York City</u> (New York: Trip Builder, 1993).

r. A Government Publication (4.6.21)

[21] United Nations, Centre on Transnational Corporations, <u>Foreign Direct Investment, the Service Sector, and International Banking</u> (New York: United Nations, 1987) 4-6.

s. The Published Proceedings of a Conference (4.6.22)

[22] Kira Hall, Michael Meacham, and Richard Shapiro, eds., <u>Proceedings of the Fifteenth Annual Meeting of the Berkeley Linguistics Society, February 18-20, 1989: General Session and Parasession on Theoretical Issues in</u>

Language Reconstruction (Berkeley: Berkeley Linguistics
Soc., 1989).

t. A Book in a Language Other Than English (4.6.23)

[23] Emanuel Poche, Prazské Palace (Praha [Prague]:
Odeon, 1977) 1-5.

u. A Book Published before 1900 (4.6.24)

[24] John Dewey, The School and Society (Chicago,
1899) 104.

v. A Book without Stated Publication Information or Pagination (4.6.25)

[25] Zvi Malachi, ed., Proceedings of the
International Conference on Literary and Linguistic
Computing ([Tel Aviv]: [Fac. of Humanities, Tel Aviv U],
n.d.).

w. An Unpublished Dissertation (4.6.26)

[26] Carol Sakala, "Maternity Care Policy in the
United States: Toward a More Rational and Effective
System," diss., Boston U, 1993, 34.

x. A Published Dissertation (4.6.27)

[27] Rudolf F. Dietze, Ralph Ellison: The Genesis of
an Artist, diss., U Erlangen-Nürnberg, 1982, Erlanger
Beiträge zur Sprach- und Kunstwissenschaft 70 (Nürnberg:
Carl, 1982) 168.

B.1.6. Sample First Note References: Articles in Periodicals

For additional information on citing the following types of sources,
consult the related sections on bibliographic entries, indicated in
parentheses after the headings.

a. An Article in a Scholarly Journal with Continuous Pagination (4.7.1)

[1] Peter Scotto, "Censorship, Reading, and Interpretation: A Case Study from the Soviet Union," PMLA 109 (1994): 65.

b. An Article in a Scholarly Journal That Pages Each Issue Separately (4.7.2)

[2] Frederick Barthelme, "Architecture," Kansas Quarterly 13.3-4 (1981): 77-78.

c. An Article in a Scholarly Journal That Uses Only Issue Numbers (4.7.3)

[3] Christoph Peters, "The Image of Thomas More in Twentieth-Century Plays: A Presentation of Five More Dramas," Moreana 109 (1992): 45-46.

d. An Article in a Scholarly Journal with More Than One Series (4.7.4)

[4] John Daniels, "Indian Population of North America in 1492," William and Mary Quarterly 3rd ser. 49 (1992): 300-02.

[5] Suzanne Gardinier, "Two Cities: On the Iliad," Kenyon Review ns 14.2 (1992): 5.

e. An Article in a Newspaper (4.7.5)

[6] Catherine S. Manegold, "Becoming a Land of the Smoke-Free, Ban by Ban," New York Times 22 Mar. 1994, late ed.: A1.

[7] Paul Taylor, "Keyboard Grief: Coping with Computer-Caused Injuries," Globe and Mail [Toronto] 27 Dec. 1993: A1.

f. An Article in a Magazine (4.7.6)

[8] Hara Estroff Marano, "Domestic Violence," Psychology Today Nov.-Dec. 1993: 48.

g. An Anonymous Article (4.7.7)

[9] "The Decade of the Spy," <u>Newsweek</u> 7 Mar. 1994:
26-27.

h. An Editorial (4.7.8)

[10] "Death of a Writer," editorial, <u>New York Times</u>
20 Apr. 1994, late ed.: A18.

i. A Letter to the Editor (4.7.9)

[11] Cynthia Ozick, letter, <u>Partisan Review</u> 57 (1990):
493-94.

j. A Review (4.7.10)

[12] Will Crutchfield, "Pure Italian," rev. of <u>Verdi:
A Biography</u>, by Mary Jane Phillips-Matz, <u>New Yorker</u>
31 Jan. 1994: 76-78.

[13] Jennifer Dunning, rev. of <u>The River</u>, chor. Alvin
Ailey, Dance Theater of Harlem, New York State Theater,
New York, <u>New York Times</u> 17 Mar. 1994, late ed.: C18.

[14] "The Cooling of an Admiration," rev. of <u>Pound/
Joyce: The Letters of Ezra Pound to James Joyce, with
Pound's Essays on Joyce</u>, ed. Forrest Read, <u>Times Literary
Supplement</u> 6 Mar. 1969: 239-40.

[15] Rev. of <u>Anthology of Danish Literature</u>, ed. F. J.
Billeskov Jansen and P. M. Mitchell, <u>Times Literary
Supplement</u> 7 July 1972: 785.

k. A Serialized Article (4.7.11)

[16] Harrison T. Meserole and James M. Rambeau,
"Articles on American Literature Appearing in Current
Periodicals," <u>American Literature</u> 52 (1981): 688-700; 53
(1981): 164-66, 348-52.

[17] Michael Winerip, "A Disabilities Program That
'Got out of Hand,'" <u>New York Times</u> 8 Apr. 1994, late
ed.: A1; pt. 3 of a series, A Class Apart: Special
Education in New York City, begun 6 Apr. 1994.

l. An Abstract in an Abstracts Journal (4.7.12)

[18] Carol Sakala, "Maternity Care Policy in the United States: Toward a More Rational and Effective System," diss., Boston U, 1993, <u>DAI</u> 54 (1993): 1360B.

m. An Article in a Microform Collection of Articles (4.7.13)

[19] Dan Chapman, "Panel Could Help Protect Children," <u>Winston-Salem Journal</u> 14 Jan. 1990: 14, <u>Newsbank: Welfare and Social Problems</u> 12 (1990): fiche 1, grids A8-11.

n. An Article Reprinted in a Loose-Leaf Collection of Articles (4.7.14)

[20] Brad Edmondson, "AIDS and Aging," <u>American Demographics</u> Mar. 1990: 28+, <u>The AIDS Crisis</u>, ed. Eleanor Goldstein, vol. 2 (Boca Raton: SIRS, 1991) art. 24.

B.1.7. Sample First Note References: CD-ROMs and Other Portable Databases

For additional information on citing the following types of sources, consult the related sections on bibliographic entries, indicated in parentheses after the headings.

a. Material Accessed from a Periodically Published Database on CD-ROM (4.8.2)

[1] Natalie Angier, "Chemists Learn Why Vegetables Are Good for You," <u>New York Times</u> 13 Apr. 1993, late ed.: C1, <u>New York Times Ondisc</u>, CD-ROM, UMI-Proquest, Oct. 1993.

[2] <u>Guidelines for Family Television Viewing</u> (Urbana: ERIC Clearinghouse on Elementary and Early Childhood Educ., 1990), <u>ERIC</u>, CD-ROM, SilverPlatter, June 1993.

[3] "U.S. Population by Age: Urban and Urbanized Areas," <u>1990 U.S. Census of Population and Housing</u>, CD-ROM, US Bureau of the Census, 1990.

b. A Nonperiodical Publication on CD-ROM (4.8.3)

[4] Orchestra, CD-ROM (Burbank: Warner New Media, 1992).

[5] "Albatross," The Oxford English Dictionary, 2nd ed., CD-ROM (Oxford: Oxford UP, 1992).

[6] Samuel Taylor Coleridge, "Dejection: An Ode," The Complete Poetical Works of Samuel Taylor Coleridge, ed. Ernest Hartley Coleridge, vol. 1 (Oxford: Clarendon, 1912) 362-68, English Poetry Full-Text Database, rel. 2, CD-ROM (Cambridge, Eng.: Chadwyck, 1993).

c. A Publication on Diskette (4.8.4)

[7] Michael Joyce, Afternoon: A Story, diskette (Watertown: Eastgate, 1987).

[8] "Nuclear Medicine Technologist," Guidance Information System, 17th ed., diskette (Cambridge: Riverside-Houghton, 1992).

d. A Publication on Magnetic Tape (4.8.5)

[9] "Agnes Scott College," Peterson's College Database, magnetic tape (Princeton: Peterson's, 1992).

[10] English Poetry Full-Text Database, rel. 2, magnetic tape (Cambridge, Eng.: Chadwyck, 1993).

e. A Work in More Than One Publication Medium (4.8.6)

[11] Perseus 1.0: Interactive Sources and Studies on Ancient Greece, CD-ROM, videodisc (New Haven: Yale UP, 1992).

B.1.8. Sample First Note References: Online Databases

For additional information on citing the following types of sources, consult the related sections on bibliographic entries, indicated in parentheses after the headings.

a. Material Accessed through a Computer Service (4.9.2)

[1] Natalie Angier, "Chemists Learn Why Vegetables Are Good for You," New York Times 13 Apr. 1993, late ed.: C1, New York Times Online, online, Nexis, 10 Feb. 1994.

[2] Guidelines for Family Television Viewing (Urbana: ERIC Clearinghouse on Elementary and Early Childhood Educ., 1990), ERIC, online, BRS, 22 Nov. 1993.

[3] "U.S. Population by Age: Urban and Urbanized Areas," 1990 U.S. Census of Population and Housing, online, Human Resource Information Network, 3 May 1994.

b. Material Accessed through a Computer Network (4.9.3)

[4] Stuart Moulthrop, "You Say You Want a Revolution? Hypertext and the Laws of Media," Postmodern Culture 1.3 (1991): par. 19, online, BITNET, 10 Jan. 1993.

[5] Bill Readings, "Translatio and Comparative Literature: The Terror of European Humanism," Surfaces 1.11 (Dec. 1991): 6, online, Internet, 2 Feb. 1992.

[6] Ken Steele, "Special Discounts on the New Variorum Shakespeare," Shaksper 2.124 (4 May 1991): n. pag., online, BITNET, 1 June 1991.

[7] Thomas Hardy, Far from the Madding Crowd, ed. Ronald Blythe (Harmondsworth: Penguin, 1978), online, Oxford Text Archive, Internet, 24 Jan. 1994.

[8] Octovian, ed. Frances McSparran, Early English Text Soc. 289 (London: Oxford UP, 1986), online, U of Virginia Lib., Internet, 6 Apr. 1994.

B.1.9. Sample First Note References: Other Sources

For additional information on citing the following types of sources, consult the related sections on bibliographic entries, indicated in parentheses after the headings.

a. A Television or Radio Program (4.10.1)

[1] "Frankenstein: The Making of the Monster," Great Books, narr. Donald Sutherland, writ. Eugenie Vink, dir. Jonathan Ward, Learning Channel, 8 Sept. 1993.

b. A Sound Recording (4.10.2)

[2] Roger Norrington, cond., Symphony no. 1 in C and Symphony no. 6 in F, by Ludwig van Beethoven, London Classical Players, EMI, 1988.

[3] Billie Holiday, "God Bless the Child," rec. 9 May 1941, The Essence of Billie Holiday, Columbia, 1991.

[4] George C. Scott, narr., World War II, audiocassette, Carmichael, 1990.

[5] D. K. Wilgus, Southern Folk Tales, audiotape, rec. 23-25 Mar. 1965, U of California, Los Angeles, Archives of Folklore, B.76.82.

[6] David Lewiston, liner notes, The Balinese Gamelan: Music from the Morning of the World, LP, Nonesuch, n.d.

c. A Film or Video Recording (4.10.3)

[7] It's a Wonderful Life, dir. Frank Capra, perf. James Stewart, Donna Reed, Lionel Barrymore, and Thomas Mitchell, RKO, 1946.

[8] Jean Renoir, dir., Grand Illusion [La grande illusion], perf. Jean Gabin and Erich von Stroheim, 1938, videodisc, Voyager, 1987.

[9] Looking at Our Earth: A Visual Dictionary, sound filmstrip, Natl. Geographic Educ. Services, 1992.

d. A Performance (4.10.4)

[10] Diana Rigg, perf., Medea, by Euripides, trans. Alistair Elliot, dir. Jonathan Kent, Longacre Theatre, New York, 7 Apr. 1994.

[11] Scott Joplin, Treemonisha, dir. Frank Corsaro, cond. Gunther Schuller, perf. Carmen Balthrop, Betty

Allen, and Curtis Rayam, Houston Grand Opera, Miller Theatre, Houston, 18 May 1975.

e. A Musical Composition (4.10.5)

[12] Ludwig van Beethoven, Symphony no. 8 in F, op. 93.

f. A Work of Art (4.10.6)

[13] Rembrandt van Rijn, <u>Aristotle Contemplating the Bust of Homer</u>, Metropolitan Museum of Art, New York.

[14] Mary Cassatt, <u>Mother and Child</u>, Wichita Art Museum, Wichita, <u>American Painting: 1560-1913</u>, by John Pearce (New York: McGraw, 1964) slide 22.

g. A Letter, a Memo, an E-Mail Communication, or a Public Online Posting (4.10.7)

[15] Virginia Woolf, "To T. S. Eliot," 28 July 1920, letter 1138 of <u>The Letters of Virginia Woolf</u>, ed. Nigel Nicolson and Joanne Trautmann, vol. 2 (New York: Harcourt, 1976) 437-38.

[16] Thomas Hart Benton, letter to Charles Fremont, 22 June 1847, John Charles Fremont Papers, Southwest Museum Lib., Los Angeles.

[17] Toni Morrison, letter to the author, 17 May 1992.

[18] Ian Lancashire, e-mail to the author, 1 Mar. 1994.

[19] Bill Moore, memo to assessment liaisons, State Board for Community and Technical Colls., Olympia, WA, 29 May 1992.

[20] Thomas Michael Shaumann, "Re: Technical German," 5 Aug. 1994, online posting, newsgroup comp.edu.languages.natural, Usenet, 7 Sept. 1994.

h. An Interview (4.10.8)

[21] Federico Fellini, "The Long Interview," Juliet of the Spirits, ed. Tullio Kezich, trans. Howard Greenfield (New York: Ballantine, 1966) 56.

[22] John Updike, interview with Scott Simon, Weekend Edition, Natl. Public Radio, WBUR, Boston, 2 Apr. 1994.

[23] I. M. Pei, personal interview, 22 July 1993.

i. A Map or Chart (4.10.9)

[24] Washington, DC, map (Chicago: Rand, 1992).

[25] The First Aid Card, chart (n.p.: Papertech, 1988).

j. A Cartoon (4.10.10)

[26] Roz Chast, cartoon, New Yorker 11 Apr. 1994: 58.

[27] Garry Trudeau, "Doonesbury," cartoon, Star-Ledger [Newark] 3 Jan. 1994: 24.

k. An Advertisement (4.10.11)

[28] Chanel for Men, advertisement, GQ Dec. 1993: 125-26.

l. A Lecture, a Speech, or an Address (4.10.12)

[29] Margaret Atwood, "Silencing the Scream," Boundaries of the Imagination Forum, MLA Convention, Royal York Hotel, Toronto, 29 Dec. 1993.

[30] Studs Terkel, address, Conf. on Coll. Composition and Communication Convention, Palmer House, Chicago, 22 Mar. 1990.

m. A Manuscript or Typescript (4.10.13)

[31] Mark Twain, notebook 32, ts., Mark Twain Papers, U of California, Berkeley, 50.

n. A Legal Source (4.10.14)

[32] Stevens v. National Broadcasting Co., 148 USPQ
755, CA Super. Ct., 1966.

B.1.10. Subsequent References

After fully documenting a work, use a shortened reference in subsequent notes. As in parenthetical references (see 5.2), include enough information to identify the work. The author's last name alone, followed by the relevant page number or numbers, is usually adequate.

[4] Frye 345-47.

If you cite two or more works by the same author—for example, Northrop Frye's *Anatomy of Criticism* and his *The Double Vision*—include a shortened form of the title following the author's last name in each reference after the first.

[8] Frye, <u>Anatomy</u> 278.
[9] Frye, <u>Double Vision</u> 1-3.

Repeat the information even when two references in sequence refer to the same work. Do not use the abbreviations *ibid.* and *op. cit.*

B.2. AUTHOR-DATE SYSTEM

The author-date system, used in the social sciences and in many of the physical sciences, requires that a parenthetical reference include the author's last name, a comma, the work's year of publication, another comma, and the page reference, preceded by the abbreviation *p.* or *pp.*: "(Wilson, 1992, p. 73)." Information cited in the text is omitted from the parenthetical reference. The authoritative guide to this documentation system is the *Publication Manual of the American Psychological Association* (see the list of style manuals in B.4), and the system is often called APA style.

Bibliographic form in APA style differs from that in MLA style in a number of ways: in APA style, only the initials of first and middle names are given; the year of publication, in parentheses, follows the author's name; for a book, only proper nouns and the first words of the title and of the subtitle are capitalized; the names of some publishers, such as university presses and associations, are spelled out; and the first line of the entry is indented, while second and subsequent lines are flush with the left margin.

> Tannen, D. (1990). <u>You just don't understand: Women and men in conversation</u>. New York: Morrow.

If the book is edited, the abbreviation *Ed.* or *Eds.*, in parentheses, precedes the year of publication.

> Tannen, D. (Ed.). (1985). <u>Gender and conversational interaction</u>. New York: Oxford University Press.

If there are two or more authors, each name is reversed, and an ampersand (*&*), not the word *and*, precedes the final name.

> Durant, W., & Durant, A. (1977). <u>A dual autobiography</u>. New York: Simon and Schuster.

Titles of essays, book chapters, and articles in periodicals are capitalized like titles of books but are neither enclosed in quotation marks nor underlined. Journal titles, however, are capitalized in a manner consistent with MLA practice (see 2.6.1) and are underlined. The volume number, also underlined, follows the journal title and a comma; the issue number, if needed, appears in parentheses after the volume number; a comma and the inclusive page numbers for the article complete the entry.

> Craner, P. M. (1991). New tool for an ancient art: The computer and music. <u>Computers and the Humanities, 25</u>, 303-13.

If the list of works cited includes more than one work by an author, the entries are arranged chronologically, and the author's name is repeated in each entry. If two or more works by the same author were published in a year, each is assigned a lowercase letter: "(1995a)," "(1995b)." For a multivolume work, the range of volume numbers is given in parentheses, preceded by the abbreviation *Vols.*: "(Vols. 1–4)."

The following parenthetical references and corresponding list of works cited demonstrate the author-date system.

Between the 1960s and the 1990s, television coverage of presidential elections changed dramatically (Hallin, 1992, p. 5).

Eighteenth-century England was a minor force in the world of music and art (Durant & Durant, 1965, pp. 214-48).

Frye defined the <u>alazon</u> as a "self-deceiving or self-deceived character in fiction" (1957a, p. 365).

In the middle of a multivolume history of modern literary criticism, René Wellek admits, "An evolutionary history of criticism must fail. I have come to this resigned conclusion" (1955-92, vol. 5, p. xxii).

There are several excellent essays in the volume <u>Sound and Poetry</u> (Frye, 1957b).

To Will and Ariel Durant, creative men and women make "history forgivable by enriching our heritage and our lives" (1977, p. 406).

Works Cited

Durant, W., & Durant, A. (1965). <u>The age of Voltaire</u>. New York: Simon and Schuster.

Durant, W., & Durant, A. (1977). <u>A dual autobiography</u>. New York: Simon and Schuster.

Frye, N. (1957a). <u>Anatomy of criticism: Four essays</u>. Princeton: Princeton University Press.

Frye, N. (Ed.). (1957b). <u>Sound and poetry</u>. New York: Columbia University Press.

Hallin, D. C. (1992). Sound bite news: Television coverage of elections, 1968-1988. <u>Journal of Communication</u>, 42 (2), 5-24.

Wellek, R. (1955-92). <u>A history of modern criticism, 1750-1950</u>. (Vols. 1-8). New Haven: Yale University Press.

B.3. NUMBER SYSTEM

Disciplines such as chemistry, mathematics, medicine, and physics use the number system, which varies from field to field (see the list of style manuals by discipline in B.4). In the number system, arabic numerals designate entries in the list of works cited and appear in parenthetical documentation followed by commas and the relevant volume and page references, which are preceded by the appropriate abbreviations: "(13, vol. 5, p. 259)." With this system, the year of publication remains at the end of the bibliographic entry, and the works are usually listed not in alphabetical order but in the order in which they are first cited in the text. Titles generally follow APA style (B.2).

But Peter Scotto has offered another view (1).

Frye defined the <u>alazon</u> as a "self-deceiving or self-deceived character in fiction" (2, p. 365).

In the middle of a multivolume history of modern literary criticism, René Wellek admits, "An evolutionary history of criticism must fail. I have come to this resigned conclusion" (3, vol. 5, p. xxii).

Eighteenth-century England was a minor force in the world of music and art (4, pp. 214-48).

To Will and Ariel Durant, creative men and women make "history forgivable by enriching our heritage and our lives" (5, p. 406).

Works Cited

1. Scotto, P. Censorship, reading, and interpretation: A case study from the Soviet Union. <u>PMLA</u> 109 (1994): 61-70.

2. Frye, N. <u>Anatomy of criticism: Four essays</u>. Princeton: Princeton University Press, 1957.

3. Wellek, R. <u>A history of modern criticism, 1750-1950</u>. 8 vols. New Haven: Yale University Press, 1955-92.

4. Durant, W., and Durant, A. <u>The age of Voltaire</u>. New York: Simon and Schuster, 1965.

5. Durant, W., and Durant, A. *A dual autobiography*. New York: Simon and Schuster, 1977.

B.4. SPECIALIZED STYLE MANUALS

Every scholarly field has its preferred style, or set of guidelines for writing. MLA style, as presented in this manual, is widely accepted in humanities disciplines. The following manuals describe other styles followed in research disciplines.

Biology

Council of Biology Editors. *Scientific Style and Format: The CBE Manual for Authors, Editors, and Publishers*. 6th ed. New York: Cambridge UP, 1994.

Chemistry

American Chemical Society. *The ACS Style Guide: A Manual for Authors and Editors*. Washington: Amer. Chemical Soc., 1986.

Geology

United States. Geological Survey. *Suggestions to Authors of the Reports of the United States Geological Survey*. 7th ed. Washington: GPO, 1991.

Linguistics

Linguistic Society of America. *LSA Bulletin*, Dec. issue, annually.

Mathematics

American Mathematical Society. *A Manual for Authors of Mathematical Papers*. Rev. ed. Providence: Amer. Mathematical Soc., 1990.

Medicine

American Medical Association. *American Medical Association Manual of Style*. 8th ed. Baltimore: Williams, 1989.

Physics

American Institute of Physics. *AIP Style Manual*. 4th ed. New York: Amer. Inst. of Physics, 1990.

Psychology

American Psychological Association. *Publication Manual of the American Psychological Association*. 4th ed. Washington: Amer. Psychological Assn., 1994.

There are also style manuals that address primarily editors and concern procedures for preparing a manuscript for publication:

The Chicago Manual of Style. 14th ed. Chicago: U of Chicago P, 1993.

United States. Government Printing Office. *Style Manual*. Rev. ed. Washington: GPO, 1984.

Words into Type. By Marjorie E. Skillin, Robert M. Gay, et al. 3rd ed. Englewood Cliffs: Prentice, 1974. New ed. projected for 1996.

For other style manuals and authors' guides, see John Bruce Howell, *Style Manuals of the English-Speaking World: A Guide* (Phoenix: Oryx, 1983).

SAMPLE PAGES OF
A RESEARCH PAPER
IN MLA STYLE

First Page of a Research Paper

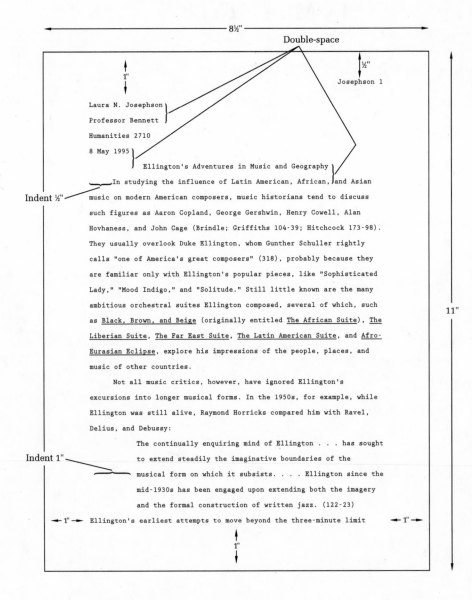

Double-space

8½"

½"

1"

Josephson 1

Laura N. Josephson

Professor Bennett

Humanities 2710

8 May 1995

Ellington's Adventures in Music and Geography

Indent ½"

In studying the influence of Latin American, African, and Asian music on modern American composers, music historians tend to discuss such figures as Aaron Copland, George Gershwin, Henry Cowell, Alan Hovhaness, and John Cage (Brindle; Griffiths 104-39; Hitchcock 173-98). They usually overlook Duke Ellington, whom Gunther Schuller rightly calls "one of America's great composers" (318), probably because they are familiar only with Ellington's popular pieces, like "Sophisticated Lady," "Mood Indigo," and "Solitude." Still little known are the many ambitious orchestral suites Ellington composed, several of which, such as Black, Brown, and Beige (originally entitled The African Suite), The Liberian Suite, The Far East Suite, The Latin American Suite, and Afro-Eurasian Eclipse, explore his impressions of the people, places, and music of other countries.

Not all music critics, however, have ignored Ellington's excursions into longer musical forms. In the 1950s, for example, while Ellington was still alive, Raymond Horricks compared him with Ravel, Delius, and Debussy:

Indent 1"

The continually enquiring mind of Ellington . . . has sought to extend steadily the imaginative boundaries of the musical form on which it subsists. . . . Ellington since the mid-1930s has been engaged upon extending both the imagery and the formal construction of written jazz. (122-23)

1"   Ellington's earliest attempts to move beyond the three-minute limit   1"

11"

1"

First Page of a List of Works Cited

8½"

1"

½"

Josephson 15

Double-space

Works Cited

Brindle, Reginald Smith. "The Search Outwards: The Orient, Jazz,

    Archaisms." <u>The New Music: The Avant-Garde since 1945</u>. New York:

Indent ½"

    Oxford UP, 1975. 133-45.

Burnett, James. "Ellington's Place as a Composer." Gammond 141-55.

Ellington, Duke. <u>Afro-Eurasian Eclipse</u>. 1971. Fantasy, 1991.

---. <u>Black, Brown, and Beige</u>. 1945. RCA Bluebird, 1988.

---. <u>The Far East Suite</u>. LP. RCA, 1965.

---. <u>The Latin American Suite</u>. 1969. Fantasy, 1990.

---. <u>The Liberian Suite</u>. LP. Philips, 1947.

---. <u>Music Is My Mistress</u>. 1973. New York: Da Capo, 1976.

Gammond, Peter, ed. <u>Duke Ellington: His Life and Music</u>. 1958. New York:

    Da Capo, 1977.

Griffiths, Paul. <u>A Concise History of Avant-Garde Music: From Debussy</u>

    <u>to Boulez</u>. New York: Oxford UP, 1978.

Haase, John Edward. <u>Beyond Category: The Life and Genius of Duke</u>

    <u>Ellington</u>. Fwd. Wynton Marsalis. New York: Simon, 1993.

Hitchcock, H. Wiley. <u>Music in the United States: An Introduction</u>. 2nd

    ed. Englewood Cliffs: Prentice, 1974.

Horricks, Raymond. "The Orchestral Suites." Gammond 122-31.

Rattenbury, Ken. <u>Duke Ellington, Jazz Composer</u>. New Haven: Yale UP,

    1990.

Schuller, Gunther. <u>Early Jazz: Its Roots and Musical Development</u>. New

    York: Oxford UP, 1968.

Southern, Eileen. <u>The Music of Black Americans: A History</u>. 2nd ed. New

    York: Norton, 1983.

Tucker, Mark, ed. <u>The Duke Ellington Reader</u>. New York: Oxford UP, 1993.

1" ---. <u>Ellington: The Early Years</u>. Urbana: U of Illinois P, 1991. 1"

1"

11"

1"

Index